CONVEYANCING 2010

CONVEYANCING 2010

Kenneth G C Reid WS

Professor of Scots Law in the University of Edinburgh

and

George L Gretton WS

Lord President Reid Professor of Law in the University of Edinburgh

with a contribution by Alan Barr of the University of Edinburgh

Avizandum Publishing Ltd
Edinburgh
2011

Published by
Avizandum Publishing Ltd
25 Candlemaker Row
Edinburgh EH1 2QG

First published 2011

ISBN 978-1-904968-45-0

British Library Cataloguing in Publication Data
A catalogue record for this book is available from the British Library.

Typeset by Waverley Typesetters, Warham, Norfolk
Printed and bound by Bell & Bain Ltd, Glasgow

CONTENTS

PREFACE

This is the twelfth annual update of new developments in the law of conveyancing. As in previous years, it is divided into five parts. There is, first, a brief description of all cases which have been reported or appeared on the Scottish Courts website (www.scotcourts.gov.uk) or have otherwise come to our attention since *Conveyancing 2009*. The next two parts summarise, respectively, statutory developments during 2010 and other material of interest to conveyancers. The fourth part is a detailed commentary on selected issues arising from the first three parts. Finally, in Part V, there are three tables. A cumulative table of decisions, usually by the Lands Tribunal, on the variation or discharge of title conditions covers all decisions since the revised jurisdiction in part 9 of the Title Conditions (Scotland) Act 2003 came into effect. Then there is a cumulative table of appeals, designed to facilitate moving from one annual volume to the next. Finally, there is a table of cases digested in earlier volumes but reported, either for the first time or in an additional series, in 2010. This is for the convenience of future reference.

We do not seek to cover agricultural holdings, crofting, public sector tenancies (except the right-to-buy legislation), compulsory purchase or planning law. Otherwise our coverage is intended to be complete.

We gratefully acknowledge help received from Alan Barr, Helen Davidson, John Glover, Bill Gordon, Adam Machray, Roddy Paisley, Andrew Steven, Neil Tainsh, Shona Wilson, and Scott Wortley.

Kenneth G C Reid
George L Gretton
15 March 2011

TABLE OF STATUTES

TABLE OF ORDERS, RULES AND REGULATIONS

TABLE OF CASES

❧ PART I ❧
CASES

CASES

MISSIVES OF SALE

(1) Hendry v Egan
2010 GWD 36-737, Sh Ct

In February 2008 the pursuers concluded missives with the defenders to buy a house near Invergordon. The missives were based on the Highland Missives, clause 9 of which says:

> So far as the seller is aware as at the date of the sellers' acceptance hereof there are no proposals for development requiring Planning Permission and/or Building Warrant nor has any such Permission or Warrant been obtained in relation to any property either adjoining or in the neighbourhood of the property. The seller has received no written intimation of any such proposals.

(On this subject, standard missives vary quite considerably in their wording. For example, compare the Glasgow and Edinburgh (Combined) Missives, clause 4, or the Borders Missives, clause 14(1)(b).) In November 2007 a developer had lodged an application to build 40 houses on the neighbouring land. At some stage – the defenders averred it was before conclusion of missives – the application was withdrawn, but in July 2009 the developer lodged a new and similar application. The sheriff's opinion does not state whether the transaction had settled by then, and does not say whether the development had gone ahead, but our impression is that the answer to both questions is affirmative. Whether, at the time when missives were concluded, the defenders knew of the first application was undetermined at the time of the hearing. The pursuers sued the defenders for damages for breach of contract. One head of damages was for 'inconvenience and discomfort'. (We would guess that there was also a crave for damages for loss of value.)

The defenders argued that at the time of missives there was no planning application before the council and that therefore there could be no question of breach of contract. The sheriff (Gordon Fleetwood) said (para 15): 'I am of the view that there is sufficient correlation between the two applications to allow the pursuers an opportunity to prove that they are, in effect, the same application.' But the pursuers' claim for damages for 'loss and inconvenience' was struck out as lacking in specification. 'They make no attempt to aver what inconvenience and discomfort the pursuers have suffered or reasonably expect to suffer' (para 16). The case has some discussion of how the two sentences of clause 9 relate to each other, but no definite conclusions emerge. Those responsible for revising standard missives may wish to consider this case.

(2) Gibson v Gibson
2010 GWD 30-614, Sh Ct

Mrs Gibson owned a property in Fraserburgh. In August 2008 she concluded missives to sell it to her daughter, Ms Gibson, and to Mr Gavryluk, in common, for the price of £35,000. Whilst the court's opinion seems not to cover the point expressly, it seems that the transaction settled and that the buyers were registered in the Land Register. Later the buyers resold the property at a considerably higher figure, and at this stage Mrs Gibson asked them for a further £23,000, on the basis that the original agreement (albeit not mentioned in the missives) had been that when the property was resold, that sum (£23,000) would be paid to her. When they did not pay, she sued them. Her case was that the property had been valued at £58,000 at the time of the original sale, but that at that time her daughter and Mr Gavryluk could raise only £35,000, so she had allowed them to defer payment of the balance. She produced the following document.

> 31–04–08
> To Peter Gavryluk,
>
> We, Bertie and Elaine Gibson offer to purchase 10 Chapelhill Road, Fraserburgh at a price of which it is valued by the surveyor. After the mortgage, and any penalties due are paid back to the mortgage company, the twenty three thousand pounds due to us by you and Leanne will be paid to us on the same day as the purchase takes place. Any equity above £58,000 will be paid directly to yourself. If the mortgage payments you have made since buying the property adds up to more than the equity, we will gladly pay you the difference on day of purchase. We guarantee no payment for rent all the while you lived there before buying it will be paid by you.

There are obviously some oddities about this document. April does not have a 31st day. The words 'offer to *purchase*' do not make sense. It is addressed only to Mr Gavryluk, and not also to Ms Gibson. There are other obscurities as well. The letter takes the form of an offer and contains no words indicating acceptance. As to signature, the sheriff principal (Sir Stephen Young) noted: 'The letter bears to have been signed by the pursuer and her husband and there is a third, illegible signature. In their answers the defenders aver that the second defender has no recollection of signing the letter.' This seems to fall short of being a positive denial of the signature.

The case was decided without hearing evidence. The sheriff held that the pursuer's pleadings were irrelevant and lacking in specification, and though the pursuer then appealed, the sheriff principal upheld the sheriff's decision. The pursuer's case was that 'this obligation was part and parcel of the original contract for the sale of the property by the pursuer to the defenders' (para 10). But that contention ran into the problem that the alleged agreement to pay a further £23,000 was not in writing (the letter dated 31 April apparently not being regarded as such), and s 1 of the Requirements of Writing (Scotland) Act 1995 requires formal writing for contracts for the sale of heritable property. The pursuer argued that the £23,000 was not part of the price but a contingent obligation, and that that fact took it outwith the 1995 Act, but (para 13):

> It is in my opinion nothing to the point that the obligation was a contingent one (contingent, that is, on a future sale of the property by the defenders), that as a matter of strict legal analysis it may not have been part of the price and that, the essential components of property, parties, price and date of entry having been stated and agreed in the missives, the contract would have been complete without this additional obligation. The fact remains that the pursuer contends that this obligation was part and parcel of the contract and, as such, it was in my opinion governed by section 1(2)(a)(i) of the 1995 Act. And I might add here that it seems to me that, even if the obligation was somehow severable from the remainder of the contract, then it must have constituted a gratuitous unilateral obligation subject to section 1(2)(a)(ii) since there is no suggestion that the pursuer gave any consideration for the obligation apart from what she undertook to do in terms of the missives.

Accordingly the pursuer's case failed. Though the point seems not to have been discussed, it might also be argued that, even if there was a valid agreement in April 2008, that agreement would have been superseded by the subsequent missives. The pursuer also had a plea about unjustified enrichment, but perhaps unsurprisingly this was dismissed.

We wonder whether other lines of argument might have been explored. If the pursuer's case was that the alleged agreement about the £23,000 was 'part and parcel' of the missives, then it might be argued that the missives had failed to reflect the common intention of the parties. If so, then it would have been possible to seek rectification of the missives in terms of s 8 of the Law Reform (Miscellaneous Provisions) (Scotland) Act 1985. As an analogy, compare another of this year's cases, *George Wimpey West Scotland Ltd v Henderson* (Case (12)) where an alleged pre-missives agreement, not satisfying the 1995 Act, was held to be a relevant basis for a rectification action. Alternatively, it might have been arguable that the alleged agreement about the £23,000 was a wholly separate contract, and thus not subject to the rules about formal writing for sales of land. Such an approach might perhaps gain support from another 2010 case, *Smith v Stuart* 2010 SC 490, 2010 SLT 1249 (Case (10)), in which it was held that an agreement to share uplift value was not an 'obligation relating to land'. Finally, one might wonder whether an argument based on 'statutory personal bar' (s 1(3) of the 1985 Act) might have been feasible. But there may have been good reasons why these lines of argument were not developed. In any event, even if the pursuer had surmounted the problems of relevancy and specification, there would still have been the hurdle of proof to overcome.

[Another aspect of this case is digested at (45) below.]

(3) Scottish Coal Company Ltd v Danish Forestry Co Ltd
[2010] CSIH 56, 2010 SC 729

The pursuer had an option to acquire the defender's land. If it did so it had to grant to the defender (ie the seller) a standard security to secure future payments. The option contract said that the seller would have to enter into a 'reasonable' ranking agreement with the buyer's bank. Was this valid? See **Commentary** p 110. This decision affirms the decision of the Lord Ordinary: [2009] CSOH 171, 2010 GWD 5-79, digested as *Conveyancing 2009* Case (9).

(4) R & D Construction Group Ltd v Hallam Land Management Ltd
[2010] CSIH 96, 2011 GWD 2-85

Hallam had an option on some land and then concluded missives to sell the land to R & D, with a condition that the sale would proceed only if the option price proved satisfactory to Hallam. When Hallam refused to proceed with their contract with R & D, the latter sued Hallam to enforce it. See **Commentary** p 109. This decision affirms the decision of the Lord Ordinary given at [2009] CSOH 128 and digested as *Conveyancing 2009* Case (8).

(5) EDI Central Ltd v National Car Parks Ltd
[2010] CSOH 141, 2011 SLT 75

This case involved a complex contract for the redevelopment of a site in central Edinburgh. It bound both parties to 'use all reasonable endeavours to achieve the Main Objectives' of the project, a key element of which was the obtaining of planning permission. Later, the parties disputed as to whether the developer had truly used 'all reasonable endeavours'. See **Commentary** p 107.

(6) Mactaggart & Mickel Homes Ltd v Hunter
[2010] CSOH 130, 2010 GWD 33-683

Mactaggart & Mickel Homes Ltd ('MML') concluded missives to buy a property near Balerno for £3.5 million. Of this £1.5 million was payable at settlement and the balance of £2 million when MML obtained planning permission for building 17 or more housing units on the site. MML was bound to use 'reasonable endeavours' to obtain such permission. Planning permission was not obtained. The case turned on whether MML had used 'reasonable endeavours'. See **Commentary** p 105.

(7) Snowie v Museum Hall LLP
[2010] CSOH 107, 2010 SLT 971

Four members of the Snowie family concluded missives to buy flats (six in all) in a development in Bridge of Allan. They then purported to resile on the ground that one of the real burdens (affecting all the properties in the development) was unusual or unduly onerous and thus contrary to the missives. (The missives are not quoted in the case, but evidently contained the standard warranty against unusual or unduly onerous burdens.) The buyers had not seen the title before concluding missives. The burden in question was a prohibition of use of a residential apartment for any trade, business or profession. The buyers raised six separate actions seeking (a) declarator that they were entitled to resile and

(b) repayment of the deposits. The defender counterclaimed for performance of the missives. **Held** that the burden was not unusual or unduly onerous. See **Commentary** p 104.

[Another aspect of this case is digested at (27) below.]

(8) AMA (New Town) Ltd v Finlay
2010 GWD 32-658, Sh Ct

When a buyer defaults on payment, the seller's usual response is to rescind, re-market the property, and claim damages. But a seller is always entitled to seek to have the contract implemented instead. That was the position here. The buyer paid an initial deposit but was unable to pay the balance of the purchase price. The seller raised an action for payment, with interest. The buyer's defence was a technical one. The proper remedy, said the buyer, was a crave for specific implement as set out in *Greens Encyclopaedia of Scottish Legal Styles* vol 8 pp 122–24 and used in *King v Moore* 1993 SLT 1117. An action for payment would not do.

This defence was rejected by the sheriff (William Holligan) and decree granted. The sheriff distinguished between implement as a general category and the particular remedy which might be sought in order to achieve it. 'The innocent party's right to seek implement of a bargain which the other party has wrongly failed to implement is, or may be, different from the particular *remedy* which the innocent party is entitled to seek from the court' (para 9). An action for payment was a form of implement, and had been approved as such, at least by implication, in *Bosco Design Services Ltd v Plastic Sealant Services Ltd* 1979 SC 189. Its competency in the present case was not open to doubt.

(9) Aberdeen City Council v Stewart Milne Group Ltd
[2010] CSIH 81, 2010 GWD 37-755

Aberdeen City Council sold some land to the defender. The missives contained a complex provision that an additional sum was to be payable in the event that the buyer resold the land at a profit. The buyer resold the land to another company in the same group at a price which was, averred the council, far below the market value. The low price would mean that the additional sum payable to the council would be zero. Had the land been resold at its market value, averred the council, the additional sum payable would have been about £1.7 million. The council raised an action for declarator that the additional sum should be calculated on market value and not on the price actually paid. The wording of the contract was less than clear on this point, but at first instance the Lord Ordinary preferred the interpretation of the pursuer: see [2009] CSOH 80, 2009 GWD 26-417 (*Conveyancing 2009* Case (6)).

The defender appealed, and the Inner House has now affirmed the Lord Ordinary's decision. Lord Clarke said (para 11):

> The defenders contended that the wording of clause 9 and the Schedule compelled a different construction. We do not think that this is so. In recent years the importance of construing contractual provisions in context, and in such a way as to give effect to

the parties' commercial objectives, has been emphasized in a large number of cases; the principal authorities are well known and scarcely require discussion. We note in passing, however, that at least in Scotland this approach is not new; it appears clearly from cases such as *Mackenzie v Liddell* (1883) 10 R 705, *Bank of Scotland v Stewart* (1891) 18 R 957, and *Jacobs v Scott & Co* (1899) 2 F (HL) 70. Following this approach, we are of opinion that clause 9 and the associated definitions in the Schedule should be construed in such a way as to give effect to the parties' clear commercial purpose in agreeing to that clause.

In *Multi-link Leisure Developments Ltd v North Lanarkshire Council* [2010] UKSC 47, 2011 SLT 184 (Case (52) below) Lord Hope, while not questioning the decision in the present case, expressed some doubt as to the value of the cases here cited (para 21). Disagreements about the way that contracts should be interpreted seem eternal.

(10) Smith v Stuart
[2010] CSIH 29, 2010 SC 490, 2010 SLT 1249

The defender had granted to the pursuer an undertaking to enter into a minute of agreement, entitling her to a share of any uplift value of certain land. No such minute of agreement was entered into, and when, more than five years later, the pursuer sought to enforce the undertaking it was held that it had prescribed. This upholds the decision of the sheriff reported at 2010 SCLR 131 (and digested as *Conveyancing 2009* Case (2)). See **Commentary** p 182.

(11) Aziz v Whannel
[2010] CSOH 136, 2010 GWD 33-682

The pursuer sold property to the defender, with the right to buy some of it back. When he claimed damages for breach of this right, the defender pled that the right was no longer enforceable because of the supersession clause in the missives. See **Commentary** p 112.

(12) George Wimpey West Scotland Ltd v Henderson
1 March 2010, Edinburgh Sheriff Court affd 2010 GWD 38-775, Sh Ct

The pursuer had a development in Renfrew. In December 2007 missives were concluded to sell one of the plots to the defender. The transaction did not settle and the developer later resold, at a lower price. In this action the developer sued the original buyer for damages based on the difference between the price in the original missives and the price achieved at the subsequent resale. Thus far the case seems a straightforward one. In fact it was far from straightforward. In the first place, whilst the present action concerned only one plot, it appears that the defender and certain business associates were buying 46 plots. (What happened in the other 45 transactions we do not know.) In the second place, the developer was anxious to conclude missives before the year end so that it could show the property in its accounts as having been sold. It pressed the defender to conclude, and (according to the defender) gave assurances that if the defender did agree to conclude, the missives would in fact not be regarded as fully binding but could be renegotiated. As evidence, the defender lodged in court copies of e-mails said to have been sent by the developer. One e-mail, of 10 December 2007, said:

> I appreciate that you are currently unable to have the 46 plots in Block B Phase 2 Ferry Village valued at the moment, primarily due to the completion dates being approximately 10 months away which I understand means that you are unable to secure funding as the date of entry is outwith the shelf life offer of loan. With this in mind I want to give you some reassurance that should the circumstances arise that there are difficulties with the valuations we will find a resolution one way or another and I suggest that against this background I would like to have a 'gentleman's agreement' that we will have the valuations carried out in the New Year with a view of having them all back early Feb which will be the basis of any negotiations (if need be). I just want to give you the comfort that in concluding missives now will still allow further negotiations should the valuation necessitate this.

Another e-mail of 19 December said that if certain circumstances did not come to pass, then 'we re-market the properties. If the question is will we come after you then I can give assurance that we won't. All I need is enough notice, ie as early in the New Year as possible to remarket. Hope this helps.' An e-mail of 21 December said:

> Should the situation arise that all bonds are in place and should the properties not achieve the values required (that is the value or closest values to those set out in the missives within 5%) an agreement will be reached by both parties where the result could be that GW will remarket all or some of the properties, in effect we would resile from the missives at no penalty to the purchaser.

When the developer sued, the defender pled (i) that the developer was personally barred and (ii) that the missives, having failed to reflect the true terms of the agreement between the parties, should be rectified, in terms of the Law Reform (Miscellaneous Provisions) (Scotland) Act 1985. The pursuer challenged the relevancy of these defences. The sheriff (William Holligan) **held** that the factual basis for the defences should be allowed to go to proof. The pursuer appealed against this decision. The sheriff principal (Edward Bowen) dismissed the appeal. We have heard that the pursuer has lodged an appeal to the Inner House.

COMMON PROPERTY

(13) B v B
2010 GWD 24-454, Sh Ct

In principle, a co-owner has an absolute right to have the property divided or, if not readily divisible, sold and the proceeds divided. But where the property is a 'matrimonial' or 'family' home, the court has discretion to postpone or even refuse an award of division and sale where the action is brought by a party to the marriage or, if the party is insolvent, by that party's trustee in sequestration. The present case deals with the first situation, the next case with the second.

The pursuer and defender were husband and wife. The defender looked after the pursuer until both he and she became too unwell. For the last two or three years the pursuer had been in hospitals and care homes. He was now suffering from dementia. He raised an action of division and sale of the matrimonial home. (Nothing is said in the case about the competency of someone with dementia raising an action. If there was a guardian this is not mentioned.) His wife invoked the court's discretion to dismiss the action, contained in s 19 of the Matrimonial Homes (Family Protection) (Scotland) Act 1981. Of the (non-exhaustive) factors which the court is directed to consider in exercising its discretion, the following were potentially relevant: (i) the conduct of the spouses, (ii) their respective needs and financial resources, and (iii) whether the pursuer had offered to make alternative accommodation available.

Holding that the onus of proof lay with the person seeking to rely on s 19 (ie the defender), the sheriff (J M S Horsburgh QC) further **held** that the onus had been discharged. In relation to (i) he found that, while the defender had looked after the pursuer for as long as possible, the pursuer for his part had (through his daughter by an earlier marriage) withdrawn most of the money from the parties' joint bank account. Now that he was in institutional care, the pursuer had no need of the capital which a sale would bring and had ample income, whereas the defender was ill and the house suited her needs (factor (ii)). Finally, no offer of alternative accommodation had been made (factor (iii)). The action therefore failed. The sheriff was unimpressed by the pursuer's argument that a refusal of decree would be a breach of the property clause of the ECHR (article 1 of the First Protocol). It is understood that the decision has been appealed to the Inner House. For a discussion, see an article by Sarah Lilley published at (2010) 55 *Journal of the Law Society of Scotland* Aug/49.

(14) Accountant in Bankruptcy v Clough
2010 GWD 35-714, Sh Ct

Mrs and Mrs Clough owned the family home in common. Following Mrs Clough's sequestration, her trustee in sequestration (the Accountant in Bankruptcy) raised an action of division and sale. Mrs Clough's defence was based on s 40 of the Bankruptcy (Scotland) Act 1985 which gives the court discretion to postpone or refuse an action for division and sale in respect of a family home. In reaching a view the court is to have regard to the criteria set out in s 40(2). Mainly these favour the bankrupt (the needs and resources of the debtor's spouse and of any child, and the length of time during which the family home was used for their residence), but the court is also to have regard to the interests of creditors.

The sheriff (Mhairi Stephen) granted decree. On the one hand, she was mindful of the interests of creditors, 'not only because it enjoys status as an enumerated heading in Section 40 but more so because it is fundamental to the purpose of sequestration – that the debtor's estate be ingathered and distributed for the benefit of the body of creditors'. On the other hand, the averments for Mrs Clough were 'woefully inadequate' in relation to factors which might assist her position. Thus:

> There is no specific information provided by way of averments relating to income or capital or other means of financial or other support provided by the second defender to her daughter. There are no specific averments which might indicate the impact on the Third Defender [the18-year old daughter] of the family home in Edinburgh being sold when she lives and studies in Aberdeen for much of the year. There are no averments in particular relating to whether alternative accommodation has been sought and is available. It would be difficult to accept that no such accommodation is available in either the public or private rented sector.

TENEMENTS

(15) Mehrabadi v Haugh
11 January 2010, Aberdeen Sheriff Court

The pursuer, the owner of the top flat in a tenement, carried out repairs to the roof of his dormer window and sought to recover a share of the cost from the owner of another flat in the building. It was **held** that he was not entitled to do so. Although the titles contained an obligation to contribute to the cost of roof repairs, this could only apply to the roof as it existed at the time when the burden was imposed. As the dormer had been added later, the responsibility for repairing its roof lay with the pursuer alone. See **Commentary** p 93.

(16) Hunter v Tindale
2010 GWD 38-776, Sh Ct

The defender owned the open pend under a tenement but without owning any of the flats. It was **held** that the pend was not part of the tenement and that, accordingly, the defender was not liable for a share of the cost of repairing the archway over the pend. See **Commentary** p 96.

(17) Kennedy v Abbey Lane Properties
29 March 2010, Lands Tr

The owner of a main-door flat sought to have a deed of conditions varied so as to relieve him of liability for maintaining the common passages and stairs. The application was refused. See **Commentary** p 97.

(17A) Patterson v Drouet
20 January 2011, Lands Tr

The owners of the two ground floor flats sought to have the deed of conditions varied so as to reduce their share of liability for the maintenance of certain parts of the building. That share was based on gross annual value, and by virtue of s 111 of the Local Government Finance Act 1992 valuations were frozen as at

1 April 1989. In 1989 the flats were used for commercial purposes and so had a high valuation but today they were in residential use and so, if revaluation were possible, would have a much lower valuation. On the merits the Tribunal thought that the applicants deserved to succeed, but continued the application to consider questions of competency. See **Commentary** p 99.

(18) Anderson v UK
[2010] ECHR 145

This is a footnote to a litigation involving a tenement which finished as long ago as 2003: see *Anderson v Express Investment Co Ltd* 2004 GWD 16-355 (*Conveyancing 2003* Case (13)). In the original case Mr Anderson, an advocate and flat-owner, sought damages of £100,000 against a commercial property company, which owned some of the flats in the same building, and against Edinburgh Council in respect of repairs which, in his view, had not been properly carried out. When the action was unsuccessful Mr Anderson raised an action against the UK Government in the European Court of Human Rights in Strasbourg seeking damages, on the basis of ECHR article 6, for the delays in the original litigation. The court accepted that some of the delay had been Mr Anderson's fault but found that nothing in the history of the case absolved the Court of Session of its 'obligation to take an active role in the management of proceedings and to make enquiries of the parties to ascertain their position in respect of the appeal' (para 28). In particular the court pointed to a period of around a year when little or nothing had happened in the appeal. Damages of €1,500 were awarded. In a trenchant commentary on this case (http://www.jonathanmitchell.info/), Jonathan Mitchell QC emphasises its sheer ordinariness, and points out wryly that the case before the Strasbourg Court took almost six years to reach a determination.

(19) Hines v King Sturge LLP
[2010] CSIH 86, 2011 SLT 2

When a fire broke out in the tenement at 73 St Vincent Street, Glasgow, in the wee small hours of 16 April 2005, it took the fire service a number of hours to trace the smoke to the affected building. As a result, the damage was substantial. The pursuers, who were tenants of premises in the tenement, sued the property manager for damages. It was averred that the telephone line for the fire alarm had been disconnected because of non-payment of the bills, that this had been made known to the defender some three weeks before the fire, and that, had the fire alarm been connected, most of the damage would not have occurred. Although they paid for the fire alarm as part of their annual charges, the pursuers had neither a contract, nor any communication, with the defender. The action was in delict and raised the apparently novel question as to whether (in Lord Carloway's words at para 77) a 'delictual duty [is imposed] upon a landlord's property agent to take reasonable care for the property of the landlord's tenant'. The pursuers argued that such a duty was indeed imposed on the basis of the tripartite test (foreseeability, proximity, and fairness, justice and reasonableness) set out in *Caparo Industries v Dickman* [1990] 2 AC 605. In addition, they argued that the parties were in a 'special relationship' and that in any event the pursuers had relied on the defender, much as in cases such as *Hedley Byrne & Co v Heller* [1964] AC 465. The pursuers were unsuccessful at first instance ([2009] CSOH 96, 2009 SLT 763), but an Extra Division (Lord Carloway dissenting) has now allowed a proof before answer. In his majority opinion, Lord Osborne expressed the view that the *Caparo* test might turn out to be satisfied.

SERVITUDES

(20) Henderson v Irvine
2010, Alloa Sheriff Court

This was a dispute about access and other rights in respect of a private road, Elistoun Drive, in Tillicoultry. A number of houses benefited from a servitude right of access over the road. These included the pursuers' houses and also house number 10, which at one time was owned by the defenders. The defenders sold number 10 to one of the pursuers but retained a small strip which they intended to use to gain access to the next-door property, number 11, on which they proposed to build a house. Number 11 had no servitude over the road. Nonetheless the plan was to access number 11 by a combination of (i) Elistoun Drive and (ii) the strip retained from number 10. The pursuers acquired title to Elistoun Drive and challenged the defenders' right to take access over it to number 11.

In the end it seems to have been conceded by the defenders that, while the strip retained from number 10 had the benefit of the servitude over Elistoun Drive, it was not permissible to use the strip as a 'bridge' to number 11. For that would be to make number 11 a dominant tenement in the servitude. The decision of the First Division in *Irvine Knitters v North Ayrshire Cooperative Society Ltd* 1978 SC 109 was conclusive on the matter. Instead the defenders' argument ultimately rested on personal bar. The pursuers had seen the work being undertaken by the defenders, and the use made of the road, and had not objected. Thus they were personally barred from denying use of the road in order to reach number 11. The sheriff allowed a proof of the parties' averments.

It might be added that personal bar could not arise in respect of works carried out on the *defenders'* property. For personal bar presupposes that a party has a right which he fails to exercise, and the pursuers could have no right to prevent the defenders carrying out work on their own property. See E C Reid and J W G Blackie, *Personal Bar* (2006) para 2-22.

(21) Orkney Housing Association Ltd v Atkinson
15 October 2010, Kirkwall Sheriff Court

In 2008 the pursuer bought the site of a former commercial garage and built four units of housing which it proceeded to let out. The site could be accessed both by a public road and by a narrow private road. The private road led to the defenders' house. Ownership of the road appears to have been uncertain, but in 2009 the defenders procured an *a non domino* disposition and were registered as owners subject to exclusion of indemnity. By that time a dispute was in progress as to the pursuer's (and its tenants') right to use the road. The A section of the pursuer's title sheet included 'a right of access for all purposes over the road commonly known as the Esgar Road'. That right, said the defenders, had been lost either by abandonment or by non-use for the period of negative prescription. This was because, when the garage was still in operation, its owner had built a wall to stop his customers from using the private road to reach the garage. That had occurred more than 20 years ago. The pursuer's action was for declarator that it had a right of access and for interdict against obstructions. The defenders counterclaimed and sought declarator that the servitude had been extinguished.

The sheriff (D W Ferguson) allowed proof before answer. If the defenders proved their averments, they would have the basis for applying to the Keeper for rectification of the Register. 'It may be', the sheriff added (p 14 of the transcript), 'that the Keeper would decline to rectify and as a result of that it may be that the defenders would be unable to ultimately obtain the remedy that they seek. But that would be speculation beyond the terms of this action.' The defender's should therefore be allowed a proof.

The correctness of this approach may be doubted. It would have been open to the defenders to add a crave for rectification of the Register. In its absence, it is hard to see how they can defend the case. For even if they can prove that, as a matter of ordinary property law, the servitude was lost by abandonment or prescription, the servitude remains on the Register and was conferred on the pursuer afresh when it registered its title in 2008. This is due to the Keeper's 'Midas touch': see s 3(1)(a) of the Land Registration (Scotland) Act 1979. Whether the pursuer *should* have a servitude is no doubt open to question. But unless or until the Register is rectified so as to remove it from the pursuer's title sheet, the servitude unquestionably exists and the pursuer is entitled to its declarator. Not even success in proving the defenders' averments would change that result.

It is worth asking whether, ultimately, the defenders could achieve rectification. Suppose that they prove loss by abandonment or prescription and obtain a declarator to that effect. The Register would then be shown to be inaccurate, and inaccuracies can, in principle, be rectified under s 9(1) of the 1979 Act. But might the pursuer be protected as a proprietor in possession? Does, in other words, the protection of s 9(3)(a) extend to the real right of servitude? On this point there is disputed authority. In *Griffiths v Keeper of the Registers*, a decision of 20 December 2002, the Lands Tribunal decided that the answer was no, but in *Yaxley v Glen* 2007 SLT 756 Lady Dorrian decided that the answer was yes. Only the latter case seems to have been cited to the sheriff in *Orkney Housing Association*. For a full discussion of the issue, see *Conveyancing 2007* pp 121–27.

(22) Parkin v Kennedy
23 March 2010 (merits), 18 May 2010 (expenses), Lands Tr

Circumstances under which the grant of 'a servitude right of way' was *held* to import a right of use by vehicles. See **Commentary** p 178.

[Another aspect of this case is digested at (38) below.]

(23) Pullar v Gauldie
25 August 2004, Arbroath Sheriff Court

By a disposition recorded in 1996 the granters disponed land but retained adjacent rights of salmon fishing at Lunan Bay in Angus. The land was

> disponed always with and under a reservation in favour of the proprietors from time to time of the adjoining lands of a right of pedestrian and vehicular access and egress over the roadway and footpaths lying through the said subjects hereinbefore disponed to said adjoining lands.

The only reasonable way of getting access to the salmon fishings, and the way established by long usage, was over the land which had just been disponed. This involved using a tractor and trailer to take a path over sand dunes. By 1996 the fishing rights had ceased to be exercised but they were later sold and the pursuer as the new owner sought to take access over the dunes. By this time the dunes belonged to the defenders, who disputed the access.

The sheriff (Ian G Inglis) **held** that a servitude of access had been successfully reserved. It was true that salmon fishings were not 'lands' in the narrow sense, and no doubt the servitude in the 1996 disposition could be explained away as referring to other land which had formerly belonged to the disponers. But it was well established in statute that 'lands' include *any* heritable property to which a title can be registered. Moreover, the reservation had to be read in the light of the surrounding circumstances:

> The principal circumstance was that although the salmon fishings had not been exercised by Johnstone's [the disponers] for about 8 years at the time of the 1996 Disposition they remained in their ownership and they presumably had in mind the possibility that either they themselves might resume fishing or that they might sell the fishings to someone else who would use them. It is clear that whoever made use of the salmon fishings would require access to them. The access which the Johnstone's had used throughout their ownership of the fishings was through what are now the defenders' subjects and the track through the dunes.

The *esto* argument for the defenders, that any servitude must be deemed abandoned by non-use, was held not to be established. See **Commentary** p 179.

As a result of an extension recently built by the defenders' predecessors, the track now passed close to their house. The pursuer's tractor would therefore cause a certain amount of disturbance. But the sheriff dismissed any suggestion that to continue to use the track would be a breach of the obligation to exercise a servitude *civiliter*:

> In my opinion if the owner of a servient tenement extends his house so that instead of being some significant distance away from the line of the right of way through his property it abuts that right of way, he cannot complain that the increased disturbance which will arise from the proximity of the building to the right of way was caused by any lack of civiliter on the part of the dominant tenement. If that was the law many rights of way could be extinguished simply by the owner of the servient tenement taking up residence very close to the right of way and then complaining that the

right of way was not being exercised civiliter. Putting it another way the increase in disturbance to the defenders' property has not been brought about by any change of activity on the part of the pursuer but by the changes made by the defenders' predecessors in title.

Another difficulty concerned the pursuer's wish to clear away sand to make the track suitable for vehicles. Of course, a servitude holder can carry out reasonable works of maintenance. But, in the defenders' view, this went beyond maintenance and altered the character of the track. This argument too was rejected by the sheriff. 'In my opinion the proprietor of the fishings is entitled to take whatever steps may be necessary to make the access which he has granted suitable for the purpose for which it was granted namely vehicular access.' In the present case there was a long practice of clearing sand at the beginning of the fishing season and the track could not be used for vehicles unless this was done.

Quite separately from the issue of servitude the sheriff also decided that an access right arose as an integral part of the right of salmon fishing. The principle here is indeed well established: see K G C Reid, *Law of Property in Scotland* (1996) para 328. The holder of fishing rights can make all uses of the adjacent banks or foreshore as are reasonably required for the conduct of the fishing. Such a right, the sheriff suggested, arose by implied reservation in the 1996 disposition.

(Although decided in 2004, this decision has only recently been brought to our attention.)

REAL BURDENS

(24) Greenbelt Property Ltd v Riggens
2010 GWD 28-586, Lands Tr

Land forming part of a residential development was feued by the developer to Greenbelt subject to a real burden which required Greenbelt to plant and maintain woodland. After feudal abolition this burden ceased to be enforceable by the developer-superior and, unless it was a facility burden, was not enforceable by anyone at all. **Held**: That the burden was not a facility burden in respect that, while the land was a facility which conferred benefit on the houses, there had not been the requisite intention to confer such benefit which is needed for a facility burden. See **Commentary** p 125.

(25) Sheltered Housing Management Ltd v Bon Accord Bonding Co Ltd
[2010] CSIH 42, 2010 SC 516, 2010 SLT 662

Until the appointed day for feudal abolition (28 November 2004), a sheltered housing development in Cults, Aberdeen, was factored by the superior, Sheltered Housing Management Ltd ('SHML'). After the appointed day, the owners exercised their powers under s 28(1) of the Title Conditions (Scotland) Act 2003 to replace SHML, choosing instead Peverel Ltd. They also drew up a new deed of conditions to replace the original one, which had been couched in feudal terms and had involved the management of the development by the superior.

One of the key changes in the new deed was a provision that certain parts of the development belonging to SHML – the warden's flat, warden's office, guest bedrooms, a garage, a potting shed and certain store rooms – were to be used only for purposes ancillary to the development. Thus the warden's flat, for example, was to be used only for occupation by the warden. In exchange, the other owners were to pay £6,000 a year, with a provision for upwards adjustments in line with the RPI.

Naturally, SHML was opposed to the change. But under s 33 of the 2003 Act – read, in the case of sheltered housing, with s 54(5)(b) – existing community burdens can be varied by the owners of two thirds of the units in the community. In the present case, two thirds of the owners had signed the deed. On the other hand, changes made under s 33 can be challenged by means of an application to the Lands Tribunal under s 90(1)(c), and SHML duly applied to have the existing deed of conditions preserved unchanged. The application was refused and £9,178 was awarded to SHML by way of compensation: see 2007 GWD 32-533 (*Conveyancing 2006* Case (35)) and decision of 11 October 2007 (*Conveyancing 2007* Case (21)).

On appeal to the Inner House, SHML argued that the new deed was incompetent in respect that variation under s 33 was only permissible in respect of properties where there was something to vary. But SHML's properties were wholly unburdened. An Extra Division of the Court of Session has now accepted this argument and allowed the application for preservation of the existing deed. See **Commentary** p 116. We understand that there is to be an appeal to the Supreme Court.

(26) Peverel Scotland Ltd v Giffen
April 2010, Elgin Sheriff Court

The pursuer was the factor in a residential development; the defender was one of the owners. Back in 2001 the defender had terminated his contract with the pursuer. In this small claims action the pursuer sought to recover its charges for the period after 28 November 2004, on the basis that, after that date, its appointment could be regarded as having been renewed by a majority of owners under s 28 of the Title Conditions (Scotland) Act 2003. It was **held** that there had been no such renewal of appointment and accordingly that nothing was due. See **Commentary** p 121.

(27) Snowie v Museum Hall LLP
[2010] CSOH 107, 2010 SLT 971

A real burden forbidding use (including ancillary use) for any trade, business or profession was interpreted as allowing such use provided it was unobtrusive in character. Furthermore, such a burden was not repugnant with ownership. See **Commentary** pp 114 and 123.

[Another aspect of this case is digested at (7) above.]

(28) Strathclyde Business Park (Management) Ltd v BAE Systems Pension
Funds Trustees Ltd
2010 GWD 39-791, Sh Ct

Clause 11 of the deed of conditions (registered in 1991) governing Strathclyde Business Park provided that:

> No proprietor shall be permitted, without obtaining the prior written consent of the Promoter (which consent shall not be unreasonably withheld or delayed) to erect upon the Site including any building thereon, any signs, logos, devices, advertisements, notices or others.

When BAE, as owner of one of the units, erected some signage, Strathclyde Business Park (Management) Ltd ('SBPM'), as 'promoter' of the Park, sought and obtained interim interdict. In this appeal, BAE sought recall.

Recall was granted by the temporary sheriff principal (Charles N Stoddart) for the following reasons. (1) As SBPM did not own any part of the Park, it had no title to sue on its own account: see s 8(1) of the Title Conditions (Scotland) Act 2003. Further, it could not be said to have been appointed as manager by a majority of the owners under s 28 of the Act because no meeting had taken place. At best, there was a stateable case that SBPM had been authorised by letter to act on behalf of the owner of one other of the units. (2) There were no averments of interest to enforce in respect of that owner. (3) Section 73(2A) of the Abolition of Feudal Tenure etc (Scotland) Act 2000 provides that 'any provision . . . to the effect that a person other than the person entitled to enforce the burden may waive compliance with, or mitigate or otherwise vary a condition of, the burden shall be disregarded'. Accordingly, the part of clause 11 providing for the promoter's prior written consent fell to be disregarded. This was 'fatal' to SBPM's invocation of the clause (para 33). (4) Particularly in view of the weakness of SBPM's *prima facie* case, the balance of convenience did not favour the granting of interim interdict.

While the decision seems correct, more might be said in relation to (3). The view that s 73(2A) excises the consent provision but otherwise leaves the clause untouched had already been reached by the Lands Tribunal in *At.Home Nationwide Ltd v Morris* 2007 GWD 31-535 (*Conveyancing 2006* Case (22)), a case that was not drawn to the attention of the court. It follows that clause 11 could not give SBPM an independent right of enforcement. But, if it could be established, SBPM's right of enforcement as agent of another owner would remain. And, shorn of the consent provision, clause 11 would continue to be enforceable on behalf of such an owner. As was said in *At.Home Nationwide Ltd* (at p 9 of the transcript), 'it seems to be accepted that section 73(2A) has the effect of simply excising the reference to the superior's consent, leaving a prohibition, enforceable at least by neighbours who can show an interest'. It may be, therefore, that SBPM will yet succeed in this litigation.

In a note published in the *Journal of the Law Society of Scotland* for January 2011 (p 53), Eric Baijal comments in relation to this case (at p 55): 'The legal principles appear straightforward in hindsight. However, their application is extremely challenging. The fact that the case made it to the sheriff principal reflects the continuing unease caused by, and the complexity found in, the 2000 and 2003 Acts.'

(29) I & H Brown Ltd, Applicants
28 April 2010, Lands Tr

A provision in a disposition requiring the disponee to pay 30% of the uplift value in the event of planning consent was **held** to be invalid as a real burden. See **Commentary** p 127.

(30) Barr v Macrae
30 November 2010, Lands Tr

By a disposition recorded in 1908 the owners of Viewfield House conveyed an adjoining area of land. Among the burdens was the following:

> Our said disponee and her foresaids in dealing with or laying out the subjects hereby disponed shall be and are hereby expressly prohibited from rearing or planting any trees opposite the south front of said Viewfield House and between such front and Viewfield Terrace on the south, which may in the opinion of us or our successors be fairly calculated to impair the light in the windows in said front or reduce the letting value of said Viewfield House.

It was **held** that the burden was enforceable by the current owners of Viewfield House (which had now been flatted) on the basis of the rule in *J A Mactaggart & Co v Harrower* (1906) 8 F 1101, not least because 'the wording of the provision appears to confirm the implication in the references to Viewfield House' (para 16). As the Tribunal pointed out, however, unless a notice of preservation is registered, the enforcement right will be extinguished on 28 November 2014 (Title Conditions (Scotland) Act 2003 s 49(2)).

PRE-EMPTIONS

(31) Howatson v Whyte
14 July 1992, Forfar Sheriff Court

Matters were so arranged that, in buying land which was subject to a right of pre-emption and also other, adjacent land, the purchaser made two separate offers through two separate companies, splitting the combined price in such a way that the price for the pre-emption land was disproportionately high. As a result the pre-emption holders could not afford to exercise their rights. They sued the seller for damages. **Held**: that in pre-emptions there was an implied term that any offer to purchase the affected property must be acceptable, at arm's length and *bona fide*, and unconnected with any other offer. That term had been breached in the present case. Damages were therefore awarded. See **Commentary** p 166. (Although decided in 1992, this decision has only recently been brought to our attention.)

VARIATION ETC OF TITLE CONDITIONS BY LANDS TRIBUNAL

(32) Tower Hotel (Troon) Ltd v McCann
4 March 2010, Lands Tr

This decision may mark a return to an approach from which the Tribunal appeared to have moved away. If so it is to be regretted.

Among the factors which the Tribunal is directed to consider by s 100 of the Title Conditions (Scotland) Act 2003 is 'the purpose of the title condition' (factor (f)). And at one time there was a tendency to tie in this purpose to the crucial factor (b) ('the extent to which the condition confers benefit on the benefited property'), with the result that a benefit was disregarded if it was not within the original purpose of the condition. This was a particular problem for burdens imposed in grants in feu. For on the one hand, the enforcement rights formerly held by superiors were, in many cases, reallocated by the Act to neighbours; but on the other hand, the purpose of such burdens, so far as discernible, was often to protect the amenity of the area in general rather than the amenity of those very neighbours who now had enforcement rights. Thus, if factor (b) was coupled with factor (f), the result was virtually to eliminate factor (b), for although neighbours took benefit it was, at it were, benefit of the wrong kind. And without factor (b), the main weapon of objectors, there was little prospect of successful resistance to an application for variation or discharge. We have criticised this approach in the past: see eg *Conveyancing 2007* p 92. There are three main objections. First, it is not sanctioned by the legislation: there is nothing in the Title Conditions Act to suggest that one factor should trump, indeed virtually eliminate, another. Secondly, it supposes that the Act, having conferred enforcement rights on neighbours, intended that such rights could be discharged without further ado by the Tribunal. In other words, it supposes a curious policy inconsistency. Thirdly, it depends on the purpose of burdens being readily discernible which, often, it is not.

The new decision illustrates some of the difficulties. Land was feued in 1965 for the building of either a hotel or a single house. A hotel was built. Further conditions in the feu disposition restricted the use of the existing building to a hotel or house, and prevented any further building without the superiors' consent. When the feudal system was abolished, enforcement rights passed to neighbours (or at least this was assumed to be the case for the purposes of the application). Wishing to sell the property and attract as much interest as possible, the owner applied to the Tribunal for the discharge of the conditions. The application was opposed by two close neighbours.

The Tribunal began by considering factor (f) (purpose of the conditions) because 'this can inform us when we consider the remaining relevant factors' (para 31). But finding the purpose, the Tribunal conceded, can be hard (para 31):

> In many cases, however, there is no clear statement of what the original intention was when putting in the conditions. In these cases, because of what we see as the importance attaching to purpose, we normally endeavour to reach a conclusion on

what this purpose might be from whatever is available elsewhere in the constitutive deed. In this particular case determining the purpose of the use restriction has not been easy. There is nothing elsewhere in the Feu Disposition which offers assistance.

Rather hesitantly, the Tribunal concluded that 'it is possible that there may have been some general amenity consideration in limiting other possible uses' (para 32). Later, however, the Tribunal seems to have changed its mind, deciding that the purpose was to ensure there was a mixed element in the development of housing in the area (para 38). But while the Tribunal seemed uncertain as to what the purpose of the conditions might be, it had no such doubts as to what the purpose was not. '[W]e are clear', said the Tribunal (para 32), 'that there is no indication of any purpose either of protecting the visual amenity of neighbours or of securing the presence of licensed facilities for the benefit of local residents.' No reason is given for a conclusion which, while expressed with confidence, seems no more than speculation.

Nothing daunted, the Tribunal proceeded to use this conclusion in its consideration of factor (b) (extent of benefit). Naturally enough, the objectors focused particularly on protection to their amenity. But, warned the Tribunal (para 30), '[m]any of their concerns falling within the amenity category might be misplaced in an objection to the discharge of a restrictive condition in a title, if these concerns are not ones which the particular condition safeguards'. More precisely (para 34):

> there is nothing in the condition which gives to the respondents the right to the view they currently enjoy from the upstairs rear of their property to the hills of Arran. There is equally no reference to a right of privacy or of protection of the extent of daylight enjoyed by them.

In reaching this view the Tribunal was influenced by the purpose of the conditions, as mentioned earlier. But it was also influenced by what it took to be their rather limited effect (para 34):

> Putting it starkly, if the applicants wished to build a multi-storeyed hotel on their grounds or to redevelop all of their land, nothing in the title condition could assist the respondents in any opposition to such plans provided the use conformed to that in the title.

This, however, seems simply incorrect, for among the burdens in the feu disposition was the following blanket prohibition of development:

> (Tertio) No outbuilding or other additional building or erection of any kind whatsoever, whether permanent or temporary, (other than the walls and fences hereinaftermentioned) shall be erected or placed on the feu without the consent of the said Trustees or their foresaids.

Factor (b) having thus been so comprehensively disposed of, it was a foregone conclusion that the applicants would be granted their discharge. The result may, of course, be correct, but the reasoning employed seems unsatisfactory.

(33) Corstorphine v Fleming
2 July 2010, Lands Tr

1 Horseleys Park, St Andrews is at the beginning of a crescent of 20 houses all built in the 1960s and all governed by identical conditions in the split-off feu dispositions. These prevent alterations and restrict the site to one house only. Wishing to extend the original house and also to build a second, the owners of number 1 applied for the discharge of these conditions. The application was opposed by their immediate neighbours at number 2 and also by seven further owners.

The Tribunal had no difficulty with the proposed new house, which would 'have virtually no impact – certainly no significant impact – on the other Horseleys Park owners, and also … fit in perfectly acceptably with the other houses in its immediate vicinity' (para 36). The extension was a different matter. This would constitute a significant increase in the building mass, create a substantially larger building with a much higher roof-line than any of the other houses in the crescent, and have some impact on number 2. Nonetheless, on balance the Tribunal was willing to grant the application, although this would only be a variation and not the complete discharge sought. The following analysis of the competing considerations is a representative example of the careful and nuanced way in which the Tribunal goes about its task (para 53):

> Ultimately … it seems to us that the effect within No.2 will be quite limited. In the garden, the mass of the extension will be quite visible, but what has particularly swayed us is the present situation with which the extension is to be compared. No.2 is a house on a narrow plot whose side aspects make little or no contribution to its amenity: it is a house which draws its amenity from the front and the back. In so far as there is an outlook to the side, it is already of a built environment, partly consisting of No.2's garage. The effect on the patio area of No.2 will also be quite limited. The existing impact of No.1 is not particularly favourable. While there will be some effect on light, there will not in our view be any significant overshadowing or loss of sunlight. As far as the more general impact on the crescent is considered, we would regard this very differently if this house was in the middle, or main part, of the crescent, but it is already at the end and slightly isolated. We have reached the view that the additional impact of the extension, while again noticeable, will also be quite limited. In these circumstances, we do not think that it will conflict in any significant way with the purpose of the conditions and we think that the degree of impediment to the applicants in not being able to carry out a development for which they have planning permission outweighs the benefit to the objectors of being able to prevent it.

In view of the approach taken in the previous case, it should be recorded that the Tribunal treats factor (f) (the purpose of the condition) as just another factor rather than one which controls the others and in particular factor (b) (extent of benefit). The Tribunal's analysis on this point deserves to be quoted in full (para 49):

> The purpose of the title condition can be of considerable significance. If a condition can be seen to have been imposed for the particular protection of another property, for example when part of a garden is sold for the development of another house

and the seller seeks to protect the particular amenity of the original house, or when something in the expression of the condition reveals a particular purpose, for example protection of a view, it is important to consider whether the condition is still achieving the particular purpose and how the proposal looks against the purpose. In this case, the condition imposed by the local authority when apparently selling individual plots in the area is more generally expressed in standard terms. However, there would, we think, have been a concept of the type of development in the area and an intention to create and then preserve its amenity. So the purpose, as we see it, was one of generally protecting the amenity of the locality, including that of the houses in the locality. It was therefore in this case a purpose not dissimilar to general planning control. The purpose, however, clearly remains relevant because the amenity has been well preserved.

(34) Corry v Maclachlan
9 July 2010 (merits), 7 October 2010 (expenses), Lands Tr

In 1984 part of the garden ground of Mansefield, Main Street, Gargunnock, was sold to allow the building of a house. In terms of the split-off disposition, there was to be built within two years 'a good and substantial dwellinghouse not exceeding one storey in height, in accordance with plans and specifications produced by our said disponees and their foresaids to us and approved by us'. The disponees now wished to add a second floor. This involved removing the existing roof and increasing the height of the walls, as a result of which the roof height would be increased by about 1.7 metres. Their application for a variation of the condition was opposed by the current owners of Mansefield.

The Tribunal emphasised that reasonableness must be viewed objectively (para 25):

The applicants' personal reasons for wishing this extension are of no particular concern. Equally, the respondents' personal feelings do not necessarily reflect an objective view. In this case, perhaps not unusually, we did feel that the respondents' concerns, both in their written submissions and in Miss Paynton's oral evidence, were somewhat exaggerated. Considering that the setting of their house is already affected to quite a degree by the applicants' house, we do not agree that the extension proposals would have a 'dramatic' effect, nor do we accept that the increased overlooking would have as much effect on the respondents' privacy as they, no doubt genuinely, think.

Nonetheless, the Tribunal accepted both that the mass and height of the extension would have a substantial effect on Mansefield (factor (b)) and also that this was exactly the sort of thing the condition was designed to prevent (factor (f)). And while the condition undoubtedly impeded the applicants' enjoyment of their property (factor (c)), they already had a large and attractive house, there was no suggestion of any need to modernise it, and it would be possible to extend at ground-floor level or at any rate in a less intrusive manner. The application was refused.

The respondents sought and were awarded expenses for preparation of and attendance at the hearing. Only the respondents, however, had used counsel and the Tribunal declined to sanction such use for what 'seemed to us to be an ordinary type of case with no legal or factual complexity' (para 8).

It may be that the applicants can go ahead with the extension in any case, a point to which the Tribunal was alert (see para 29). The burden takes the form of an affirmative obligation and not a restriction: it says what the disponees must do and not what they must not. As the single-storey house was built in accordance with the burden's terms, the burden appears to be spent, and, unless there is some other restriction in the disposition, it is arguable that there is nothing to prevent the extension. In that connection it should be borne in mind that, in the law of real burdens, restrictions need to be express and cannot usually arise by implication: see K G C Reid, *The Law of Property in Scotland* (1996) para 417.

(35) Kennedy v Abbey Lane Properties
29 March 2010, Lands Tr

The owner of a main-door flat sought to have a deed of conditions varied so as to relieve him of liability for maintaining the common passages and stairs. The application was refused. See **Commentary** p 97.

Among the reasons given by the Tribunal was that purchasers buy properties with their eyes open (para 42):

> [P]urchasers were, of course, free to form their own view as to the extent of any unfairness and to walk away from a purchase. We can therefore assume that all current owners must have formed the view that the allocation percentages were acceptable in the context of their purchase.

This, however, must always be true of applicants to the Tribunal, except for those who received the property by gift or inheritance.

(36) Co-operative Group Ltd v Propinvest Asset Management
17 September 2010, Lands Tr

This was a preliminary hearing in an application by the tenant under a 125-year lease of a unit in a shopping centre in Paisley for the variation or discharge of a number of conditions, including a keep-open clause. The unit required to be used as a 'high quality retail departmental store' and the applicants (the Co-op), having withdrawn from the department store market, wanted to maximise the unit's value for the purposes of sale.

The respondent, who was the landlord, raised some preliminary points. One concerned competency. While most Tribunal applications involve real burdens or servitudes, the Tribunal has power, under s 90(1)(a)(i) of the Title Conditions (Scotland) Act 2003, to vary or discharge any title condition; and among the obligations listed in s 122(1) as 'title conditions' is 'a condition in a registrable lease if it is a condition which relates to the land (but not a condition which imposes either an obligation to pay rent or an obligation of relief relating to the payment of rent)'. This provision did not change the law although the former legislation was differently worded: under the Conveyancing and Feudal Reform (Scotland) Act 1970 s 1(2) the Tribunal had jurisdiction in respect of obligations 'relating to land'. It was argued for the respondent that a distinction must be made between (i) conditions which benefited the fundamental or 'property' interest of the land and (ii) those which benefited only the landlord's 'commercial' interest for as long as the lease subsisted. Only the former could be said to 'relate to land'. Unsurprisingly, this submission was rejected by the Tribunal, on the basis that it was necessary to consider the interest of the tenant as well as that of the landlord, and that from the tenant's perspective it was plain that the conditions in question (like other conditions in a standard lease) related to land. Indeed (though no one seems to have made the point), given that conditions which relate to land, in the Tribunal's sense, are precisely those which run with the lease and bind successors, it would be surprising if some of them were exempt from the Tribunal's jurisdiction.

Another issue raised for the respondent was the proper meaning of factor (c) ('the extent to which the condition impedes enjoyment of the burdened property'). The applicant had made averments as to the effect of the conditions on the marketability or value of the lease, but, in the respondent's view, ability to dispose of the land was not 'enjoyment' of it. The Tribunal disagreed. It had always taken a wide view of what constituted 'enjoyment', and that certainly included making the property more marketable or valuable.

(37) Chisholm v Crawford
17 June 2010 (merits), 12 August 2010 (expenses), Lands Tr

Two end-terraced council houses, numbers 32 and 34 Dunn Place, Winchburgh, West Lothian, were separated by a strip of land some 16 feet in width. The boundary was the half-way point. An access driveway leading, ultimately, to the garage to the rear of number 32 ran down the centre of the strip. When the houses came to be sold under the right-to-buy legislation, the acquirer of number 32 was given a servitude right of vehicular access over that part of the driveway which belonged to number 34. No matching servitude was conferred on the acquirer of number 34.

The owner of number 34 sought the discharge of the servitude. The application, which was opposed by the owners of number 32, was refused. The Tribunal found (factor (b)) that the servitude conferred considerable benefit on number 32 in respect that, without it and so by using only their own land, the owners would have difficulty in reaching their garage. Conversely, the burden on number 34 was relatively slight (factor (c)) and, while the absence of a reciprocal right was certainly a matter worthy of consideration, the applicant had made clear that she was not seeking such a right. A change in circumstances (factor (a)), namely the growth in car ownership which had put a premium on off-street parking, was another factor which favoured the respondents. Expenses were awarded against the applicant.

(38) Parkin v Kennedy
23 March 2010 (merits), 18 May 2010 (expenses), Lands Tr

An end-terraced house in Port Charlotte, Islay, was subject to a servitude right of way in favour of the other houses in the terrace over a road which ran immediately at the back of the house. Wishing to extend the house, the owners applied to have the servitude (i) re-routed round the back of the proposed extension and (ii) restricted to a right of pedestrian access. The immediately adjacent owner objected.

There was no difficulty as to (i). In the Tribunal's words (para 31):

> There have been several applications to us involving such a proposal to move the line of a right of way, most notably from former local authority houses where similar rights of way exist in favour of the mid-terraced houses. In such cases, it can often be seen that the purpose of the servitude is just as well fulfilled by the proposed alternative route as by the existing prescribed route, so that preserving the existing route is of no, or at least extremely slight, benefit to the dominant proprietor. Such applications therefore often go in favour of the applicant, principally on the basis that the impediment of not being able to proceed with an extension for which a planning consent has been granted far outweighs the extent of the benefit to the benefited proprietor in retaining an existing access route.

But (ii) was a different matter. Having a right of vehicular access benefited the adjacent house 'to a considerable degree' (para 44) and no doubt added value to the house (factor (b)). In the absence of such a right (para 43), 'the respondent would be unable to bring his car to the back door of his house. While the servitude no doubt does not itself involve a right to park, it does enable the respondent to park near the back door of his house. It also facilitates other deliveries, such as coal or oil or other bulky items.' Alternative accesses were far less attractive. Of course, to refuse the application would involve hardship to the applicants (factor (c)) and would prevent a development for which they had planning permission (factor (g)). But the balance of advantage lay with refusing the application. Indeed, this was one of those cases where not even an award of compensation would allow the application to be granted. Expenses were awarded against the applicants.

[Another aspect of this case is digested at (22) above.]

(39) ATD Developments Ltd v Weir
14 September 2010, Lands Tr

The site of a former school was divided into plots in 2002 and sold. The plot owned by the applicant included a part of the former playground, still in its original state, over which the owners of other plots had a servitude right of access. The applicant obtained planning permission for the erection of six houses, but their gardens would encroach to a significant extent on to the former playground. The application was to restrict the servitude to the non-garden area. This left a route 5.5 metres wide at the road end and 3 metres wide at the other end. In addition, the benefited proprietors had a right to take access over the rest of the former playground (which was not the property of the applicant).

Although the application was initially opposed, it was now unopposed. Nonetheless, as it concerned servitudes and not real burdens (for which unopposed applications can generally be granted without further inquiry: see Title Conditions (Scotland) Act 2003 s 97), the Tribunal was obliged to consider the application on its merits. The Tribunal had little difficulty in granting the application. On the one hand, the servitude constituted a severe restriction on the applicant's enjoyment of its property (factor (c)); on the other hand, the benefited proprietors would suffer little disadvantage from the proposed restriction.

(40) Scott v Teasdale
19 April 2010, Lands Tr

The applicants had lost on the merits (decision of 22 December 2009 (*Conveyancing 2009* Case (32)) but asked the Tribunal to modify the expenses on the basis that their application had been both reasonable in itself and conducted in a reasonable way. The Tribunal rejected this argument and awarded expenses against the applicants. As the Tribunal pointed out (para 11), applications 'may very often be characterised as reasonable, particularly no doubt where they [the applicants] have planning permission, but that in itself is of little or no avail if they do not succeed. The rationale of the expenses rule is that the party who does not succeed has caused expense to the successful party.'

The applicants and also one of the respondents had used counsel. The Tribunal was narrowly persuaded to sanction the respondent's use of counsel partly because of the significance of the issues to the respondents and partly because the title conditions were slightly outside the usual run of building restrictions.

(41) Gibb v Kerr
12 March 2010, Lands Tr

When this case was first heard, the applicant was awarded expenses but reduced by 50% to take account of the applicant having already carried out the works and the fact that she did not achieve complete success. See decision of 26 November 2009 (*Conveyancing 2009* Case (41)). As taxed, this amounted to £1,556.06. The respondent, who received legal aid in respect of her own expenses, enrolled a motion under s 18(2) of the Legal Aid (Scotland) Act 1986 to have the award of expenses modified. Section 18(2) provides that, in awarding expenses against a person who was legally assisted, the court should restrict the amount to what is reasonable for the person to pay having regard to all the circumstances including the means of all the parties and their conduct in connection with the dispute. The Tribunal had considered conduct in making its original award. It now fell to it to consider the parties' means.

Neither party was well-off, although on the limited evidence available it seemed that the applicant was slightly better placed. The Tribunal concluded that, while weight had to be given to the respondent's very limited resources, the fact was that she had persisted with very little real grounds in opposing the application. The Tribunal reduced the award of expenses to £1,000.

(42) G v A
10 February 2010 (compensation), 24 August 2010 (expenses), Lands Tr

In an earlier hearing, the Tribunal discharged a servitude of way on the basis that compensation would be paid: see decision of 26 November 2009 (*Conveyancing 2009* Case (40)). Compensation was needed because, while the respondent had an alternative access to his property, the now discharged route was needed if he was to gain access to his garage by vehicle. The garage could still be reached on foot and so used as a store but it could not be used to park the respondent's car.

By s 90(7)(a)(i) of the Title Conditions (Scotland) Act 2003 the sum to be awarded was 'to compensate for any substantial loss or disadvantage suffered by … the owner, as owner of the benefited property … in consequence of the discharge or variation'. Normally, compensation would be measured by reference to reduction in value (para 9). But the respondent wanted the cost of cure and proposed three possible bases: (i) repositioning of the garage door so as to be accessible from another access route; (ii) demolition and replacement of the garage; and (iii) retention of the existing garage but construction of a new one. All three options were expensive, and numbers (ii) and (iii), the Tribunal noted, would lead to 'such substantial betterment as to make an award on this basis unjust'. There could also be no guarantee that the respondent would use the money for the claimed purpose. Instead the Tribunal made an award of £7,500 to reflect diminution in value.

Although the applicant was successful on the merits and the respondent in relation to compensation (at least in the sense of having beaten a 'tender'), no expenses were awarded to either side (para 11):

> Had the applicant acknowledged that the discharge would cause loss to the respondent and proceeded on the basis that he should receive appropriate compensation, we would in all probability have awarded expenses of the merits stage in her favour, but she did not. Had the respondent claimed compensation at an earlier stage, we may well have made some award of expenses in his favour, but he did not. Having considered, other, more discriminating disposals on expenses, we have reached the view that no award either way properly reflects the parties' respective conduct of these proceedings.

Sanction for counsel was refused.

(43) Faeley v Doull
19 November 2010, Lands Tr

This case is a successor to *Faeley v Clark* 2006 GWD 28-626 (*Conveyancing 2006* Case (29)). That case mainly concerned a burden in a disposition of 1967 of an area which included but extended beyond the applicants' property. The burden prohibited further building. The original application having been refused, the applicants brought a new application with a revised proposal for the second house which they wished to build. Agreement was reached in respect of the application except for this claim for compensation by one of the benefited proprietors. This concerned a similar burden in a later disposition, of 1990, of the land belonging to the applicants.

The claim was made under s 90(7)(b) of the Title Conditions (Scotland) Act 2003 ('a sum to make up for any effect which the title condition produced, at the time when it was created, in reducing the consideration then paid or made payable for the burdened property'). The Tribunal refused the claim. In order for such a claim to succeed it was necessary to show (i) that there was 'hope value' in the prospect, however distant, of being able to build a second house, (ii) that the imposition of the condition, as a direct impediment to the possible development, had the effect of reducing the price paid for the property, and (iii) that the reduction could be properly valued. But no evidence had been brought in support of (i) and indeed the access difficulties at the site were so severe as to make a second house rather unlikely. Similarly, there was no evidence as to (ii) (para 25):

> A burden such as this is commonly created when land is sold to build a house. ... [T]here is nothing to indicate that the building restriction was not simply a standard imposition of such a burden in such circumstances. There is no evidence of any valuation of this land, with or without hope value, at the time of this transaction. There is no evidence of any acknowledgement or appreciation of this hope factor. It was a transaction between friends, without any exposure to the market. Speculation about conscious consideration at the time of this transaction of the possibility of another house does not, as it seems to us, necessarily lead in the direction of supporting this claim.

As to (iii), the figure claimed – £7,500 (10% of the value of the land (£3,500) as adjusted for inflation) – was just plucked from the air and was not supported by valuation evidence. In any event (para 15), 'the legislation does not apparently allow for such inflation so that the most we could award if we upheld the claim would be £3,500, apparently without interest'.

PUBLIC RIGHTS OF WAY AND ACCESS RIGHTS

(44) Hamilton v Nairn
[2010] CSIH 77, 2010 SLT 1155

The pursuers were in the process of buying land near Aberdeen. The land abutted a public road but was separated from it by a verge of up to 7 or 8 metres. Part of this verge was grassed and maintained by the council, but closer to the pursuers' land the verge was rough grassland and scrub and overgrown in places. A track, capable of taking vehicles, led from the pursuers' land across the verge to the public road. The junction was marked by a bell mouth. The defender, apparently opposed to the use to which the pursuers now proposed to put the land (a cattery and livery stables), bought the verge and challenged the pursuers' right to take access over it. The access had not been in place for long enough for a servitude to have been established by prescription.

The extent of the public road, as listed, included the whole of the verge right up to the boundary of the pursuers' land, and it was conceded for the defender that the whole verge was a 'verge' for the purposes of the Roads (Scotland) Act 1984 and hence, by s 151(1), part of the road. After a proof it was **held** that a public right of passage had been constituted over the verge by use for the prescriptive period (eg for horse riding or by vehicles having to move to the side of the (narrow) road to let an oncoming vehicle past). Hence the pursuers (as members of the public) were entitled to take access in that way. More controversially, Lord Glennie further indicated that, if a road is subject to a public right of passage and adopted, that right must be taken to extend to the whole road as adopted, including the verge: see [2009] CSOH 163, 2010 SLT 399 (*Conveyancing 2009* Case (51)).

The defender appealed but an Extra Division adhered. Both of the Lord Ordinary's grounds of decision were **held** to be correct, the Extra Division emphasising the practical importance of allowing those whose land fronted a public road to take direct access to that road. The Extra Division continued (para 22):

> It is understandable why Parliament considered it appropriate to include the verge in the definition of a road, thereby conferring a public right of passage over the verge. There will be many situations where it is in the interests of safety that road users should have a right of passage over verges. Indeed in the present case, where the metalled carriageway is too narrow to permit the safe passage of two vehicles, one or both vehicles may need to mount a verge to enable them to pass in safety. Moreover, in the context of a country road, pedestrians might elect to walk on the verge in the interests of their own safety. We reject the suggestion by counsel for the reclaimer that, if they did so, they would be trespassing. A verge is an integral part of the road. It may accommodate utilities, traffic signs and sight lines for farm vehicles exiting fields or farm tracks. As in this case, it may be essential for the drainage of the road including the accommodation of a ditch to remove surface water draining from the road on to the verge.

Two points may be added. First, the question of what is or is not verge may be a matter of dispute, as it initially was in this case. For an example of where disputed land was held *not* to be part of the verge, thus denying the frontager access, see *Elmford Ltd v City of Glasgow Council (No 2)* 2001 SC 267 (*Conveyancing 2000* Case (17)). Secondly, one of the reclaimer's arguments was (para 10) that 'the Lord Ordinary had erred in suggesting that the listing of a road under section 1 of the 1984 Act is conclusive of the issue whether there is a public right of way'. In the event, this argument was not discussed by the appeal court but, standing the decision in *Hamilton v Dumfries and Galloway Council (No 2)* 2009 SC 277, it seems plainly correct (see *Conveyancing 2009* p 157).

EXECUTION OF DEEDS

(45) Gibson v Gibson
2010 GWD 30-614, Sh Ct

In 2006 the pursuer sold a house to the defenders (her daughter and her daughter's boyfriend) for £35,000. Formal missives were concluded. The figure of £35,000 was used as being the maximum amount the defenders were able to borrow at that time. As, however, the house was valued at £58,000, there was, the pursuer averred, an additional, unwritten agreement that the defenders would pay the 'balance' of £23,000 in the event of a future sale. It was this agreement that the pursuer now sought to enforce.

The agreement was **held** to be unenforceable due to lack of formality. It was either an additional term of the missives or a gratuitous unilateral obligation. If the first, it required to be in formal writing just like the missives themselves (Contract (Scotland) Act 1997 s 1(4)); if the second, it, equally, required to be in formal writing unless in the course of business, which it was not (Requirements of Writing (Scotland) Act 1995 s 1(2)(a)(ii)).

[Another aspect of this case is digested at (2) above.]

(46) Low & Bonar plc v Mercer Ltd
[2010] CSOH 47, 2010 GWD 16-321

A pension scheme could only be altered by 'deed'. In deciding that the minutes of a board meeting signed by the chairman were a 'deed' for this purpose, Lord Drummond Young discussed the meaning of 'deed' in Scots law (para 16):

> [I]t is clear that the word 'deed' has no technical meaning in Scots law. In *Henderson's Trs v IRC* 1913 SC 987, a case dealing with the question of whether a minute of acceptance of office by trustees engrossed upon a trust disposition and settlement was a deed for the purposes of the Stamp Act 1891, LP Dunedin stated (at 989):

>> 'Now the Stamp Act does not define what a deed is, and I think it unnecessary to consider whether the word "deed" is there used as a term of art, because in any case it is only in England that it is so used. I am quite content to take "deed" as being used in the popular sense. The statute has not defined what a deed is, nor am I tempted to give a definition, but I am certainly clearly of opinion that, whatever is a deed, this acceptance of trust is not.'

> Lord Kinnear stated (at 990):

>> 'I am entirely of the same opinion, and I agree with your Lordship that for the purpose of this case the word "deed" is a word of ordinary language, because it is not in our system a term of art. I agree also that it is unnecessary to attempt any exact definition of what the word "deed" means; but I take the definition which was suggested in the ingenious argument for the Inland Revenue, in which it was said that a deed was any formal instrument which creates a legal relation.'

> In *Lennie v Lennie's Trs* 1914 1 SLT 258, Lord Dewar quoted from the last case and continued (at 260):

>> 'In the absence of any definition of what a deed is, the question just comes to be whether it is reasonable to suppose that a business man would regard a pencil jotting on the back of an envelope as a "deed". I do not think that he would. He would never think of calling it a deed in ordinary conversation or speak of it as he would of his title "deeds" or trust "deed" or "deed" of co-partnery. The word "deed" would, I think, suggest to his mind some document his solicitors prepared, or at all events something of a much more formal character that we have here.'

It is unnecessary for present purposes to attempt any definition of the word 'deed'. Nevertheless, I take from these cases that the significant characteristics of a deed are first that it should have some degree of formality and secondly that it must demonstrate an intention to create a legal relation. These are the two features highlighted by Lord Kinnear, and it seems to me that they convey the essence of the expression.

TRANSFER OF OWNERSHIP

(47) Marquess of Linlithgow v Commissioners for HM Revenue and Customs
[2010] CSIH 19, 2010 SC 391

It has long been accepted that for the purposes of tax law, the way that the transfer of property is analysed does not necessarily match the ordinary rules of the law of property. In particular, the effective date of a transfer tends to be treated as the date on which the disposition is delivered rather than – as in ordinary property law – the date on which it is registered. See *Thomas v Lord Advocate* 1953 SC 151 and, more generally, K G C Reid, 'Ownership on delivery' 1982 SLT (News) 149. *Marquess of Linlithgow* is the latest case in this line, and the first after the landmark decision of the House of Lords in *Burnett's Tr v Grainger* 2004 SC (HL) 19 (discussed in *Conveyancing 2004* pp 78–79).

In order to gain an exemption from inheritance tax it was necessary that a 'transfer of value' was made before 22 March 2006. But while a (gratuitous) disposition was delivered before that date it was not recorded until after. Did the disposition attract the exemption? By s 3(1) of the Inheritance Tax Act 1984 'a transfer of value is a disposition made by a person (the transferor) as a result of which the value of his estate immediately after the disposition is less than it would be but for the disposition', and a person's 'estate' is defined, in s 5(1), as 'the aggregate of all the property to which he is beneficially entitled'.

Following *Burnett's Tr v Grainger*, the argument for the Revenue was based on orthodox principles of property law. As summarised by Lord Reed, giving the Opinion of an Extra Division of the Court of Session, it was as follows (para 11):

> The Revenue's argument ... was based primarily on the contention that the granter remains beneficially entitled to the property, and that it therefore continues to form part of his estate. In support of that contention, counsel for the Revenue submitted that the delivery of a disposition did not have the effect of vesting any right of property in the disponee; nor did it make the granter of the disposition a trustee of the subjects. It followed that the granter remained 'beneficially entitled' to the 'property', as those expressions were understood in Scots law. The concept of beneficial entitlement, in particular, had no meaning in Scots law outside the context of the law of trusts. Reliance was placed on Lord Hope's statement in *Burnett's Tr* (para 51) that, following the delivery of an unrecorded disposition, 'the real right in the property of which [the granter] was the beneficial owner remained vested in her'.

But such an approach, the court said, was 'misconceived' (para 12), being based 'upon the premise that the words "property" and "beneficially entitled" in section 5(1) of the 1984 Act, bear the same meaning as in the Scots law of property' whereas they have their own special meaning. Indeed counsel on both sides were taken to task for focusing on the Scots law of property instead of 'the correct approach to the interpretation of the statute' (para 7). In England, the court said, there could be no question that, on facts such as the present, a transfer of value would have been made. The result in Scotland was the same. According to s 5(2) of the Act, a person is beneficially entitled to property if he 'has a general power which enables him … to dispose of [the] property, or to charge money on [the] property'. Following the analysis by Lord Rodger at paras 101 and 102 of *Burnett's Tr*, there could be no doubt that an 'uninfeft' proprietor could do these things. It was the transferee, therefore, and not the transferor, who must be treated as 'beneficially entitled' to the property for the purposes of the statutory provision. The claim for the exemption therefore succeeded.

COMPETITION OF TITLE

(48) McGraddie v McGraddie
[2010] CSOH 60, 2010 GWD 21-404

The pursuer and his wife had lived for many years in Albuquerque, New Mexico. When his wife became seriously ill, the pursuer determined to return to Glasgow and commissioned his son, the first defender, to buy a flat. Money was sent for that purpose. The flat was duly bought and the pursuer came home to live in it. The son had, however, taken title in his own name. A year or so later, the pursuer gave his son a second sum of money and again a house was bought, and this time taken in the name of the son and his wife (the second defender). The litigation was a result of disagreement as to the basis on which the money was handed over. The pursuer's case was that his son was simply being appointed as agent, to buy the houses on the pursuer's behalf. Accordingly, the pursuer sought an order that the houses be conveyed to him. The defenders' position was more complicated but in its essentials amounted to saying that the first house was to be used for the benefit of the defenders' family, and that the second cheque was an outright gift. In a decision issued last year Lord Brodie found for the pursuer: see [2009] CSOH 142, 2009 GWD 38-633 (*Conveyancing 2009* Case (60)). The current phase of the litigation was concerned with remedies. It appears that, given the result of the litigation, the defenders were likely to be insolvent.

As the son had acted as his father's agent, it followed, said Lord Brodie, that all of the first house and a one half share in the second were held in trust for the pursuer. Unexpectedly, Lord Brodie described the pursuer's right as 'a real right' (para 3), overlooking the settled principle that the right of a trust beneficiary is a personal right and not a real right: see eg *Inland Revenue v Clark's Trs* 1939 SC 11 at 22 per Lord President Normand. (Such a right defeats personal creditors of the trustee not because it is real but because personal creditors have no rights in respect of the trust patrimony.) As for the second defender, the pursuer was said to have a (personal) remedy in unjustified enrichment.

See Andrew J M Steven, 'Property issues in lien' (2010) 14 *Edinburgh Law Review* 455 for discussion of an aspect of this decision.

LAND REGISTRATION

(49) Burr v Keeper of the Registers of Scotland
12 November 2010, Lands Tr

Circumstances in which **held** that the correct date for assessing possession for the purposes of the proprietor-in-possession exception is either the date of application for rectification of the Register or the date on which the application is disposed of by the Keeper. See **Commentary** p 160.

[Another aspect of this case is digested at (76) below.]

RIGHT-TO-BUY LEGISLATION

(50) Robb v Tayside Joint Police Board (No 3)
1 March 2010, Lands Tr

Tayside police allowed one of their officers to occupy a house rent-free. The officer, now retired, applied to purchase it under the right-to-buy legislation. The request was refused, whereupon the case went to the Lands Tribunal, which found in favour of the applicant. (See 2009 SLT (Lands Tr) 23 (*Conveyancing 2008* Case (46), not followed in *Cochrane v Grampian Joint Police Board* 2010 SLT (Lands Tr) 19, 2010 Hous LR 57, Case (000) below.) A further procedural skirmish was fought in 2009, in which it was held that the application had lapsed but it was also held that a fresh application could be made. (Tribunal decision dated 12 August 2009.) A fresh application was made, and the Tayside police issued an offer whose terms the applicant objected to. **Held** (i) that the condition in the offer requiring the applicant to pay rent for the period since he retired was reasonable; (ii) that the offer should not have excluded an area used as a drying green; and (iii) that the offer was right to exclude a parking area.

(51) Cochrane v Grampian Joint Police Board
2010 SLT (Lands Tr) 19, 2010 Hous LR 57

If a public sector tenant 'is a constable of a police force ... who in pursuance of regulations under section 26 ... occupies the house without obligation to pay rent or rates' then there is no right to buy: Housing (Scotland) Act 1987 sch 2 para 7(a)(i). On this ground the application was refused, the Tribunal declining to follow its own decision in *Robb v Tayside Joint Police Board* 2009 SLT (Lands Tr) 23 (*Conveyancing 2008* Case (46)).

LEASES

(52) Multi-link Leisure Developments Ltd v North Lanarkshire Council
[2010] UKSC 47, 2011 SLT 184

This was one of two Supreme Court cases on property law this year, the other being *Royal Bank of Scotland plc v Wilson* (Case (66) below). The defender owned grazing land near Cumbernauld and entered into a 50-year lease with the pursuer. The pursuer was to develop the land as a pay-and-play golf course, and that duly took place. The lease contained a purchase option. When, after a few years, the pursuer exercised the option, the parties could not agree how the price should be calculated. The pursuer considered that the correct price was £500,000. The defender considered that the correct price was £5.3 million, in view of the land's potential for development. The pursuer was successful at first instance (2009 SLT 1170). The defender appealed, successfully (2010 SC 302, *Conveyancing 2006* Case (70)). The pursuer then appealed to the Supreme Court, which has affirmed the decision of the Inner House, ie in favour of the defender.

The lease provided:

> The Option price, if the Option to purchase is exercised subsequent to the first year of let, shall be equal to the full market value of the subjects hereby let as at the date of entry for the proposed purchase (as determined by the Landlords) *of agricultural land or open space suitable for development as a golf course* but, for the avoidance of doubt, shall be not less than the sum of ONE HUNDRED AND THIRTY THOUSAND POUNDS (£130,000) STERLING. In determining the full market value (i) the Landlords shall assume (a) that the subjects hereby let are in good and substantial order and repair and that all obligations of the Landlords and the Tenants under this Lease have been complied with, and (b) that the subjects hereby let are ready for occupation, and (ii) the Landlords shall disregard (a) any improvements carried out by the Tenants during the period of this Lease otherwise than in pursuance of an obligation to the Landlords, and (b) any damage to or destruction of the subjects hereby let.

As Lady Hale said (para 39):

> The puzzle is what those italicised words are meant to mean. There are at least four possible meanings of the term taken as a whole: (i) the value of the land as agricultural land or open space suitable for development as a golf course, without any hope value; (ii) the same but with any hope value; (iii) the value of the land with the golf course which has now been constructed on it, without any hope value; and (iv) the same but with any hope value.

Given 'the poor quality of the drafting' (Lord Hope at para 19), the court sought to arrive at a commonsensical interpretation. Although the court ended up agreeing with the decision of the Inner House, it managed to disagree with what was said in the Inner House, and indeed the Justices of the Supreme Court themselves do not approach the task of interpretation with one mind.

(53) Forbes v Cameron
[2010] CSIH 25, 2010 SLT 1017

This case was about the meaning of 'Whitsunday', the validity of a notice to quit depending on the answer. The Term and Quarter Days (Scotland) Act 1990 s 1(4) provides that in pre-Act leases, any reference to the term or quarter days 'without further specification as to date or month' would be deemed a reference to the 28th of the month.

In the present case a lease granted in 1915 ran from year to year, the annual ish being 'Whitsunday'. Notice to quit had to be served at least one year before the ish, because the tenancy was agricultural. The landlord served a notice on 22 May 2007 to take effect as at Whitsunday 2008. If the 'Whitsunday' in the lease meant 28 May, the notice was timeous, but not if it meant 15 May. The body of the lease merely said 'Whitsunday' without further specification, but the lease had a schedule headed 'General Conditions' which said, in relation to payment of rent, that Whitsunday meant 15 May.

The Land Court held that the annual ish was 15 May, and that because of the specification in the schedule, the date of the ish had not been altered by the 1990 Act, and that accordingly the notice had been served too late (27 October 2008, Scottish Land Court, unreported). The landlord appealed, and the Inner House, reversing the Land Court, has now **held** that the notice was timeous. The Lord Justice-Clerk (Gill) said (para 17):

> [T]he decision in this case begins and ends with section 1(4) of the 1990 Act. Section 1(4) applies to 'a reference' to Whitsunday that is without further specification as to date or month. I consider that, regardless of the specification of Whitsunday in article 3 [of the schedule], the reference to Whitsunday in the entry clause is a reference without further specification as to date or month. On that straightforward ground, I conclude that section 1(4) applies to that reference.

We are not convinced that the approach taken by the Land Court was entirely lacking in merit.

(54) Batt Cables plc v Spencer Business Parks Ltd
[2010] CSOH 81, 2010 SLT 860, 2010 Hous LR 43

Leases often involve the giving of notices, such as notices to quit, notices to exercise break options, and so on, and it is often in the interest of the recipient to argue that the notice is for one reason or another invalid. *Forbes v Cameron* (Case (53) above) and *McGrath v Nelson* (Case (55) below) are other examples from this year. In the current economic climate, break options are being invoked by tenants and challenged by landlords.

In the present case there was a lease from 1995 to 2020 with break options in favour of both parties at the 10, 15 and 20 year points. Spencer Business Parks Ltd was the landlord. But as so often happens with corporate groups, there was confusion between different companies, in this case between Spencer Business Parks Ltd and Spencer Holdings Plc. A key figure was a Mr Dempsey, who was an employee of another company in the group, Spencer Property Asset Management Ltd. The notice exercising the break option was addressed to Mr Dempsey at Spencer Holdings Plc. Spencer Holdings Plc was not the landlord, and Mr Dempsey was employed neither by that company nor by the actual landlord, Spencer Business Parks Ltd. The landlord denied that the break option had been validly exercised, and the tenant raised an action for declarator that the lease had been validly terminated.

It was found that Mr Dempsey was in fact the agent of Spencer Business Parks Ltd. The fact that the letter referred to Spencer Holdings Plc was held not to be fatal. Accordingly, the Lord Ordinary (Hodge) **held** that the notice had been validly served.

(For other recent conveyancing cases involving muddles as to corporate identity, see *Ben Cleuch Estates Ltd v Scottish Enterprise* 2008 SC 252 (*Conveyancing 2007* Case (47)) and *A W D Chase de Vere Wealth Management Ltd v Melville Street Properties Ltd* [2009] CSOH 150, 2009 GWD 38-652 (*Conveyancing 2009* Case (72)).)

(55) McGrath v Nelson
[2010] CSOH 149, 2010 GWD 40-824

This was a crofting case and we do not generally cover crofting law. But it illustrates the problems that can easily arise in relation to the transfer of a lease on death. The subject is complex and full of pitfalls. Here the tenant of a croft at Achaleven in Connell in Argyll, Mrs MacLean, died and her executors dative notified the landlord that they were nominating Mrs McGrath as the successor to the croft. The landlord then purported to terminate the tenancy on the ground that the nomination had been invalid, because it was in the wrong form and because the executors had not confirmed. This was an action of declarator that Mrs McGrath was the lawful tenant, and for reduction of the landlord's notice of termination. **Held**: action dismissed. Both of the landlord's arguments were sound.

(56) Them Properties LLP v Glasgow City Council
[2010] CSIH 51, 2010 SC 690, 2010 Hous LR 69

The owners of a flat let it out to students and thereafter applied for a HMO licence. Neighbours objected. See **Commentary** p 180.

(57) Crieff Highland Gathering Ltd v Perth & Kinross Council
[2010] CSOH 67, 2010 GWD 22-431

The Crieff Highland Gathering has been held at the Market Park since about 1880. The park is owned by Crieff Highland Gathering Ltd. It recently granted a six-year lease to the local authority, for no rent, but placing on the local authority obligations of upkeep. It alleged that the local authority had failed in its obligations, and it sent a notice rescinding the lease for material breach of contract. The local authority defence was (i) that the upkeep provisions were too vague to be enforceable, (ii) that it was maintaining the property to a satisfactory standard, and (iii) even if the provisions were enforceable, and even if there had been breach, the 'no fair and reasonable landlord' test in s 5 of the Law Reform (Miscellaneous Provisions) (Scotland) Act 1985 barred the landlord from rescission. **Held:** that the action was relevantly pled, and proof before answer allowed.

(58) Cramaso LLP v Viscount Reidhaven's Trs
[2010] CSOH 62, 2010 GWD 20-403

'Mr Alastair Erskine, a successful businessman and a keen shot, decided to take on the lease of the grouse moor at Castle Grant', writes the Lord Ordinary (Hodge) at para 3 of a highly readable Opinion. Though Mr Erskine invested several hundred thousand pounds the shooting proved disappointing. He claimed that he had been 'induced to enter into the lease as a result of fraudulent or at least negligent misrepresentations by an employee of the trustees, namely Mr Sandy Lewis, the chief executive of the trust and of other Seafield family estates and entities' (para 4). He sought reduction of the lease and damages.

After proof, the Lord Ordinary held that there had indeed been a negligent misrepresentation, which had led Mr Erskine to take on the lease. But the lease had not been taken on by Mr Erskine himself. He had formed an LLP, Cramaso LLP, and it was this LLP that had taken on the lease. The representation had been made to Mr Erskine in September 2006, and Cramaso LLP had not even been created until December 2006. 'For a defender to be liable in delict for a careless representation, he must have broken a pre-existing duty of care to prevent the pursuer sustaining economic loss as a result of his negligent misrepresentation' (para 116). 'In my view there was not sufficient proximity between Mr Lewis and any as yet uncreated vehicle for the lease for there to be a duty of care to that entity' (para 118). 'Thus, unfortunately, Mr Erskine's decision to create Cramaso to take the lease deprives him of a remedy in law. While it may appear a harsh decision at first sight, I observe that Mr Erskine, who is an experienced businessman and is familiar with corporate transactions, chose to transact through Cramaso for his own reasons' (para 119).

(59) Warren James (Jewellers) Ltd v Overgate GP Ltd
[2010] CSOH 57, 2010 GWD 17-348

The lease of a unit in a shopping centre had an 'exclusivity' clause, ie one limiting the landlord's right to let other units to competing businesses. The drafting of the clause was poor, and previous litigation had been necessary in order to determine its meaning: see *Warren James (Jewellers) Ltd v Overgate GP Ltd* [2005] CSOH 142 (*Conveyancing 2005* Case (26)), [2007] CSIH 14 (*Conveyancing 2007* Case (35)). In the present action the pursuer sought additional damages for breach by the landlord. The landlord pled prescription. Under para 2(e) of sch 1 of the Prescription and Limitation (Scotland) Act 1973 the prescriptive period for an 'obligation relating to land' is 20 rather than five years, so that if the pursuer's claim concerned an 'obligation relating to land' the defence of prescription would fail. **Held:** that the obligation did not 'relate to land' within the meaning of the Act and accordingly the landlord's defence was sustained. See **Commentary** p 184.

(60) Geoffrey (Tailor) Highland Crafts Ltd v G L Attractions Ltd
2010 GWD 8-142, Sh Ct

As in the previous case, a tenant sued the landlord for allegedly wrongful use of part of the retained premises. The landlord was trading in competition with the tenant, but here there was no exclusivity clause. The tenant argued its case not on the basis that the landlord was competing in a way that was contrary to the lease. Rather, the tenant argued that the retained area was excluded, by the terms of the lease, from being used for any retail purposes whatsoever, whether or not in competition with the tenant's business.

The building was a former water tower near the top of Edinburgh's Royal Mile, and the landlord had reserved an office (the 'Control Office') within it. After some years the landlord company came into new ownership, whereupon it began to use the office for retail business. Tempers rose (para 20):

> Mr Taylor recollected when those presently in control of the defenders began trading from the 'Control Office'. The only way they could have got stock to the 'Control Office' was over property leased to the pursuers. They were selling like for like with the pursuers ... The defenders were asked to stop and declined. The pursuers erected tartan strips over the entrance to the 'Control Office' in an attempt to discourage business. The defenders cut them down within a few minutes. The pursuers then fixed spotlights to the external facings of the 'Control Office'. Servants of the defenders smashed them with a hammer. Servants of the defenders took to standing in the corridor leased by the pursuers trying to usher customers into the 'Control Office' ... Mr Taylor said that Mr Nicholsby [director of the tenant company] had been ... assaulted by Malap Singh, a person associated with the defenders.

The pursuer had in fact three leases, of different parts of the building. These leases did not expressly limit the use to which the landlord could put the 'Control Room'. But the tenant argued that the only reasonable interpretation of the leases was that such a limitation must have been intended by the parties. The sheriff (G W M Liddle) agreed, and granted interdict against the defender.

(61) The Mount Stuart Trust v McCulloch
[2010] CSIH 21, 2010 SC 404, 2010 SLT 409

This was a dispute about the tenancy of two farms at Kilmichael and Glecknabae, Linniehullen, Isle of Bute. The lease had an irritancy clause. In the event of any breach by the tenant:

> it shall be in the power of the Proprietors (provided always that in the case of an alleged breach which is capable of being remedied the Proprietors or their factor have first served written notice on the Tenant by recorded delivery post requiring the Tenant to remedy the alleged breach within a period of two months from the date of the said notice and the Tenant has failed to remedy the same) by written intimation addressed

to the Tenant and posted in a registered or recorded delivery letter forthwith to put an end to this lease and immediately to resume possession of the Farm. . . .

The tenant missed a rent payment and the landlord sought his removal, without having first served any written notice calling on the tenant to remedy the breach. **Held:** that the breach was remediable and that therefore the landlord's action failed. The case proceeded upon the interpretation of the quoted clause. It should be noted that s 4 of the Law Reform (Miscellaneous Provisions) (Scotland) Act 1985 does not apply to agricultural tenancies: see s 7. Section 20 of the Agricultural Holdings (Scotland) Act 1991 was not discussed.

(62) Coatbridge Retail No 1 Ltd v Oliver
2010 GWD 19-374, Sh Ct

There was a lease of a retail unit in a shopping centre in Coatbridge, running from 2002 to 2012. The question at issue was whether the lease still existed. The tenant argued that there had been an oral agreement to vary the lease from a ten-year lease to a year-to-year lease and that he had validly brought that lease (as so varied) to an end. The landlord sought declarator that the 10-year lease was still in existence, unvaried. The tenant's difficulty lay in the fact that s 1(2) of the Requirements of Writing (Scotland) Act 1995 requires writing for 'a contract or unilateral obligation for the creation, transfer, *variation* or extinction of a real right in land' and s 1(7) says that 'real right in land' includes leases, other than leases for a year or less. So the tenant sought to found on what are sometimes called the 'statutory personal bar' provisions of s 1(3). But as the sheriff (Peter Hammond) noted, under these provisions 'the defender must aver and prove (firstly) that any acting or refraining from acting upon which he founds must be specifically referable to the lease as varied, and (secondly) that the specific acting or refraining from acting in reliance on the lease as varied was with the knowledge and acquiescence of the pursuers' (para 38). The defender's written pleadings did not contain the necessary averments, and accordingly the defence failed for lack of relevancy. (Proof was allowed on certain other matters at issue between the parties.)

(63) Primary Healthcare Centres (Broadford) Ltd v Humphrey
[2010] CSOH 129, 2010 GWD 35-730

This protracted and complex litigation is about liability for rent in relation to a lease of premises to a (now dissolved) medical partnership. The present action was against three former partners. The action failed against two of them ([2009] CSOH 46, 2009 SLT 673, *Conveyancing 2009* Case (69)) but the landlord continued the action against the third. Although liability was in principle joint and several, the Lord Ordinary (Lord Hodge) **held** that the fact that the action against the two others had failed meant that the third partner could not be made liable for more than one third of the rent. The Lord Ordinary's opinion is graced by apt quotations from Stair, Erskine, Bankton and Bell on the right of relief between co-obligants.

For a previous, connected, action see [2008] CSOH 14, 2008 Hous LR 24 (*Conveyancing 2008* Case (52)).

(64) Cheshire West and Cheshire Borough Council, Ptrs
[2010] CSOH 115, 2010 GWD 33-684

This was an insolvency case concerning property in England, but is nevertheless worth noting. A Scottish company had a lease of property in High Street, Worcester. It went into administration, and the question was whether the rent accruing between (i) the date of administration, and (ii) the date when the lease was terminated should be treated as an expense of the administration. The answer to this question can make a great deal of difference to landlords. After reviewing the authorities on this issue, both in relation to administration and in relation to liquidation, including the decision of the House of Lords in *In re Toshoku Finance UK plc* [2002] 3 All ER 961, Lord Glennie **held** that the rent was to be treated as an expense of the administration. There is a valuable discussion of the case by Alistair Burrow at (2010) 55 *Journal of the Law Society of Scotland* Oct/47.

(65) Almondale Investments (Jersey) Ltd v Technical & General
Guarantee Co SA
2010 GWD 31-651, Sh Ct

The pursuer owned land at Europark, Bellshill, which it leased to Lowland Rubber Co Ltd. The lease provided that the property was to be used 'as an engineering workshop to shred and granulate tyres and materials and as a processing plant for the manufacture and distribution of rubber products'. It was also provided that when the lease came to an end the property was to be restored. A guarantee for the tenant's restoration obligations ('the restoration security') was provided by Technical & General Guarantee Co SA.

In December 2008 the tenant went into liquidation and in January 2009 the lease was terminated. The tenant having failed to restore the site, the pursuer called on the defender to pay for the restoration, and when payment was not made the present action was raised. The case turned on the interpretation of the guarantee. The defender argued that the restoration guarantee did not include removing rubber from the site. **Held:** (by Sheriff Principal Bowen) that on a proper interpretation the defender's obligation did extend to the obligation to pay for removal of the rubber from the site.

STANDARD SECURITIES

(66) Royal Bank of Scotland plc v Wilson
[2010] UKSC 50, 2010 SLT 1227, 2010 Hous LR 88

The bombshell decision from the Supreme Court on enforcement of standard securities, reversing *Royal Bank of Scotland plc v Wilson* 2009 SLT 729 (*Conveyancing 2009* Case (75)). See **Commentary** p 129.

(67) Royal Bank of Scotland plc v Carlyle
[2010] CSOH 3, 2010 GWD 13-235

In August 2007 a bank advanced to the defender, a property developer, £1,405,000 to buy a development site in Gleneagles. Repayment was due in August 2008. When the developer failed to repay the loan, the bank sued. The defence was that the bank had undertaken to advance a further £700,000 to enable the development to be completed, that it had failed to advance that further sum, and that it was liable in damages to the defender for breach of its obligation, the amount of damages exceeding the sum sued for. After proof, the Lord Ordinary (Glennie) **held** that the undertaking had indeed been given and that the bank had indeed been in breach of that undertaking. A reclaiming motion has been lodged, and preliminary aspects of this reclaiming motion can be found at [2010] CSOH 108.

(68) Stewart v Accord Mortgages Ltd
2010 SCLR 435, Sh Ct

This was an application under the Mortgage Rights (Scotland) Act 2001 to suspend the creditor's enforcement rights. The property had been bought for £213,000 with a £180,000 loan. Because of the recession the property was now worth only about £170,000, and moreover the sum due to the lender had risen above £180,000 because of arrears. Hence there was negative equity. If the owner sold the property within two years of the loan there would be an exit penalty of £11,000. Hence voluntary sale would be problematic.

The court refused the application. There was little prospect that the debtor would be able to begin paying the full monthly sum, let alone make inroads into the arrears.

SEXUAL PROPERTY

(69) Esposito v Barile
2010 GWD 23-447, Sh Ct

An unmarried couple co-owned the house where they lived. They broke up and there was an action of division and sale. The parties disagreed as to how the proceeds of sale should be divided. See **Commentary** p 171.

(70) Souter v McAuley
2010 SLT (Sh Ct) 941, 2010 Hous LR 73

The pursuer, a mature student, was tenant of a council house in Dundee. He formed a relationship with the defender, and in December 2008 the landlord, Dundee City Council, acceded to his request that the tenancy should henceforth be a joint tenancy. No civil partnership was entered into between the parties. In February 2009 they split up. It was not an amicable parting. As for the pursuer, he 'assaulted the defender ... and ... pled guilty to a charge of assault' (findings in fact, para 4). As for the defender, 'he pled guilty ... to a contravention of section 127(1)(a) of the Communications Act 2003 in relation to text messages sent by him to the pursuer' (findings in fact, para 8). (The provision in question prohibits emails etc that are 'grossly offensive or of an indecent, obscene or menacing character'.) The pursuer moved out. Each party then applied to the court for an order vesting the tenancy solely in him. Such requests are competent in terms of s 18 of the Matrimonial Homes (Family Protection) (Scotland) Act 1981. The sheriff noted: 'the rental for the property is £48.68 per week for 48 weeks per annum. Equivalent property available in Dundee for private rent would be at a rental of approximately £350 per month' (findings in fact, paras 16 and 17). This generosity from the public purse no doubt explains why both parties were so keen to have the tenancy.

The court found the claims about equal. 'In relation to suitability to become the tenant, there is little to choose between the parties; the pursuer can demonstrate a history of ten years as a council tenant without ever having been evicted and with any difficulty in relation to rent arrears having been resolved; he is, however, noisy and a disturbance to his neighbours; the defender has been rendered bankrupt and has abused the housing benefits system, but is a quiet and friendly neighbour' (findings in fact and law, para 7). 'In the absence of any other clear distinction between the parties, it seemed to me that there was merit in falling back on the person considered to be the less troublesome neighbour, given the misery which can be suffered by decent tenement dwellers when they have to put up with the noisy and inconsiderate, especially when that includes both threats of and the noise of actual violence' (Note, para 22). Accordingly the court ordered that the tenancy be vested solely in the defender.

(71) Adams v Adams
2010 SLT (Sh Ct) 2, 2010 Fam LR 30

If spouses co-own a house, and then split up, it may be that the question of what happens to the house can be dealt with consensually. If not, in a divorce action the court can order that one party must transfer his/her share to the other: s 8 of the Family Law (Scotland) Act 1985. It can also order the sale of the property: 1985 Act s 14. An action of division and sale is also competent, but only with the consent of the court: Matrimonial Homes (Family Protection) (Scotland) Act 1981 s 19.

In the present case the pursuer and defender were married and co-owned the house. They became estranged. The wife moved out while the husband stayed in the house. Nevertheless the monthly mortgage payments continued to be made solely by the wife. She raised an action of divorce, and, while the action was still in court, sought an order for sale in favour of herself at a value to be determined by an independent expert. The order was sought under s 14 of the 1985 Act. See **Commentary** p 169.

SOLICITORS

(72) Bird v Bank of Scotland plc
[2010] CSOH 162, 2011 GWD 1-34

An extraordinary story of misconduct by a conveyancing solicitor, leaving others to try to pick up the pieces. See **Commentary** p 162.

(73) Credential Bath Street Ltd v DLA Piper Scotland LLP
[2010] CSOH 26, 2010 GWD 17-347

This case arises out of an earlier case, *Credential Bath Street Ltd v Venture Investment Placement Ltd* [2007] CSOH 208, 2008 Hous LR 2 (*Conveyancing 2007* Case (66)). Credential Bath Street Ltd was the landlord of Callpoint Europe Ltd in respect of a property in Bath Street, Glasgow. The lease was from 2001 to 2026 and the initial rent was £328,320 per annum. A further £103,680 per annum was payable to cover the costs of works carried out at the tenant's request. The rent and other obligations were guaranteed by another company in the same group as the tenant, Venture Investment Placement Ltd.

The tenant went into insolvent liquidation. The guarantee had a time limit: 'The guarantor shall be deemed to be released from its obligations under these presents on 1 January 2005 save in respect of any antecedent breach of the guarantee occurring prior to 1 January 2005.' During 2004 the landlord had served on both tenant and guarantor a schedule of dilapidations, but no actual demand was made on the guarantor to pay for the repairs prior to 1 January 2005. By the time that such a demand was made, the time limit had passed. The landlord sued for payment. The guarantor argued that the demand came too late. The landlord argued (a) that the phrase 'breach of the guarantee' really meant 'breach of the terms of the lease', and (b) that even if that were not the correct reading, the service of the schedule of dilapidations could be deemed to be a demand against the guarantor.

In the earlier case the Lord Ordinary (Reed) held against the landlord on both arguments. Now the landlord sued the law firm that had acted for it for having drafted the guarantee in unsatisfactory terms, and also for having failed to take proper steps to enforce it. The defender attacked the relevancy and specification of the pursuer's pleadings in a number of respects, and also averred that the guarantor would not have been good for the money and so the failure of the action against the guarantor had not in fact caused the landlord loss. The Lord Ordinary (Glennie) **held** that the pursuer's pleadings were sufficiently relevant. Proof before answer was allowed.

BOUNDARIES, ENCROACHMENT AND PRESCRIPTION

(74) Allen v Thomson
2010 SLT (Sh Ct) 60

In building four holiday lodges and an access driveway on land on the north shore of Loch Tay, the owner demolished a stone dyke. Later, when the lodges and also the neighbouring land had changed hands, the owners of the latter sought interdict against the owners of the former on the basis that the lodges, or at least the driveway, encroached on their land. Whether they did so depended on the location of the now-demolished dyke, for, in terms of the titles, this marked the mutual boundary. After a proof the sheriff **held** that there was some encroachment, at least in respect of the driveway, and remitted the position to a person of skill to plot the precise boundary.

In cases like this, there is often personal bar on the part of the person whose land is encroached upon. We do not know whether personal bar was pled in this case, but in any event the orthodox view is that it is personal to the person who stood by and watched the encroachment and so would not bind successors such as the pursuers.

(75) Welsh v Keeper of the Registers of Scotland
2010 GWD 23-443, Lands Tr

The applicant had a registered title to property in Nethanfoot, Lanarkshire. The Land Register was, he claimed, inaccurate, in that one of the boundaries as set out in the title sheet was slightly misplaced, giving him too little land. Having failed to persuade the Keeper to rectify the Register, he appealed to the Lands Tribunal. The neighbour on that boundary entered appearance. The case turned on the proper interpretation of the earlier Sasine deeds on which the Land Register title was based. After hearing evidence the Tribunal refused the appeal. See **Commentary** p 158.

(76) Burr v Keeper of the Registers of Scotland
12 November 2010, Lands Tr

The Keeper accepted that an additional strip should be included in the applicants' title plan but refused rectification on the basis that the neighbour in whose title plan the strip appeared claimed to be a proprietor in possession. The applicants appealed. After a proof, the Lands Tribunal found that the neighbour was not in possession. See **Commentary** p 160.

[Another aspect of this case is digested at (49) above.]

MISCELLANEOUS

(77) Luminar Lava Ignite Ltd v Mama Group plc
[2010] CSIH 1, 2010 SC 310, 2010 SLT 147

Luminar Liquid Ltd owned premises in Edinburgh's Lothian Road and sold them to Mama Group plc. The missives bound the buyer not to compete with Luminar Lava Ignite Ltd (a company in the same group as the seller) in its business at nearby premises. The latter then claimed that the defender was in breach of the undertaking and sought interdict. The Lord Ordinary refused interdict ([2009] CSOH 68, 2009 GWD 19-305 (*Conveyancing 2009* Case (91)), and the pursuer reclaimed. **Held** (the Lord President dissenting): that the decision at first instance should be reversed. The case contains valuable discussion of the way in which contracts should be interpreted.

PART II

STATUTORY
DEVELOPMENTS

STATUTORY DEVELOPMENTS

Home Owner and Debtor Protection (Scotland) Act 2010 (asp 6)

Apart from debtor protection in respect of residential standard securities (for which see **Commentary** p 150), the Act also, in part 2, implements one of the recommendations of the Final Report of the Debt Action Forum (see *Conveyancing 2009* p 179), namely that a trust deed for creditors should be able to exclude the family home. The creditors can reject such a trust deed, but if they do not reject it, the result is that the family home is outwith the ambit of the trust deed. These provisions came into force on 15 November 2010: see the **Home Owner and Debtor Protection (Scotland) Act 2010 (Commencement) Order 2010, SSI 2010/314** art 6. Consequential amendments are made to the Protected Trust Deeds (Scotland) Regulations 2008, SSI 2008/143, by the **Protected Trust Deeds (Scotland) Amendment Regulations 2010, SSI 2010/398.** Something comparable has for some time been competent in England and Wales in respect of IVAs.

Crofting Reform (Scotland) Act 2010 (asp 14)

In this series we do not cover crofting law, but nevertheless mention major changes. Among other things this Act establishes a new Crofting Register, under the auspices of the Keeper, which will gradually supersede the existing Register of Crofts kept by the Crofters Commission (which is renamed by the Act, becoming the Crofting Commission). It is intended that the new register will result in accurate and reliable public information about crofts, their boundaries, and their holders. There are currently around 18,000 crofts. Under the legislation, registration in the new register will be required on a 'trigger' event, such as a transfer of tenancy or of ownership. However, the Scottish Government apparently intends that, during the first year of the register, the triggers will not apply and registration will be voluntary. To encourage such voluntary registration, the Government will subsidise registration fees for groups of 10 or more crofters who submit community applications during this initial period. See (2010) 55 *Journal of the Law Society of Scotland* Sept/15.

Some other aspects of the legislation are discussed in the *Journal of the Law Society of Scotland* for 2010 by Adele Nicol and Alasdair G Fox (March/49) and by David Findlay (Aug/52). Some provisions of the Act are already in force and others will be brought into force during 2011 by the **Crofting Reform (Scotland) Act 2010 (Commencement, Savings and Transitory Provisions) Order 2010, SSI 2010/437.**

Separate from the new Act, reg 2 of the **Crofting (Designation of Areas) (Scotland) Order 2010, SSI 2010/29**, made under the Crofters (Scotland) Act 1993, extends crofting tenure to:

(a) that part of the local government area of Highland that is outwith the crofting counties;
(b) the local government area of Moray;
(c) in the local government area of Argyll and Bute, the parishes of Kingarth, North Bute and Rothesay; and
(d) in the local government area of North Ayrshire, the islands of Arran (including Holy Island and Pladda), Great Cumbrae and Little Cumbrae.

Maps of the areas designated by this Order can be found at http://www.scotland.gov.uk/Topics/farmingrural/Rural/crofting-policy/new-crofting-areas.

Housing (Scotland) Act 2010 (asp 17)

The Housing (Scotland) Act 2010 was passed by the Scottish Parliament on 3 November and received Royal Assent on 9 December 2010. Its main concern is the regulation of social landlords but it also contains important provisions restricting the right to buy and on a number of other subjects. So far almost none of the Act has been brought into force.

Regulation of social landlords

'Social landlords', in the sense used in the Act, comprise (i) registered social landlords, (ii) local authority landlords, and (iii) local authorities which provide housing services (s 165). Paragraph 5 of the *Policy Memorandum* which accompanied the Bill notes that the term 'social housing' is considered as stigmatising by some, but that it did not prove possible to agree on a different term.

The Act puts the Scottish Housing Regulator (SHR) on a statutory footing as a body corporate that is independent of Ministers (see s 7) but staffed by civil servants. It is to have a minimum of three members (s 8(1)). The SHR's formal objective is to safeguard and promote the interests of the homeless, of tenants of social landlords, and of recipients of housing services provided by social landlords (s 2). The SHR has been in existence since 2008, but only as an executive agency (see www.scottishhousingregulator.gov.uk). Under the Act, the SHR is given a range of functions in relation to the regulation of social landlords, many of which are based on functions that the Scottish Ministers exercise at present – in practice, through the SHR (replacing Communities Scotland) – in respect of the safeguarding of good governance, financial wellbeing and assets. The idea is to separate the public policy role of setting standards for social landlords, which remains with the Scottish Government, from that of measuring performance against those standards, which is now to be undertaken by an independent regulatory body.

Part 2 of the Act (ss 22–30) provides for the SHR to assume functions, broadly equivalent to those exercised at present by the Scottish Ministers under part 3 of the Housing (Scotland) Act 2001, in relation to the registration of social landlords. The policy objective is to encourage improvements in the level and quality of social housing by allowing for a wider range of bodies to be registered and regulated by the SHR. This part of the Act does not extend to local authority landlords, which will continue to provide housing services without the requirement to register with the SHR. The 2001 Act focused on structure and status by stipulating that to be eligible to register as a social landlord the body must be non-profit distributing and either an industrial and provident society or a registered company. Under the new Act, eligibility for registration is no longer tied to structure and status but is based on what the body is established to do (ss 24–26).

Part 3 (ss 31–41) provides for the new Scottish Social Housing Charter for social landlords which is to be devised by the Government following consultation. Among the illustrative 'standards and outcomes' set out in s 32 are the maintenance of housing accommodation, its method of allocation, participation of tenants in formulating policy, the alleviation of homelessness, and the provision and management of sites for gypsies and travellers. The idea is that the Charter should be ready by April 2012. It will then be used to inform the assessment of social landlords by the SHR in the form of annual performance reports (ss 40 and 41). The SHR is required to issue a code of conduct setting out standards of financial management and governance (s 36).

Much of the rest of the Act is taken up with ancillary matters. Part 4 (ss 42–51) provides the SHR with powers to carry out inquiries and obtain information from social landlords. Part 5 (ss 52–67) confers powers to intervene where the SHR has concerns about a social landlord's performance, governance arrangements, or financial viability. Accounting requirements are to be set (part 6, ss 68–72). Part 7 (ss 73–91) provides the SHR with powers to deal with an insolvent registered social landlord, and part 8 (ss 92–106) deals with the constitution, rule changes, amalgamation, and dissolution of registered social landlords. The provisions for disposal of land in ss 66–68 and sch 9 of the Housing (Scotland) Act 2001 are re-enacted in parts 9 (ss 107–112) and 10 (ss 113–124), while part 11 (ss 125–136) replicates the 'tenant's choice' provisions at ss 56–64 of the Housing (Scotland) Act 1988 (which allow a person to seek ministerial approval to purchase a house belonging to a public sector landlord which is let under a Scottish secure tenancy). Finally, part 12 (s 137) makes provision for regulation of charitable registered social landlords.

Ending the right to buy: new houses and new tenancies

Hitherto tenants holding a Scottish secure tenancy (SST) from a social landlord have usually had some form of right-to-buy (RTB) entitlement. This allowed them to purchase the property they were renting at a discount. The level of discount varied and depended primarily on the length of time they had rented property from a social landlord and the type of RTB entitlement they had. There are two forms of RTB entitlement: (i) 'preserved', for tenancies starting before 30 September 2002; and (ii) 'modernised', for tenancies starting on or after 30 September 2002.

'Preserved' RTB entitlements typically have more generous discounts than those under 'modernised' RTB terms. The main provisions are found in part III of the Housing (Scotland) Act 1987, and in particular in s 61.

Since its introduction RTB has resulted in the sale of about half a million properties. That means that more properties have been lost from social rented stock than have been built – a depletion of social housing stock which, the Scottish Government has concluded, is unsustainable in the face of continued high levels of demand. Some of the problems are brought out in a study by Heriot-Watt University commissioned by the Scottish Government and published in November 2010: see Glen Bramley et al, *A Study into the Capacity of Registered Social Landlords and Local Authorities to Build Housing across Scotland* (available at http://www.scotland.gov.uk/Publications/2010/11/11115938/0). The Executive Summary points out that:

> In Scotland, as elsewhere in the UK, the past few years have seen further increases in the demand for affordable housing. For example, in the period 2006–2009 the number of households registered on local authority waiting lists increased by 13% to 156,000. More importantly, social landlords have needed to gear up to meet their widened rehousing responsibilities towards homeless people legislated under the Housing (Scotland) Act 2003 and due for full implementation in 2012.

The study projects a capacity to develop some 6,400 homes per year for social housing over the period to 2034.

Against this background, part 14 of the Act, once in force, will bring the right to buy to an end, although without changing the RTB entitlements of existing tenants (including those subsequently moving on to new tenancies). There are two main provisions, one directed at the housing stock and the other at tenants. First, a new s 61F is inserted into the Housing (Scotland) Act 2007 (by s 143) which exempts 'new supply social houses' from the RTB. These are defined as houses which were not let under a SST on or before 25 June 2008 (being the date of the Parliamentary announcement that the Scottish Government intended to legislate to end RTB on new social housing) and which were let under a SST on or after the day in which the provision comes into force (s 61F(3)). Notice that there is no right to buy must be given to tenants in the form prescribed by the **Limitation on Right to Purchase (Form of Notice) (Scotland) Regulations 2010, SSI 2010/468**. There are various exemptions. Secondly, a new s 61ZA, inserted into the 2007 Act (by s 141), removes the RTB for those becoming tenants for the first time after the provision comes into force, and also for those returning to social housing after a voluntary break. Again there are some exemptions.

Suspending the right to buy: pressured areas

Section 61B of the Housing (Scotland) Act 1987, as inserted by s 45 of the Housing (Scotland) Act 2001, provides that a local authority can apply to the Scottish Ministers to designate an area as a 'pressured area' for a period of up to five years. Ministers may decide to designate the area as 'pressured' if a great deal more social rented housing is (or is likely to be) needed than is available, and if the RTB would worsen the situation. The effect of a designation is to suspend all 'modernised' RTB entitlements in the designated area. Those tenants with 'preserved' RTB entitlements are unaffected. As at 27 May 2010 there were 15 pressured areas across 12 local authority areas (see http://www.scottish.parliament.uk/business/pqa/wa-10/wa0527.htm and, for specification of areas and villages, *Conveyancing 2008* pp 61–62):

1. East Renfrewshire (Eastwood area): 7 October 2005 to 6 October 2010.
2. Highland (all areas excluding Caithness, Sutherland and some estates in Inverness and Fort William): 15 November 2005 to 14 November 2010.
3. South Ayrshire (29 letting areas comprising much of Prestwick and Ayr, and rural settlements): 10 February 2006 to 9 February 2011.
4. Moray (Elgin, Lossiemouth and Forres rural): 7 March 2006 to 6 March 2011.
5. Fife (for St Andrews and East Neuk): 8 May 2006 to 7 May 2011.
6. Dumfries and Galloway (69 villages of population less than 400 across the local authority area): 5 June 2006 to 4 June 2011.
7. Fife (13 West Fife villages): 15 January 2007 to 14 January 2012.
8. Perth and Kinross (21 letting areas across Highland Perthshire and in the rural areas around Perth): 2 February 2007 to 1 February 2012.
9. Aberdeen City (35 letting areas across the city): 5 September 2007 to 4 September 2012.
10. North Ayrshire (11 letting areas): 14 May 2008 to 13 May 2013.
11. Aberdeenshire (88 letting areas): 6 November 2008 to 5 November 2013.
12. North Lanarkshire (Cumbernauld and Moodiesburn): 2 February 2009 to 1 February 2014.
13. Moray (Forres letting area): 17 February 2009 to 16 February 2014.
14. Stirling (35 letting areas): 25 March 2009 to 24 March 2014.
15. Moray (Speyside and Cairngorm National Park areas): 18 May 2010 to 17 May 2015.

The designation in respect of Highland has since been expanded and renewed for a further five years, and now affects around 6,000 tenancies.

Some important changes are introduced by s 142 of the 2010 Act, which amends ss 61B and 61C of the 1987 Act. Once in force, this will extend the maximum designation period from five to ten years, allow particular housing types as well as particular areas to be designated as 'pressured', and allow local authorities themselves (rather than Scottish Ministers) to designate, revoke or amend pressured-area and housing-type designations. Section 61C as amended sets out various requirements in relation to consultation, decision-making, and publicity.

Miscellaneous

Section 152, which provides certain protections to tenants in the event that the property is subject to a standard security which is being enforced, is discussed at p 155 below. Other changes introduced by the 2010 Act include:

- The rule in s 8 of the Land Tenure Reform (Scotland) Act 1974, which restricts leases of dwellinghouses to 20 years, is disapplied to leases *to* (but not *by*) social landlords, their connected bodies, and rural housing bodies (s 138).
- Social landlords, their connected bodies, and rural housing bodies are empowered to renounce the right conferred by s 11 of the Land Tenure Reform (Scotland) Act 1974 to redeem a standard security over a dwellinghouse after 20 years (s 139).
- Section 50 of the Housing (Scotland) Act 2006, which allows local authorities to pay the share of maintenance costs (typically in tenements) due by a defaulting owner (see *Conveyancing 2005* pp 120–22), is extended from 'can't pay' to 'won't pay' cases (s 150(1)).
- Where a social landlord in a Scottish secure tenancy wishes to remove a tenant on grounds of rent arrears, it will be necessary to comply with certain pre-action requirements, such as providing advice to the tenant as to eligibility for housing and other benefits, and attempting to agree a 'reasonable plan' for payment of rent, including arrears (s 155, amending s 14 of the Housing (Scotland) Act 2001 and inserting a new s 14A).

Finance Act 2010 (c 13)

The first of the three Finance Acts passed in 2010 makes changes in stamp duty land tax. See **Commentary** p 184.

Equality Act 2010 (c 15)

A primary aim of this substantial and wide-ranging Act is to prevent discrimination on the grounds of any of the 'protected characteristics', which are defined in s 4 as 'age; disability; gender reassignment; marriage and civil partnership; pregnancy and maternity; race; religion or belief; sex; sexual orientation'. Of particular interest to conveyancers is the power given to Scottish Ministers, by s 27, to make regulations allowing disabled persons to carry out appropriate alterations to the common parts in tenements and other buildings. See **Commentary** p 102.

Increase in registration fees

New rates of fees are set by the **Fees in the Registers of Scotland Amendment Order 2010, SSI 2010/404**. This substitutes a new schedule for the existing schedule to the Fees in the Registers of Scotland Order 1995, SI 1995/1945. Details of the main changes are given below. In certain cases (eg registration of a standard security, where the fee is increased from £30 to £60) the existing fee is doubled or more than doubled. The new fees came into effect on 10 January 2011. Some discussion of the changes will be found in Register of Scotland's *Update 30* (available at http://www.ros.gov.uk/pdfs/registers_update_30.pdf), where it is explained that the original proposal to charge an *additional* fee of £400 for a deed imposing real burdens is not being proceeded with for now but may be revisited at a later date.

	Current fee (£)	New fee (£)
Part I, Section 1, Head A (Land Register registration fees in respect of interests in land other than heritable securities)		
Additional fee per each additional title sheet affected (in addition to the fee specified in Table A in Part IV of the Schedule) where a single application affects a number of title sheets	30	60
Application made to give effect to a survivorship destination	30	60
Application made by certain statutory authorities seeking to complete title	30	60
Part I, Section 1, Head B (Land Register registration fees in respect of heritable securities)		
Registration fee (per title sheet affected) for the creation of a heritable security over a registered interest in land under section 2(3) of the Land Registration (Scotland) Act 1979	£30 (£20 for ARTL System application)	£60 (£50 for ARTL System application)
Registration fee (per title sheet affected) for any other dealing with a heritable security under section 2(4) of the Land Registration (Scotland) Act 1979	£30 (£20 for ARTL System application)	£60 (£50 for ARTL System application)
Part I, Section 2 (Land Register report fees)		
Form 10 application for a report prior to first registration	28.50	32.00
Form 11 application for continuation of report prior to first registration	16.50	19.00
Form 12 application for a report over registered subjects	28.50	32.00
Form 13 application for continuation of report over registered subjects	16.50	19.00
Form 14 application for a report to ascertain whether or not subjects have been registered	28.50	32.00
Form P16 application for comparison of a bounding description with the Ordnance Map separate from Form 10 application	28.50	29.50
Form P17 application for comparison of the boundaries of the title plan with the Ordnance Map separate from Form 12 application	28.50	32.00

	Current fee (£)	*New fee (£)*
Combined fee for a Form P16 for comparison of a bounding description with the Ordnance Map in conjunction with Form 10 application	41.00	45.00
Combined fee for a Form P17 for comparison of the boundaries on the title plan with the Ordnance Map in conjunction with Form 12 application	41.00	45.00
Part I, Section 3 (Land Register miscellaneous services)		
Form 5 application for noting an overriding interest etc (for each title sheet affected)	30.00	60.00
Form 9 application for rectification of the register	30.00	60.00
Application for checking the boundaries of adjoining properties	20.00	60.00
Application for withdrawal of an application under rule 11 of the Land Registration (Scotland) Rules 2006	30.00	Equivalent to applicable registration fee, up to a maximum of £400
Application for the provision of information from a deed or document in the Land Register archive (for each deed/document)	8.00	16.00
Application for registration of a tree preservation order or a compulsory purchase order (for each title sheet affected)	30.00	60.00
A rejected application under rule 13 of the Land Registration (Scotland) Rules 2006	30.00	Equivalent to applicable registration fee, up to a maximum of £400
A rejected application prior to being accepted for the Land Register under section 4 of the Land Registration (Scotland) Act 1979	N/A	30.00
Part II (Register of Sasines recording fees)		
Application to record notice of title (a) along with another deed granting a long lease or servitude over the whole or part of same subjects, (b) on behalf of certain statutory authorities seeking to complete title, or (c) on behalf of a Health Board or Special Health Board completing title under an order made under section 2 of the National Health Service (Scotland) Act 1978	30.00	60.00

	Current fee (£)	New fee (£)
Recording a heritable security	30.00	60.00
Recording of a writ by memorandum (per memorandum)	30.00	60.00
Part III (fees for registrations and recordings in both the Land and the Sasine Registers)		
Recording and registration fees for single transactions effected by more than one deed and/or application where, as a result of a single transaction concerning interests in land other than heritable securities, an application is made for registration in the Land Register and recording in the Register of Sasines	Fee calculated in accordance with Table A, Part IV of Schedule plus fee of £30 for each related deed presented for recording or for every other title sheet affected by an application for registration in the Land Register	N/A
Recording and registration fees for single transactions effected by more than one deed and/or application where, as a result of a single transaction concerning heritable securities, an application is made for registration in the Land Register and recording in the Register of Sasines	£30 in respect of transaction plus £30 for every other title sheet affected or deed recorded	N/A
Application for registration or recording of miscellaneous deeds not referred to elsewhere in Parts I to III of the Schedule to this Order	£30	£60 (or £50 for ARTL System application)
Application for registration or recording comprising an application for dual registration or an application for variation of a title condition where no fee is provided in respect of such an application elsewhere in Parts I to III of the Schedule to this Order	£30 plus £30 for each other title sheet affected and for each deed recorded	£60 plus £60 for each other title sheet affected and for each deed recorded
Applications personally presented at a Registers of Scotland customer service centre (per title affected, in addition to recording/registration fee)	N/A	15.00
Part IV – Table A – Registration and recording fees (based upon consideration or value)		
£50,000 (up to and including)	30.00	60.00
£100,000 (up to and including)	100.00	120.00

	Current fee (£)	New fee (£)
£150,000 (up to and including)	200.00	240.00
£200,000 (up to and including)	300.00	360.00
£300,000 (up to and including)	400.00	480.00
£500,000 (up to and including)	500.00	600.00
£700,000 (up to and including)	600.00	720.00
£1,000,000 (up to and including)	700.00	840.00
Part IV – Table B – Registration and recording fees for ARTL System applications (based upon consideration or value)		
£50,000 (up to and including)	20.00	50.00
£100,000 (up to and including)	75.00	90.00
£150,000 (up to and including)	150.00	180.00
£200,000 (up to and including)	225.00	270.00
£300,000 (up to and including)	300.00	360.00
£500,000 (up to and including)	375.00	450.00
£700,000 (up to and including)	450.00	540.00
£1,000,000 (up to and including)	550.00	660.00
Part XI, Section 1 (fees for the provision of information)		
Section 1, Head A (Register of Sasines)		
Presentment book – per search against a name, an address or a minute number	1.80	3.00
Minute book – per search against a name, an address or a minute number	1.80	3.00
Search sheet – per search against a search sheet number; per view of any individual search sheet; or the provision of information from any other index, volume, document or process	1.80	3.00
Section 1, Head B (Land Register of Scotland)		
Application record – per search against a name, an address, an application number, or a title number	1.80	3.00

	Current fee (£)	New fee (£)
Title sheet – per search against a name, an address or a title number, or per view of the title sheet affecting one interest in land	1.80	3.00
Index map – per seed rectangle search or per seed point search	1.80	3.00
Provision of information from any other index, volume, document or process	1.80	3.00
Section 1, Head C (Books of Council and Session)		
For each search in the Register or Deeds or Register of Judgments Index against a name, a pursuer/petitioner, a defender/respondent, or a judgment number	1.80	3.00
Section 1, Head D (Register of Inhibitions and Adjudications)		
For each group of six names or fewer searched against	1.80	3.00
For provisions of a copy of the daily minutes (per day)	19.50	21.00
Per search of a specified minute number	1.80	3.00
Section 1, Head E (Searches of Registers Direct service conducted by Registers of Scotland)		
Search request submitted by email, letter or fax	N/A	£8.00 plus £3.00 Registers Direct service search fee per search
Search request made in person at a Registers of Scotland Customer Service Centre	N/A	£12.00 plus £3.00 Registers Direct service search fee per search
Section 1, Head F (Miscellaneous)		
Per copy deed recorded in the Register of Sasines via the Registers Direct service	N/A	3.00
Pre-registration enquiries service (per enquiry)	N/A	50.00
Part XI, Section 2 (Extracting and copying fees)		
For a plain copy or duplicate	8.00	16.00
For an official extract or certified copy	15.00	30.00

	Current fee (£)	New fee (£)
For an official extract obtained from the National Archives of Scotland (NAS) (to be charged as official extract – see above)	5.00 plus NAS fee	30.00
For an office copy	15.00	30.00
For each additional extract of any deed or document requested at the same time as recording in the Register of Sasines or registration in the Books of Council and Session	8.00	10.00

Amendment to the Building (Scotland) Regulations 2004

Minor amendments to the Building (Scotland) Regulations 2004, SSI 2004/406 (for which see *Conveyancing 2004* p 37) are made by the **Building (Scotland) Amendment Regulations 2010, SSI 2010/32**. Among other matters, these affect the description of works not requiring a building warrant, and the standards applicable to the design and construction of buildings set out in schedule 5 of the 2004 Regulations.

Licensing of houses in multiple occupation

Mandatory licensing of HMOs (with some exceptions) was introduced in phases from 2000, and since 1 October 2003 has extended to all properties occupied by three or more people (being members of different families). The current rules, contained in the Civic Government (Scotland) Act 1982 (Licensing of Houses in Multiple Occupation) Order 2000, SSI 2000/177, are to be replaced with effect from 31 August 2011 by the revised rules contained in part 6 (ss 124–66) of the Housing (Scotland) Act 2006. See the **Housing (Scotland) Act 2006 (Commencement No 8, Transitional Provisions and Savings) Order 2010, SSI 2010/159**. The 2010 Order also sets out some transitional provisions, so that for example (art 4) most licences granted under the 2000 Order will be deemed to have been granted under the 2006 Act.

Disposal of land by local authorities at undervalue

Under section 74 of the Local Government (Scotland) Act 1973, a local authority required the consent of the Scottish Ministers (formerly the Secretary of State) to dispose of land for a consideration less than the best that could reasonably be obtained. Section 74 was amended by the Local Government in Scotland Act 2003 s 11(1) by the addition of subsection (2A), permitting disposals at less than best consideration where either the best consideration that could reasonably be obtained was less than the 'threshold amount', or the difference between that consideration and the proposed consideration was less than the 'marginal amount'. The **Disposal of Land by Local Authorities (Scotland) Regulations 2010, SSI**

2010/160, reg 2 now sets the 'threshold amount' at £10,000 and the 'marginal amount' at 25% of the best consideration. By reg 4, an undervalue disposal may only take place if the local authority is satisfied that the disposal is reasonable and is likely to contribute to one or more of the following purposes: economic development or regeneration, health, social well-being, or environmental well-being. This new facility for undervalue disposal came into force on 1 June 2010: see the **Local Government in Scotland Act 2003 (Commencement No 5 and Saving) Order 2010, SSI 2010/119** art 3.

Continuing validity of repair notices under the Housing (Scotland) Act 1987

The Housing (Scotland) Act 2006 (Commencement No 7, Savings and Transitional Provisions) Order 2009, SSI 2009/122 (for which see *Conveyancing 2009* p 61) commenced the repeal of ss 108–12 of the Housing (Scotland) Act 1987, which make provision about repair notices, the carrying out of repair work and the recovery of expenses. These are now replaced by the new work notice introduced by s 30 of the Housing (Scotland) Act 2006 (in force from 1 April 2009). The 2009 Order is amended by art 2 of the **Housing (Scotland) Act 2006 (Commencement No 7, Savings and Transitional Provisions) Amendment Order 2010, SSI 2010/114** so as to save ss 108–12 in relation to repair notices served before the repeal.

PART III
OTHER MATERIAL

OTHER MATERIAL

Regulation of property managers

After several years of discussion, it now seems that something is to be done to regulate property managers (or factors). As yet, however, it is unclear what form that regulation will take.

There has been much public assertion and discussion as to the quality of factorial services. In a statement issued on 2 June 2010 and rich in metaphor, Mike Dailly, principal solicitor at Govan Law Centre, said:

> Govan Law Centre is inundated with complaints from clients who are unhappy with their property factor. From concerns about poor quality repairs, unnecessary work, poor value for money, serious overcharging, to problems around unfair charging practices and substandard service, nothing has changed in Scotland over the last few years in this sector. ... Scottish property factors are as unregulated as the old Wild West, and it's incredible to think that cowboy companies still have a free hand to rip-off vulnerable households.

More measured, both in tone and in content, was the Office of Fair Trading's study on *Property Managers in Scotland*, published in February 2009 (see *Conveyancing 2009* pp 72–75), with its conclusion that, while 70% of those surveyed were happy with their property manager, a significant minority was not, especially with regard to the way in which complaints were handled. The OFT's conclusion was to offer provisional support for the self-regulation scheme then being floated by the Scottish Government, although adding (p 9) that 'if an effective scheme is not in place and operating successfully within two years, proposals for a statutory scheme should be brought forward and implemented'.

Voluntary accreditation scheme

The cowboy metaphor had been in evidence back in July 2008 when the Communities Minister, Stewart Maxwell MSP, announced that an 'industry-led' accreditation scheme would be set up which (rather puzzlingly to the literally-minded) 'will help weed out the cowboys' (see *Conveyancing 2008* p 70). Following consultation with the property factor sector, a consultation draft was issued on 10 May 2010, *Quality in Common: Residential Property Managers and Land Maintenance Companies in Scotland: Core Standards for a Voluntary Accreditation Scheme* (http://www.scotland.gov.uk/Publications/2010/05/06171828/0). Its introduction sets the scene:

In order to join the accreditation scheme, property managers must agree to comply with the core standards. Membership of the scheme will help homeowners identify managers who provide high standards of service. The accreditation scheme also allows property managers to assure their customers of the standard of service provided and gives those who join the scheme the recognition and support they deserve. Compliance with the standards is intended to promote a positive relationship between property managers and consumers, with good communication and fewer misunderstandings and disputes.

In order to build and enhance the reputation of the scheme, the accreditation body will be prepared to take action against any property manager who breaches the standards, including expulsion from the scheme if high standards of service are not being maintained. The accreditation body will also approve any changes to the standards and ensure that they evolve to reflect the experience of operation, as well as changes in practice and legislation.

At the centre of the proposals are the rather detailed 'core standards' which are set out in draft in the consultation document and which cover eight topics: property management services, communication and consultation, financial obligations, debt recovery, insurance, contractors and repairs, complaints resolution, and staff training. These standards, it is explained, 'are informed by a combination of current legislation and good practice. They are designed to be reasonable and realistic. Compliance is not expected to place a burden on property managers who already follow good management practices.'

The response to this document was modestly positive although there was disagreement on points of detail: see John Scott and Steven Reid, *Consultation on Core Standards for a Voluntary Accreditation Scheme for Property Managers and Land Maintenance Companies in Scotland: An Analysis of Responses* (http://www.scotland.gov.uk/Resource/Doc/326090/0105070.pdf). For some, however, the idea of a voluntary code of conduct is unacceptable, Mike Dailly, for example, commenting that 'the Scottish Government's "self-regulation" strategy is wholly inadequate to providing consumer protection in Scotland'.

Property Factors (Scotland) Bill

By this time an alternative approach was in the frame. As early as 26 March 2007, Gordon Jackson MSP had lodged a proposal in the Scottish Parliament for a Property Factors (Scotland) Bill but this fell shortly afterwards with the dissolution of Parliament. The idea was taken up again immediately after the 2007 election by another Labour MSP, Patricia Ferguson. Following a consultation launched in October 2007, and a debate on factoring services on 4 March 2010 (see *Official Report* cols 24219 ff), a Property Factors (Scotland) Bill was introduced on 1 June 2010 as a Member's Bill. Help with the drafting was provided by the Govan Law Centre. The initial response of the Government was to express interest and sympathy but to continue with its support for a voluntary scheme. However, in oral evidence to the Local Government and Communities Committee at Stage 1 of the Bill (*Official Report* col 3478 (22 September 2010)), Alex Neil, the Minister for Housing and Communities, stated: 'Where the scheme eventually goes depends on what happens to the Bill. We will not spend more money on it until we get clarification on the progress of the Bill.' There matters rest for the moment.

The Bill completed Stage 3 of the Parliamentary process on 3 March 2011, and is awaiting Royal Assent. In coming out in support of a legislative solution the Local Government and Communities Committee, in its Stage 1 Report (http://www.scottish.parliament.uk/s3/committees/lgc/reports-10/lgr10-10.htm), was influenced particularly by the thought that it was those very factors who give substandard service – the 'rogue' factors – who would refuse to sign up for a voluntary scheme (see paras 36–45).

The Bill seeks to do three main things. In the first place it sets up a public register of property factors for the estimated 140 to 200 factors (including local authorities and housing associations) currently in business. An application for registration will be accepted only if the Scottish Ministers (who are to administer the register) are satisfied that the applicant is 'a fit and proper person to be a property factor' (ss 4(4)(a) and 5). Registration is essential for continuing in the business: it would be an offence for an unregistered person to operate as a property factor (s 12). One model for these provisions seems to have been the system of registration of private-sector landlords contained in part 8 of the Antisocial Behaviour etc (Scotland) Act 2004.

Secondly, the Bill provides for a Code of Conduct, to be prepared by the Scottish Ministers (s 13). No doubt the work already done on the 'core standards' for the voluntary scheme could be re-used for this purpose.

Finally, there is a new system of ADR. While the Government would apparently have preferred an ombudsman, the Bill makes use of the system set up by ss 21–26 of the Housing (Scotland) Act 2006 in relation to repairs defaults by landlords in the private rental sector. The intention is to use the same structure and personnel as under the 2006 Act, but when acting in relation to property factors the private rented housing panel is to be known as the 'homeowner housing panel', and private rented housing committees are to be known as 'homeowner housing committees' (s 15). So this is ADR funded from the public purse. Under the Bill, the panel acts as a screening mechanism for cases to be heard by one of the committees. Applications can be made where the factor fails to comply with either a contractual obligation or with the Code of Conduct (s 16). If it regards the application as made out, the committee issues a 'property factor enforcement order' (ss 18 and 19). This cannot be enforced directly by the home-owner, but failure to comply is both a criminal offence and a ground for the factor being removed from the register (ss 22 and 23).

Private Rented Housing (Scotland) Bill

The Housing (Scotland) Act 2010 (discussed at p 50 above) is mainly about public sector housing. But an Executive Bill focusing on the private sector is currently before the Scottish Parliament. The Private Rented Housing (Scotland) Bill was introduced on 4 October 2010 and, at the time of writing, had completed Stage 1 of the parliamentary procedure. It follows on from the Scottish Government's recent *Review of the Private Rented Sector* (for which see *Conveyancing 2009* pp 75–77).

The Bill comprises four main parts. Part 1 makes a number of further amendments to the system of registration of private landlords first introduced by part 8 of the Antisocial Behaviour etc (Scotland) Act 2004 (for which see *Conveyancing 2004* pp 92–95). For example, some alterations are made to the 'fit and proper person' test (ss 1 and 2), and when advertising housing to let landlords will have to disclose their registration number (s 6, inserting a new s 92B into the 2004 Act). Part 2 contains a number of (mainly minor) amendments to the regime of licensing of houses in multiple occupation set out in part 5 of the Housing (Scotland) Act 2006 (itself not yet in force). A new statutory notice – the 'overcrowding statutory notice' – is created by part 3. This can be served on landlords by local authorities where a house is overcrowded to the extent that this has an adverse effect on the health or wellbeing of any person or on the amenity of the house or its locality (s 17). Failure to comply is a criminal offence (s 25). Finally, among the miscellaneous changes made by part 4 are the introduction of tenant information packs, which are to be provided by landlords before the start of an assured tenancy (s 29, inserting new ss 30A and 30B into the Housing (Scotland) Act 1988), and a new facility allowing landlords who are having trouble gaining access to the property in order to check on its state of repair or to carry out work (see Housing (Scotland) Act 2006 s 181(4)) to seek the assistance of the private rented housing panel (s 31, inserting new ss 28A–28C into the 2006 Act).

Long Leases (Scotland) Bill

The Long Leases (Scotland) Bill is a Government Bill, introduced to the Scottish Parliament on 10 November 2010. It is based on the Scottish Law Commission's *Report on Conversion of Long Leases* (Scot Law Com No 204, 2006; available at www. scotlawcom.gov.uk). The aim is to convert 'ultra-long' leases into ownership. The scheme is modelled on the Abolition of Feudal Tenure etc (Scotland) Act 2000, the idea being that the landlords of ultra-long leases are in functional terms akin to superiors, while the tenants are in functional terms akin to vassals. An ultra-long lease is defined as one with a term of more than 175 years, and with not less than 100 years left to run. Leases that are for less than the minimum period but which contain renewal options can qualify, such as a 99-year lease granted in 1920 that is renewable at the tenant's option.

Conversion would be automatic, just as under the 2000 Act the conversion of *dominium utile* into full ownership happened automatically. However, unlike the 2000 Act, a tenant holding an ultra-long lease could opt out. Further, the Bill excepts leases where the rent is £100 *per annum* or over. There are also some exceptions for pipeline leases and mineral leases.

In feudal abolition, it was the estate that was the lowest unit of the feudal chain that was converted into full ownership, and all superiorities disappeared. The same principle is to apply to leasehold conversion. To quote the explanatory notes to the Bill: 'If A, the owner of land, leases 10 hectares to B for 999 years and B in turn sublets 4 of these hectares to C for 920 years, C is the qualifying tenant in relation to the 4 hectares and B in relation to the remaining 6 hectares.' But if C's lease had been for 99 years then that lease would not be a qualifying lease, whereas B's would be, so it would be B who would become owner of all 10 hectares.

Conversion would not in general affect third-party rights, such as servitudes. Any standard security over a converted lease would become a standard security over the land. Conditions in the converted lease would convert into real burdens provided that certain requirements were satisfied. For some lease conditions (about maintenance, management, reinstatement or use of facilities) conversion would be automatic. With others, conversion would require the service and registration of a notice, nominating benefited property. The rules here are similar to those that applied to feudal burdens, some of which were converted automatically into non-feudal burdens, while others had to be saved by the service and registration of a notice. No leasehold condition can become a real burden unless it satisfies the requirements for real burdens under the Title Conditions (Scotland) Act 2003.

Reserved mineral rights are to be converted automatically into separate tenements, vested in the ex-landlords. The same would apply to reserved game rights, but with the difference that the conversion would not be automatic, but would require the service and registration of a notice.

In feudal abolition, the vassal had to pay the superior a sum to compensate for the loss of any feuduty, and likewise the Bill requires the tenant to make a 'compensatory payment' to compensate the landlord for loss of rent. Since, however, the Bill excludes leases where the rent is over £100, such payments will range from the small down to the microscopic. And since the ex-landlord has to serve a notice to claim this money, and do so within two years of conversion, it is likely that few such notices will in fact be served.

In certain cases an ex-landlord can, within two years of conversion, serve a notice claiming a further 'additional payment' to compensate for the loss of ownership. This would cover the loss of the right to resume possession at the ish of the lease, but only if the ish is less than 200 years into the future. In relation to the 'additional payment', as in relation to other matters, jurisdiction is given to the Lands Tribunal.

Two differences between the Bill and the Scottish Law Commission recommendations have already been mentioned: the exclusion from the conversion scheme of leases where the rent is over £100 and of leases 'for the sole purpose of allowing access (including work) to pipes or cables'. A third is that there is included in the conversion scheme any 'lease which is continuing by tacit relocation as if any provision (however expressed) (a) included in the lease prior to it so continuing, and (b) requiring the landlord to renew the lease, had been complied with'. We quote the explanatory notes:

> To give an example, some leases in Blairgowrie are for 99 years but contain provisions requiring the landlords to renew them in perpetuity for further periods of 99 years. The effect of section 69 is that where such leases have not been renewed but continue on tacit relocation, the renewal is deemed to have taken place, including conditions about further renewals. This means that the durational requirements for leases to convert to ownership are met.

Historic Environment (Amendment) (Scotland) Bill

This Executive Bill, which is expected to be passed by the Scottish Parliament on 20 January 2011, makes a number of amendments to the Historic Buildings and Ancient Monuments Act 1953, the Ancient Monuments and Archaeological Areas Act 1979, and the Planning (Listed Buildings and Conservation Areas) (Scotland) Act 1997. The Bill amends the 1979 Act in relation to aspects of the 'scheduling' of monuments as well as in respect of provisions related to properties held in the guardianship or ownership of Scottish Ministers. The 1997 Act is amended in relation to certain grant-making powers and aspects of 'listing'. For further details, see an article by Alastair McKie at p 43 of the *Journal of the Law Society* for July 2010.

Consultation on Building Repairs (Scotland) Bill

A proposal for a Building Repairs (Scotland) Bill was lodged with the Scottish Parliament on 16 December 2010 by David Stewart MSP and put out for consultation. The consultation document, *Keeping Scotland Safe* (http://www.scottish.parliament.uk/s3/bills/MembersBills/documents/BuildingRepairsConsultationPaperFinal.pdf), asks for responses by 11 March 2011. The Bill aims to improve recovery rates for local authorities which carry out work following service of a defective building notice or a dangerous building notice under ss 28 and 30 of the Building (Scotland) Act 2003. At present there is estimated to be £1.3 million of unrecovered debt. The recovery rate for defective building notices – a mere 48% – is so low that many local authorities do not use them. Since the 2003 Act came into force, only six out of 32 local authorities have served such notices. The main solution proposed is that local authorities should be able to use charging orders to recover costs.

Among a number of interesting statistics in the paper is the information that Edinburgh Council issues more building notices than all of the other local authorities combined, amounting to an annual output of some 2,800 notices.

Lloyds Banking Group: cuts in residential conveyancing panel

Following similar moves in England and Wales and in Northern Ireland, Lloyds Banking Group has introduced new criteria for solicitors to remain on its residential conveyancing panel, based on the volume of transactions carried out for Group lenders within the past year. The volume threshold, not specified, is apparently in single figures and is slightly lower in rural areas. This threshold is being applied irrespective of the size of the firm. Affected firms received a letter in November 2010 and have the opportunity to appeal against their removal from the panel (though this is not mentioned in the letter). Apparently a limited number of appeals have been successful. The Group's lenders are Lloyds TSB Bank plc, Bank of Scotland, Cheltenham & Gloucester, Halifax, Birmingham Midshires, Intelligent Finance, St James' Place Bank, Lloyds TSB Scotland plc, and Scottish Widows Bank.

Both the Law Society of Scotland and the Scottish Law Agents Society have been vocal in their opposition to this move, with the latter describing it as 'anti-Scottish and anti-small business': see www.slas.co.uk and also Ian C Ferguson, 'Lloyd's panel cuts – a survival guide' (2010) 78 *Scottish Law Gazette* 82. The Law Society is to obtain counsel's opinion on whether Lloyds' decision contravenes EU competition law, on the basis that it effectively restricts consumer choice. The Society is also continuing to canvass MPs and MSPs on the issue.

Lloyds Banking Group: no discharge until payment

Departing from its previous practice, and the practice of most other lenders, Lloyds Banking Group no longer releases signed discharges of standard securities until repayment of the loan has been received. Discharges will, however, be released within 14 days of repayment, thus – in theory at least – allowing firms to comply with an undertaking to deliver a signed discharge within 21 days.

Changes to the *CML Lenders' Handbook*

There have been a number of changes to the *CML Lenders' Handbook*. A helpful summary is given on the CML website at http://www.cml.org.uk/cml/handbook.

New provisions have been inserted on account of increasing concern about conveyancing fraud (paras 3.2 and 3.3):

3.2   If you are not familiar with the seller's solicitors or independent qualified conveyancers, you must verify that they appear in a legal directory or they are currently on record with the Law Society of Scotland or other supervisory body as practising at the address shown on their notepaper. Check part 2 to see whether we require you to notify us of the name and address of the solicitors firm or licensed conveyancers firm acting for the seller.

3.3   If the seller does not have legal representation you should check part 2 to see whether or not we need to be notified so that a decision can be made as to whether or not we are prepared to proceed.

After the changes were announced, the Law Society of Scotland posted this notice (http://www.lawscot.org.uk/members/member-services/professional-practice/professional-practice-updates-):

CML have produced a 'Summary of Amendments'. ... One critical amendment which has not been highlighted is the change to the wording of paragraph 4.1.1 of the *Handbook*. The Conveyancing Committee has obtained clarification from CML that the effect of this change is that a valuation report must be examined in every case where there is a mortgage. If a copy is not supplied by the lender, solicitors will have to obtain one from their clients. Solicitors should ensure that they see the valuation report that is being relied on by the lender (which for the avoidance of doubt is not the Home Report). This is essential to comply with the requirements on solicitors, under paragraphs 4.1.2 and 4.1.3 of the *Handbook*, to check that there are no discrepancies in the description of the property as valued and that any assumptions made by the valuer about the title are correct.

Registers of Scotland

Increased registration fees

Increased fees for registration and other services provided by Registers of Scotland came into effect on 10 January 2011. For details, see p 54 above. A main reason for the increase is the financial pressure on RoS as a result of the recession.

£50 for pre-registration inquiries

One of the fee changes is the introduction of a fee of £50 (post-paid) for pre-registration inquiries. Telephone inquiries are no longer accepted. For further information, see *Update 31* (http://www.ros.gov.uk/pdfs/registers_update31.pdf). RoS will endeavour to deal with inquiries within five days of receipt. Contact details remain as before:

> Pre-Registration Enquiries
> Registers of Scotland
> Meadowbank House
> 153 London Road
> Edinburgh EH8 7AU
> DX 550907 LP55 EDINBURGH 5
> Email: pre-reg@ros.gov.uk
> Fax 0131 479 3675
> Phone 0845 607 0163   0845 607 0163 (for messages only)

Voluntary registrations

We understand that the Keeper is now more willing to accept voluntary registration applications than hitherto, and that around 95% of voluntary applications made in the last year have been accepted, amounting to over 1,600 in all. Where agents are considering making such an application, the contact point is Eric Willis (eric.willis@ros.gov.uk, 0131 528 3831).

Use of ARTL

As Peter Nicholson wryly observes, in the August *Journal of the Law Society* (at p 5), 'It must have come as something of a surprise to those involved in the ARTL (automated registration) project ... to learn that sections of the profession appear to be resolutely opposed to having anything to do with it.' Although around 35,000 transactions have now been completed using ARTL, all but a few of these have involved securities only, with no property transfer, and therefore only a single solicitor acting. See (2010) 55 *Journal of the Law Society of Scotland* Jan/24.

As of 1 September 2010 Lloyds Banking Group is requiring panel members to use ARTL wherever appropriate at least for the security: see (2010) 55 *Journal of the Law Society of Scotland* June/32. So for example the version of the *CML Lenders' Handbook* for Bank of Scotland says this:

18.2.1. Does the lender allow completion and registration of standard security on ARTL?

Any transaction in which you are instructed by us, and which is capable of being initiated via ARTL, must be carried out using that system, unless there are valid reasons why ARTL cannot be used.

Much depends, of course, on what is meant by 'capable of being initiated'. At the least, however, all panel solicitors will need to have signed up to ARTL. Unsurprisingly, this move has not been universally popular among solicitors. For critical discussion of this and indeed of ARTL more generally, see the letters in the *Journal of the Law Society* for July (p 8), August (p 8), September (p 10), November (p 10), and December 2010 (p 8), one of them referring to ARTL as 'clunky' and predicting lax security and a breakdown in the system, another complaining that it is neither fast nor user-friendly, a third expressing herself 'amazed at the primitive processes'. A letter published at (2010) 78 *Scottish Law Gazette* 75 describes an attempt to use ARTL for an intra-office sale/purchase, where the technical problems proved 'insurmountable' in a system which is 'poorly designed'. The attempt had an unhappy ending:

> Acting for the purchaser, I discovered that I could not progress the transaction because I could not supply the 'effective date' for Stamp Duty Land Tax. As any conveyancer will know, the effective date cannot be provided until the actual date of settlement. At this point my colleague and I gave up trying to effect this transaction through ARTL and reverted to the conventional system of paper drafts.

A response by David Preston to some of these issues was published in the *Journal* for October 2010 (p 9). See also the account of an ARTL training session by Graham Gibson in the same issue (p 56).

Photocopies of death certificates no longer accepted

Death certificates sometimes have to be submitted to the Keeper, eg to update the title sheet following the death of an owner whose title is affected by a survivorship clause. For reasons of Crown copyright, the Keeper will no longer accept photocopies of death certificates but requires an official extract.

Submission of digital plan data

Although digital data – using Geographical Information Systems or Computer Aided Design and Drafting software – are not a substitute for a deed plan, this information can usefully be submitted with applications for registration. According to a note by RoS in the November 2010 edition of the *Journal of the Law Society* (p 11): 'In cases where the area of ground in an application for registration is large, or the delineation on the Ordnance Survey map is difficult, we particularly welcome being provided with digital data, as this allows us to process the application more efficiently as we can carefully compare the digital data with the deed plan.'

Rejection rates

From 1 January to 30 November 2010, 160,942 applications were submitted for registration of which 16,728 (10.39%) were rejected. Since 10 January 2011, rejections have attracted a fee of £30. For further details, see *Update 33* (http://www.ros.gov. uk/pdfs/registers_update%2033.pdf).

Applications will be rejected, and the new fee incurred, where, for example, the application:

- is not accompanied by the appropriate, duly completed, application form(s) and inventory form 4;
- does not provide the appropriate fee payment and/or supporting fee information;
- is not accompanied by the relevant Stamp Duty Land Tax certificate (if required);
- does not enclose the deed (or deeds) that is to be registered;
- is for the registration of a deed containing a plan that is not docketed in conformity with section 8 of the Requirements of Writing (Scotland) Act 1995;
- is for the registration of a Disposition by the granter(s) to themselves in the same capacity (A to A, A and B to A and B etc) other than to discharge or waive a survivorship destination;
- is to register a deed from which the requisite Title Number has been omitted (this will not apply to a Discharge of a Standard Security that was recorded in the General Register of Sasines);
- is made by a party other than a solicitor or licensed conveyancer and is not accompanied by the requisite RoS ID Form;
- is to register a constitutive deed in terms of the Title Conditions (Scotland) Act 2003 and only some, but not all, of the requisite forms and/or registration fees are provided;
- is made in respect of a Deed of Variation of a Standard Security that was recorded in the General Register of Sasines but no application is made to register the Standard Security in question;
- affects more than one registered interest but is not accompanied by the requisite application forms and/or registration dues in respect of all of the affected titles;
- is an application for voluntary registration that has not been agreed in advance with the Keeper (in these circumstances, the Keeper may exercise her discretion as to whether such applications are to be rejected);
- is made in respect of a creditor who no longer has a legal right in the security assets (for example following a transfer of engagements).

Payment by direct debit

Errors in cheques were formerly another common reason for rejection. However, since 1 April 2010 RoS has moved to direct debit for pre-paid registration fees.

That means that no cheques are now accepted. RoS are also considering whether direct debit might be made available for post-paid business.

The Law Society has issued guidance that the principal client bank account should never be subject to variable direct debit and a separate account should be opened instead. This will reduce the risk of an error causing a shortage on the client bank account and assist in the ease of reconciling the account.

Revised rules for requisitions

Where an application has an omission or defect falling short of one which would require rejection, the practice is for RoS to operate a requisition process with the submitting party, usually involving the return of a deed for amendment or a request for supplementary evidence. Meanwhile the application is put into 'standover'. In 2009, 36% of first registration applications went into standover. The corresponding figures for transfers of part of a registered title and dealings with whole were 29% and 16% respectively. In many cases this could be avoided by taking greater care in the preparation of the application.

To reduce the incidence and costs of requisitions for transactions, RoS made some changes in its practice with effect from 1 September 2010. These are explained in *Update 28* (http://www.ros.gov.uk/pdfs/update28.pdf):

- We will no longer delay registration pending receipt of a discharge that has been marked 'to follow'. This may result in a land certificate being issued showing an outstanding standard security by the previous owner. However, it is possible to demonstrate that the prior standard security has been removed from the title sheet by obtaining a Form 12 report or a copy of the title sheet from Registers Direct. . . . If an application to register the discharge is submitted before the related application is completed we will process them together.
- We will no longer issue a reminder once the 60-day standover period has elapsed. Failure to respond to a request within this period will result in the application being cancelled or progressed with an exclusion of indemnity. However, if a solicitor is experiencing particular difficulty in meeting a requisition, we will consider extending the compliance period if, during that period, we are asked to do so in writing with a full explanation of the reasons for the delay.

This may not be the end of the matter. 'If', it is warned, 'standover rates remain high, RoS may have to introduce further measures. These range from seeking legislative change to reduce the standover period from the current 60 days, through to the withdrawal of the facility for certain transaction types and/or certain errors and omissions.' See (2010) 55 *Journal of the Law Society of Scotland* Sept/15.

Scan and create

Since November 2008 all non-ARTL application forms have been scanned by RoS and key information captured by means of Optical Character Recognition. *Update 29* (http://www.ros.gov.uk/pdfs/update29.pdf) gives further guidance on the completion of application forms in an OCR-friendly way:

To allow these efficiencies to be realised, an important element in this process is the quality of application forms received by solicitors. The Keeper recommends that solicitors use the RoS Forms which are available from our website ros.gov.uk using our eForms services or downloadable pre-printed forms. The use of these forms results in a 95% success rate within our recognition software.

The Keeper also issues 3rd party licences to companies who produce forms for solicitors. It is important that these comply with the required standards to allow our OCR software to operate at the efficiency levels required. A large number of the 3rd party forms we receive do not meet the required standard. Due to this our acceptance rate within the recognition software is 69% which then requires additional resource to correct the errors on these forms.

Common issues that occur with 3rd party licensed forms are:

Lower case. All text must be typed in UPPER CASE only (no lower case characters should be used) and all characters must fit within the confines of the text boxes. The use of £ signs and commas in monetary fields is also not allowed.

Font. It is important that correct font is used. The following font styles should be used for populating the form:

- OCR-B font (9pt) (available for download from website adobe.com)
- Courier 12pt
- Arial 10pt

Please do not use any other font.

Handwritten forms. Any forms with handwriting cannot be captured by OCR.

Reform of the law of land registration

Overview

In February 2010 the Scottish Law Commission published its Report on *Land Registration* (Scot Law Com No 222, available at www.scotlawcom.gov.uk). The Scottish Government decided to carry out a consultation on the recommendations, and asked the Keeper to do this. The Keeper's consultation paper was published in September 2010, and the consultation period closed on 30 November 2010.

Whether and when legislation will follow depends – as is always the case – on the politicians. But at the time of writing it seems reasonably likely that a Government Bill will be introduced to the Scottish Parliament before the end of 2011. If that happens, Royal Assent might be expected before the end of 2012. Commencement would probably take place at least 12 months after Royal Assent, to allow time for the Keeper to make the necessary preparations, to allow the necessary statutory instruments to be put in place, and so on. At the moment the betting for commencement date is centring on 4 January 2014. But it may be that there will be pressure from some quarters of the profession for early commencement of two aspects of the eventual Act, namely (i) the advance notice system, which would allow letters of obligation to become a thing of the past, and (ii) the possibility of having all conveyancing documents, including missives, in electronic form.

The Scottish Law Commission's Report recommends the complete repeal of the Land Registration (Scotland) Act 1979 and its replacement with a new statute. That is less dramatic than it sounds. The central functional features of the current system would remain. There would continue to be a map-based Land Register. Existing registered titles would carry on. Title sheets would retain their familiar four sections. Titles would continue to be guaranteed by the Keeper, though, as now, there would be certain exceptions and qualifications. Whilst the 1979 Act has its faults, it was also a progressive measure, and the new legislation would build on its successes. The watchword of the Commission's Report is evolution, not revolution. Throughout the process the Commission was aware of the importance of not causing unnecessary inconvenience to conveyancers.

The report is a long one, running to two volumes, and what follows does no more than take a peep at a few of the recommendations. Some further details can be found in an article published at (2010) 55 *Journal of the Law Society of Scotland* March/22.

Completing the Register

The Registration Act 1617 set up the Register of Sasines. It said that all deeds had to be recorded there. Yet today, nearly 400 years later, there are still a few properties that have never entered the Register of Sasines (for example, some university properties, some local authority properties and some Crown properties). The Land Register is less ambitious than the Register of Sasines: only dispositions trigger first registration, and even then only dispositions for value. Unless the law changes, in 400 years from now there will probably still be properties not yet in the Land Register. Currently about 55% of individual titles in Scotland, relating to about 20% of the land mass, appear on the Land Register, increasing at two to three per cent a year.

There are two reasons for speeding things up. One is that it is inconvenient for conveyancers, and for the Keeper, to have two separate registers in operation. The second is that the Land Register brings with it transparency as to land titles and boundaries, information that is of value to a multitude of interest groups. So the Law Commission's Report recommends a programme for the completion of the Land Register. One step is that all dispositions of unregistered property, not only dispositions for value, will trigger first registration. Another is that the Keeper will have the power to register any unregistered property without the owner's consent. This is not so dramatic a power as might at first appear. The proprietor would be charged no fee, and the way that the new legislation would be constructed means that any error by the Keeper, eg as to boundaries, would not prejudice anybody's rights.

The Report recommends several other measures aimed at closing the Register of Sasines as soon as possible and hastening the day when all land in Scotland is in the Land Register. One of them is that, whereas under current law the Keeper has a discretion to refuse applications for voluntary registration, that discretion would disappear. However, since the publication of the Report the Keeper's practice in this area has changed. Hitherto the Keeper usually refused to accept applications for voluntary registration. Now the Keeper will usually accept such applications. (See p 72 above.)

Electronic conveyancing

ARTL was introduced in 2006. Though a valuable step forward, it is by no means a complete package for electronic conveyancing. First, it does not allow for electronic deeds in the Land Register unless they are being used in an ARTL transaction. Secondly, ARTL can only be used for certain types of deed. For example it cannot be used for split-off deeds. Thirdly, documents that are not registered in the Land Register cannot be in electronic form. Examples include missives and non-registrable leases. Finally, the Register of Sasines cannot take electronic deeds, and the Books of Council and Session, equally, is open only to paper deeds.

The Report recommends that all conveyancing documents should be capable of being in electronic form. This will require extensive amendments to the Requirements of Writing (Scotland) Act 1995. However, the position taken by the Commission was that parties who wish to use electronic documents should be free to do so, and it did not recommend any element of compulsion. The Keeper's consultation paper did, however, pose this question (number 38): 'Do you agree that a provision should be included in the Bill delegating power to the Scottish Ministers to prescribe the use of ARTL (and its successors in eRegistration)?'

Electronic documents mean electronic signatures. At present the Keeper is the issuing authority for e-signatures for use in ARTL. But if electronic documents are permitted in all cases (ie including cases not involving a registrable deed), the question arises as to who would issue such signatures. That question has yet to be resolved.

Inaccuracy, rectification, indemnity

A persistent criticism of the 1979 Act is that its rules about inaccuracy, rectification, and indemnity are highly complex and, moreover, too often fail to deliver reasonable solutions when problems arise. The Commission agreed with that criticism, and recommends a complete overhaul of the rules. We will not go into the details here. But we would stress that the basic principle of guaranteed title would continue.

Duty of care to the Keeper?

To what extent those involved in land registration transactions owe a duty of care to the Keeper is uncertain. The Report recommends that there should be such a duty of care, but limited to what is reasonable in the circumstances. Thus a conveyancer who acts to the standard of an ordinarily competent conveyancer would have nothing to fear. The effect of the reform may be that application forms can be simplified, for the duty of care would mean a duty to disclose to the Keeper any problems.

Advance notices and letters of obligation

Many countries have a system whereby an advance notice of a transaction can be noted on the register. Then, as and when the transaction is registered, it will take priority over any other entry that may have been made in the intervening period. Take an example from England. X is selling to Y. A priority entry is made in HM Land Registry on 1 May. On 10 May a mortgage by X to Z is registered. On 12 May the conveyance by X to Y is submitted for registration. The conveyance has priority over the mortgage. The Commission recommends that a comparable scheme be adopted in Scotland. The details are based in part on the English system but also in part on the system that exists in Germany. The scheme has been designed to ensure that in ordinary transactions letters of obligation would become unnecessary. Although advance notices would be optional, the possibility exists that the CML might require their use.

A *non domino* dispositions

The 1979 Act is silent on how the Keeper is to handle *a non domino* cases in the Land Register. The Keeper has, as a result, developed a non-statutory scheme. The Report recommends a statutory scheme.

Uncompleted titles, deduction of title, and notices of title

The Report recommends that clauses of deduction of title should no longer be required in dispositions inducing first registration granted by 'uninfeft' proprietors. But in the cases where a notice of title is needed in the Register of Sasines it would also be needed in the Land Register.

Deadlines for the Keeper

Delays in registration have been a persistent issue. The Commission recommends that Ministers should be able to prescribe maximum periods during which applications can sit in the Keeper's in-tray. Different periods could be set for different types of case.

Tough love

One cause of delay is that applications for registration are too often defective. As well as affecting the application in question, this takes up staff time at Registers of Scotland in correspondence to see if the application can be put right. The Report recommends a 'tough love' policy whereby defective applications would simply be rejected – though the applicant would be free to make a new, and better, application. So no more 'requisitions'. Indeed the Keeper has already made a significant step in this direction: see p 75 above.

Exclusion of professional liability for environmental law matters

In April 2003 the Law Society of Scotland issued guidance regarding con-taminated land: see http://www.journalonline.co.uk/magazine/48-4/1000481.

aspx. The Society's Professional Practice and Conveyancing Committees have recently reconsidered that guidance in the light of the complexity of this area and the availability of specialist advice from solicitors accredited in environmental law. The Committees' view is that if a solicitor does not feel qualified to comment on environmental matters, whether in general or in regard to contaminated land matters, then, whatever the nature of the property in the transaction, that solicitor is entitled to seek to exclude liability for environmental law matters or contaminated land matters provided that this is made clear in the initial terms of business issued to the client with respect to the transaction in question.

14-day limit for 'classic' letters of obligation

Originally 14 days, the specified maximum period for 'classic' letters of obligation was extended to 21 days to take account of various factors inhibiting prompt submission of applications for registration, particularly delays in obtaining Stamp Duty Land Certificates following the introduction of SDLT in 2003. However, the introduction and refinement of the facility to submit SDLT returns online has greatly speeded up this process. Accordingly the Law Society has taken the decision to restore the original period with effect from the beginning of the current practice year (1 November 2010). The new requirement does not apply to undertakings to deliver a discharge of the seller's standard security, and such undertakings may continue to specify a 21-day time limit. For the meaning and scope of a 'classic' letter of obligation, see *Conveyancing 2002* pp 42–43 and (2003) 48 *Journal of the Law Society of Scotland* April/26.

Consumer Code for Home Builders

An industry-led Consumer Code for Home Builders has been developed by NHBC and MD Insurance Services Ltd (trading as Premier Guarantee and LABC New Home Warranty) in respect of new-build houses. All builders and developers registered with these organisations are required to adopt the Code, which came into effect on 1 April 2010. This initiative follows on from the Barker Review of 2004 and the Office of Fair Trading market study into the house building industry of October 2008 and is, in part, an attempt to head off the legislative regulation ultimately supported by the OFT. For further background see http://www.consumercodeforhomebuilders.com/index.html, and also an article by Rod MacEachrane at p 56 of the *Journal of the Law Society of Scotland* for March 2010.

The Code is sufficiently short for it to be reproduced below. Conveyancers will be particularly interested in rules 2 and 3 – for example, the clear provisions in respect of reservations (r 2.6) (a matter which was the subject of recent litigation: *McDougall v Heritage Hotels Ltd* [2008] CSOH 54, 2008 SLT 494, discussed in *Conveyancing 2008* pp 81–83), or the requirement that the contract must be 'clear and fair' and comply with the Unfair Terms in Consumer Contracts Regulations, SI 1999/2083 (r 3.1).

1 ADOPTING THE CODE

1.1 Adopting the Code

Home Builders must comply with the requirements of the Code and have regard to the good-practice guidance.

1.2 Making the Code available

The Home Builder must display the Code and give, without charge, a copy to customers who ask for it and to all Home Buyers who reserve a Home. The Home Builder should also inform their customers that further guidance is available and how they can get this.

1.3 Customer Service

The Home Builder must have suitable systems and procedures to ensure it can reliably and accurately meet the commitments on service, procedures and information in the Code.

1.4 Appropriately trained customer service staff

The Home Builder must provide suitable training to all staff who deal with Home Buyers about their responsibilities to them and what the Code means for the company and its directors.

1.5 Sales and advertising

Sales and advertising material and activity must be clear and truthful.

2 INFORMATION – PRE-CONTRACT

2.1 Pre-purchase information

Home Buyers must be given enough pre-purchase information to help them make suitably informed purchasing decisions. In all cases this information must include:

- a written Reservation agreement;
- an explanation of the Home Warranty cover;
- a description of any management services and organisations to which the Home Buyer will be committed and an estimate of their cost.

Also, if a Home is not yet completed, the information must include:

- a brochure or plan reliably showing the layout, appearance and plot position of the Home;
- a list of the Home's contents;
- the standards to which the Home is being built.

2.2 Contact information

Home Buyers must be told how their questions will be dealt with and who to contact during the sale, purchase and completion of the Home.

2.3 Warranty cover

Home Buyers must be given accurate and reliable information about the insurance-backed warranty provided on the Home.

2.4 Health and safety for visitors to developments under construction

Home Buyers must be informed about the health and safety precautions they should take when visiting a development under construction.

2.5 Pre-contract information

Home Builders must advise Home Buyers to appoint a professional legal adviser to carry out the legal formalities of buying the Home and to represent their interests.

2.6 Reservation

Home Buyers must be given a Reservation agreement that sets out clearly the terms of the Reservation, including, but not limited to:

- the amount of the Reservation fee;
- what is being sold;
- the purchase price;
- how and when the Reservation agreement will end;
- how long the price remains valid;
- the estimated cost and nature of any management services the Home Buyer must pay for.

The Reservation fee must be reimbursed if the Reservation agreement is cancelled. The Home Buyer must be told of any deductions that may be made. While the Reservation agreement is in force, the Home Builder must not enter into a new Reservation agreement or sale agreement with another customer on the same Home.

3 INFORMATION – EXCHANGE OF CONTRACT

3.1 The contract

Contract of sale terms and conditions must:

- be clear and fair;
- comply with the Unfair Terms in Consumer Contracts Regulations 1999;
- clearly state the contract termination rights.

3.2 Timing of construction, completion and handover

The Home Buyer must be given reliable and realistic information about when construction of the Home may be finished, the date of Legal Completion, and the date for handover of the Home.

3.3 Contract termination rights

The Home Buyer must be told about their right to terminate the contract.

3.4 Contract deposits and pre-payments

The Home Builder must clearly explain how Home Buyers' contract deposits are protected and how any other pre-payments are dealt with.

4 INFORMATION – DURING OCCUPATION

4.1 **After-sales service**

The Home Builder must provide the Home Buyer with an accessible after-sales service, and explain what the service includes, who to contact, and what guarantees and warranties apply to the Home.

4.2 **Health and safety for Home Buyers on developments under construction**

Home Buyers must be told about the health and safety precautions they should take when living on a development where building work continues.

5 COMPLAINTS AND DISPUTES

5.1 **Complaints handling**

The Home Builder must have a system and procedures for receiving, handling, and resolving Home Buyers' service calls and complaints. The Home Builder must let the Home Buyer know of this, and of the dispute resolution arrangements operated as part of this Code, in writing.

5.2 **Co-operation with professional advisers**

The Home Builder must co-operate with appropriately qualified professional advisers appointed by the Home Buyer to resolve disputes.

Treasury Committee Report on the Crown Estate

In March 2010 the Treasury Committee of the House of Commons published a two-volume report on *The Management of the Crown Estate* (HC 325, available at http://www.publications.parliament.uk/pa/cm/cmtreasy.htm), the second volume of which comprises evidence to the Committee. The main interest for Scotland lies in the discussion of the marine estate (vol 1 ch 7) which, while accounting for only 7% of the total value of the UK Crown estate, produces the largest gross revenue surplus in Scotland (£7.4 million in 2008–09). The foreshore managed by six councils in the Highlands and Islands is nearly 30% longer than the foreshore in all of England and Wales; and in the UK as a whole the Crown Estate Commissioners (CEC) manage 55% of the foreshore. As well as foreshore, the marine estate includes the bed of the territorial sea (to 12 nautical miles), the sovereign rights of the UK in the continental shelf (vested by the Continental Shelf Act 1964, but excluding oil, gas and coal), and rights to salmon fishings, mussels and oysters. The report focuses on the latest and least mature uses – tidal and wave power, and gas and carbon storage – and records some frustration with the CEC's monopoly position and slowness to react. In a brief separate chapter on Scotland (ch 8), the report notes that the CEC has been criticised for being Anglo-centric and for failing to put enough back into the Scottish economy. Overall, the report recommends that the CEC should not focus so much on short-term economic gain but should consider both the longer-term outlook as well as the wider public interest. In relation to

Scotland there is a recommendation that a memorandum of understanding be drawn up between the CEC and the Scottish Government.

Home reports

Despite the abolition of home information packs (HIPs) in England and Wales by the new UK Government, the Scottish Government has made plain that home reports are here to stay in Scotland. One justification is that home reports are different from HIPs, not least because the latter did not include a single survey.

Meanwhile an *Interim Review of the Home Report*, commissioned from independent researchers, was published by the Scottish Government (http://www.scotland.gov.uk/Publications/2010/09/27113029/0). This comprises research findings and also a fuller report. During the first year of operation 77,000 home reports were produced. Initially these might take several weeks to generate but this was soon brought down to around ten days. 'Overall', the *Interim Review* concludes, 'buyers found the Home Report to be helpful.' But it is reluctant to reach firm conclusions on many of the important issues. 'It is too early', we are told, 'to determine whether the Home Report has impacted on the housing market. The credit crisis, recession and collapse in the housing market have been major market influences, and it is not possible to isolate any additional impacts from the Home Report.' It is also 'too early to determine whether the Home Report will impact positively on the overall condition of Scotland's housing'. On multiple surveys, the *Interim Review* says:

> The incidence of individuals commissioning multiple surveys on successive properties was already falling prior to the introduction of the Home Report, as buyers started to make their offers 'subject to survey' over recent years. However, with the introduction of Home Reports, buyers are now making informed bids – they do not have to wait until after their offer is accepted to obtain information about the property, as this is available in the Home Report. Additional reports are sometimes required for a property (funded either by the seller or the buyer) – principally to meet lenders' requirements, but sometimes also to provide buyers with additional or specialist information.

More information is given about lenders:

> Lenders are clear that the information in the Home Report must meet their lending criteria if it is to be used for mortgage purposes. The criteria applied vary between lenders, but often include the following elements:
>
> - The surveyor (and surveyor who undertakes any subsequent reports) must be on a panel of chartered surveyors whose valuations they will trust *in that area;*
> - Any refreshed Home Report must be undertaken by the surveyor who undertook the original Home Report;
> - A three month deadline for acceptance of a Home Report for any mortgage;
> - Shorter timescales for mortgages over 60% of the valuation.

The *Interim Review* notes that 'the practice of fixing unrealistically low asking prices has now ended' and while this is 'largely due to the shift to fixed price sales during the recession', home reports are also playing a part. Some concern was expressed about the accuracy of home reports, particularly the single survey:

> Maintaining confidence in the Home Report is important if these benefits are to be sustained. The study identified a small number of areas where there were perceptions of (possible) inaccuracy. These were principally around the role of the draft Single Survey, where it was felt sellers had the opportunity to influence the report; the use of so-called 'beauty parades' where it was felt that sellers had the opportunity to select a high valuation for their home; and inconsistencies between Single Surveys for very similar properties.

Among the recommendations made are the following:

- Guidance should be provided on what constitutes reasonable charges for providing a Home Report.
- Further guidance should be provided on access to Home Reports – to maximise prospective buyers' access to Home Reports, and to limit sellers' agents' access to personal information about prospective buyers.
- Some revision of the content of the Home Reports is recommended, to better tailor the Energy Report and access information to specific properties; and it is recommended that a tick box is included to indicate if the seller has not lived in the property being sold.
- Further guidance should be provided on the role of the Property Questionnaire, and how it should be completed.
- Further information on commissioning Home Reports should be provided.
- A review of the Energy Performance Certificate database should be undertaken, to ensure it will support an increased volume of registrations, when the property market improves.
- The potential to reduce the incidence of additional reports should be explored.

A persistent criticism of home reports has been cost, and the consequential reluctance of at least some people (including speculative or timorous sellers) to put their property on the market. The *Interim Review* notes that: 'The cost depends on the value of the property and the supplier, and can vary substantially, but prices tend to start at around £400 for a property worth up to £100,000, and rise in increments of around £100 for every £100,000 thereafter. Deferred payment may be an option, but is not well used.' Since that was written, the only provider of the deferred-payment option, Close Payment Services, has withdrawn the service with effect from the end of 2010. It had given sellers a nine-month loan repayable on the sale of the house.

Meanwhile, conveyancers have continued to divide as to the merits of home reports (a topic discussed in *Conveyancing 2009* pp 68–69). A letter by Jim Craig published at (2010) 78 *Scottish Law Gazette* 74 presents the case against, while Scott Brown is quoted in the *Journal of the Law Society* for June 2010 (p 58) as saying: 'Home reports have actually been very positive for Scotland, so axing them would be a bad move for the property sector. They have created a greater sense of realism among buyers and sellers. ... It also means that more homes are being sold for "offers around" prices, which is helping provide even more transparency in the market.'

Books

Mark Higgins, *The Enforcement of Heritable Securities* (W Green 2010; ISBN 9780414017818)

Colin T Reid, *Nature Conservation Law*, 3rd edn (W Green 2010; ISBN 9780414016958)

Kenneth G C Reid and George L Gretton, *Conveyancing 2009* (Avizandum Publishing Ltd 2010; ISBN 9781904968405)

Andy Wightman, *The Poor Had No Lawyers: Who Owns Scotland and How They Got It?* (Birlinn; ISBN 9781841589077)

Articles

Ross Gilbert Anderson, 'Fax and email in corporate completions' 2010 SLT (News) 73

Ross Gilbert Anderson, 'Subscription and settlement by fax and email' 2010 SLT (News) 67 (considering *Park Ptr (No 2)* 2009 SLT 871)

Eric Baijal, '*Sheltered Housing Association Ltd v Bon Accord Bonding Co Ltd:* principle prevails over equity?' 2010 SLT (News) 117

Lorraine Barrie and Lindsay Paterson, 'Only a civil matter?' (2010) 55 *Journal of the Law Society of Scotland* Nov/9 (discussing the crime of unlawful eviction of tenants)

Stewart Brymer, 'Title insurance – does more than it says on the tin' (2010) 104 *Greens Property Law Bulletin* 4

Alistair Burrow, 'Expensive business' (2010) 55 *Journal of the Law Society of Scotland* Oct/47 (discussing *Cheshire West and Cheshire Borough Council* 2010 GWD 33-684)

Alistair Burrow, 'Tenancy or bust' (2010) 55 *Journal of the Law Society of Scotland* April/44 (considering *Goldacre (Offices) v Nortel Networks UK Ltd (in Administration)* [2010] Ch 44, in relation to the liability of the administrator of a tenant for payment of rent)

Alistair Burrow, 'Uncertain security' (2010) 55 *Journal of the Law Society of Scotland* Jan/47 (considering the use of the landlord's hypothec on the tenant's insolvency)

Malcolm M Combe, 'Crofting, nominee sales and the separation of powers' (2010) 14 *Edinburgh Law Review* 458

Gillian Craig, 'Wriggle room' (2010) 55 *Journal of the Law Society of Scotland* Sept/56 (considering *Snowie v Museum Hall LLP* 2010 SLT 971)

Andrew Duncan, 'Pre-emptions as real rights: lost in the fog' (2010) 105 *Greens Property Law Bulletin* 4

David Edwin, 'Environmental risks' (2010) 108 *Greens Property Law Bulletin* 1

Ian C Ferguson, 'Lloyds panel cuts – a survival guide' (2010) 78 *Scottish Law Gazette* 82

David Findlay, 'A future for crofting' (2010) 55 *Journal of the Law Society of Scotland* Aug/52 (considering the Crofting Reform (Scotland) Act 2010)

Jacqueline Fordyce, 'Land Reform (Scotland) Act 2003 – pushing the boundaries' 2010 *Juridical Review* 263 (considering the ways in which land might be exempted from access rights)

Alasdair G Fox, 'Creating a jigsaw' (2010) 55 *Journal of the Law Society of Scotland* Dec/49 (considering changes to the Agricultural Holdings (Scotland) Acts which may be made by a 2011 SSI)

Alasdair G Fox, 'Win some, lose some' (2010) 55 *Journal of the Law Society of Scotland* June/48 (considering *Coulston Trust v A C Stoddart & Sons* 2010 SC 399 and *Forbes v Cameron* 2010 SLT 1017)

Alasdair G Fox and Fiona M Stephen, 'Courting controversy' (2010) 55 *Journal of the Law Society of Scotland* Sept/50 (considering *Loudon v Hamilton* 2010 SLT 984, *Mount Stuart Trust v McCulloch* 2010 SC 404, *Morison-Low v Paterson* 2 June 2010, Scottish Land Court, and *Salvesen v Riddell* 29 July 2010, Scottish Land Court)

Sandy Grant, 'Advice on HMO legislation' (2010) 106 *Greens Property Law Bulletin* 3

George L Gretton, 'Missives by fax or PDF?' (2010) 14 *Edinburgh Law Review* 280

George L Gretton, 'The shape of things to come' (2010) 55 *Journal of the Law Society of Scotland* March/22 (explaining the Scottish Law Commission's proposals for reform of the law of land registration)

Mark Higgins, 'An orchestra of instruments' (2010) 55 *Journal of the Law Society of Scotland* Oct/22 (considering the SSIs which flesh out the Home Owner and Debtor Protection (Scotland) Act 2010)

Gordon Junor, 'Acquiescence – and the singular successor' 2010 *Juridical Review* 217

Gordon Junor, 'Expert and/or arbiter?' 2010 SLT (News) 5 (considering *Macdonald Estates plc v National Car Parks Ltd* [2009] CSOH 130)

Gordon Junor, 'Pre-emptions, promises and prospective liabilities' 2010 SLT (News) 95 (considering *Braes v Keeper of the Registers of Scotland* 2010 SLT 689)

Gordon Junor, 'Ransom strips – paying the price!' (2010) 78 *Scottish Law Gazette* 84

John Kerrigan, 'Separation agreements, survivorship destinations and succession' 2010 SLT (News) 25

Richard Leslie and Andrew Steven, 'Cool drafting' (2010) 55 *Journal of the Law Society of Scotland* Nov/54 (considering climate change burdens)

Sarah Lilley, 'A burden discharged' (2010) 55 *Journal of the Law Society of Scotland* Aug/49 (considering *B v B* 2010 GWD 24-448)

Angus McAllister, 'The landlord's hypothec: down but is it out?' 2010 *Juridical Review* 65

Gavin McEwan and Emma Ledsom, 'An easy way to give?' (2010) 55 *Journal of the Law Society of Scotland* Aug/56 (considering the granting of standard securities by charities in favour of substantial funders)

Alastair McKie, 'Links with the past' (2010) 55 *Journal of the Law Society of Scotland* July/43 (considering the Historic Environment (Amendment) (Scotland) Bill)

Peter Nicholson, 'Default position' (2010) 55 *Journal of the Law Society of Scotland* Dec/56 (considering *Royal Bank of Scotland plc v Wilson* 2010 SLT 1227)

Adele Nicol and Alasdair G Fox, 'The future of crofting' (2010) 55 *Journal of the Law Society of Scotland* March/49 (considering the Crofting (Scotland) Bill)

Tim Power, 'Forecast cloudy' (2010) 55 *Journal of the Law Society of Scotland* July/52 (reviewing the state of the property market)

Donald B Reid, 'Rectification of deeds: part 2' (2010) 104 *Greens Property Law Bulletin* 1

Robert Rennie, 'Law v practice: *Royal Bank of Scotland plc v Wilson*' 2010 SLT (News) 219

Robert Rennie, 'Solicitors' negligence – new developments' 2010 SLT (News) 159

Robert Rennie, 'The ice cream man cometh' 2010 SLT (News) 165 (considering *Snowie v Museum Hall LLP* 2010 SLT 971)

Lynn Richmond, 'Signed, sealed and ... delivered?' 2010 SLT (News) 63 (considering *Kodak Processing Companies Ltd v Shoredale Ltd* 2009 SLT 1151)

Kenneth Ross and Colin McIntosh, 'To grant or not to grant?' (2010) 55 *Journal of the Law Society of Scotland* April/ 56 (replying to the article by Todd and Oliphant mentioned below)

Anna Scott, 'Mini hydro schemes' (2010) 108 *Greens Property Law Bulletin* 6

Euan Sinclair, 'Rights of passage' (2010) 55 *Journal of the Law Society of Scotland* May/56 (considering *Hamilton v Dumfries and Galloway Council* 2009 SC 277)

Sarah Skea and Andrew J M Steven, 'The landlord's hypothec: difficulties in practice' 2010 SLT (News) 120

Adrian Stalker, '*Todd v Clapperton*: the evolving law on repairing obligations and claims against landlords of residential property' 2010 SLT (News) 31

Andrew J M Steven, 'Property issues in lien' (2010) 14 *Edinburgh Law Review* 455

Ken Swinton, 'Can *Braes* bank on the Keeper's promise' (2010) 78 *Scottish Law Gazette* 15 (considering *Braes v Keeper of the Registers of Scotland* 2010 SLT 689)

Ken Swinton, 'Enforcing standard securities: *Royal Bank v Wilson (No 2)*' (2010) 78 *Scottish Law Gazette* 87

Ken Swinton, 'Unequal division and sale' (2010) 78 *Scottish Law Gazette* 86 (considering *Esposito v Barile* 2010 GWD 23-447)

Ken Swinton, 'Varying community burdens' (2010) 78 *Scottish Law Gazette* 38 (considering *Sheltered Housing Management v Bon Accord Bonding Co Ltd* 2010 SLT 662)

Andrew Todd, 'Supersession clauses – a reminder' (2010) 109 *Greens Property Law Bulletin* 3

Andrew Todd and Rachel Oliphant, 'No guarantees?' (2010) 55 *Journal of the Law Society of Scotland* Feb/54 (considering the granting of warrandice where buying from or selling to an insolvency practitioner)

Andrew Todd and Robbie Wishart, 'Can servitudes be granted in favour of tenants under a long lease?' (2010) 105 *Greens Property Law Bulletin* 1

Andrew Vennard, 'Land registration: the next 30 years?' 2010 SLT (News) 1

Lu Xu, 'Managing and maintaining flatted buildings: some Anglo-Scottish comparisons' (2010) 14 *Edinburgh Law Review* 236

☙ PART IV ☙
COMMENTARY

COMMENTARY

TENEMENTS

The first decisions on the Tenements (Scotland) Act 2004 are now beginning to appear. In 2010 there were two. Neither, however, shows a close acquaintanceship with the legislation, and indeed the first decision largely ignores it. Two further cases noted here explore whether it is possible to escape an unfair allocation of maintenance liabilities by means of an application to the Lands Tribunal.

Repairing dormers

A tenement is built and the flats sold. In the titles of each a maintenance burden provides for a rateable contribution to the cost of roof repairs. Later, the owner of a top floor flat adds a dormer window. Later still, the slates fall off the dormer and need replaced. Who is responsible for the cost – all the proprietors in the building or only the proprietor of the top floor flat?

This was substantially the question which arose in *Mehrabadi v Hough*. The tenement, at 20 Summerfield Terrace in Aberdeen, was built in the 1960s. The split-off writs imposed an obligation on the proprietors of each of the eight flats to pay 'a one-eighth share of the cost of maintaining, upholding and if need be renewing ... the roof'. The roof was also made the common property of everyone. Dormer windows were added in 1972 and, much later, had to be repaired, the cost being £4,000. The top floor proprietor paid the bill and then sought to make recovery from the other proprietors in the building. The present action was an action for payment against the proprietor of a flat on the second floor.[1]

At common law, the pursuer's position looked rather weak. If a real burden imposes an obligation to contribute to the maintenance of the 'roof', it is arguable that this means the roof as it existed when the burden was first imposed.[2] Later additions, therefore, would not be included, and the dormer was, of course,

---

1 No question was raised as to the legality of altering a roof which was the common property of everyone, but the issue is not without difficulties. After such a long interval, the problem may have been resolved by positive prescription or acquiescence: see K G C Reid, 'The law of the tenement: three problems' (1990) 35 *Journal of the Law Society of Scotland* 368.
2 That is the view expressed by one of us in a passage cited by the sheriff principal at para 8: see K G C Reid (1990) 35 *Journal of the Law Society of Scotland* 368 at 370. There are also counter-arguments. Professor W M Gordon has suggested to us that, at least where all owners agree to the alteration, or can be taken to have acquiesced in it, there is much to be said for it being included within the scope of the burden.

just such a later addition. It was on this basis that the pursuer failed before the sheriff.[1]

The pursuer appealed to the sheriff principal.[2] His argument was both simple and ingenious. When the dormer was added, he said, its roof became part of the tenement roof by accession. As the tenement roof was common property, it must follow that the dormer roof was common property too. And if something is common property, it falls to be maintained by all of its owners in proportion to the size of their *pro indiviso* shares. In the present case, everyone had an equal share in the roof and so everyone had to contribute equally to the cost.

This argument was brushed aside rather more easily than it deserved and the appeal refused.[3] The sheriff principal's logic is indeed hard to follow. The pursuer had founded on a passage from an article by Professor (now Sheriff) D J Cusine for the – hardly controversial – proposition that co-owners of a part of a tenement are liable for its maintenance.[4] The context for Professor Cusine's remarks was the case where maintenance was not already provided for by the titles – for the obvious reason that, if it was so provided, there was no need to consider liability arising out of common property. The sheriff principal, however, placed on this context a weight which it cannot bear:[5]

> [I]t is clear that the conclusion of Sheriff Cusine in the passage which I have quoted … was based on the premise that the titles were silent on the question of repairing obligations. … In this case the titles do contain express provision both as to the extent of those parts of the building which are to be the common property of the proprietors of the individual flats within the building and as to the extent of the obligations of these proprietors to contribute to the cost of repairing the common property. It follows that the pursuer's solicitor's alternative submission based on the common law must be rejected.

In fact no such thing 'follows'. The operation of accession is not affected by the presence or absence of a maintenance burden. And even if the interaction of maintenance burdens and the rules of common property in respect of maintenance can sometimes be awkward, such awkwardness was avoided in the present case by the simple fact that there was no such interaction. For, by the unchallenged finding of the sheriff, the maintenance burden did *not* apply to the dormer roof.

This is not, however, to say that the pursuer's argument was necessarily correct. In tenements the normal rules of accession are often suspended,[6] and the allocation of ownership then determined by the law of the tenement. That law, of course, is now statutory. By s 2(3) of the Tenements (Scotland) Act 2004 'a top flat

---

1 June 2009, Aberdeen Sheriff Court (*Conveyancing 2009* Case (17)).
2 11 January 2010, Aberdeen Sheriff Court. The sheriff principal was Sir Stephen S T Young QC.
3 Except in relation to one of the defenders in respect of whose flat, it was now discovered, the burdens were imposed *after* the dormers had been added.
4 D J Cusine, 'Maintenance of tenement roofs' (1993) 38 *Journal of the Law Society of Scotland* 402 at 403.
5 Paragraphs 12 and 13.
6 K G C Reid, *The Law of Property in Scotland* (1996) para 585.

extends to and includes the roof over that flat'. Of course, the law of the tenement does not apply to the extent that the titles make provision on the topic in question.[1] In the present case, however, the declaration in the titles that the roof was common property could not apply to a portion of roof added after the declaration. On this view, the dormer roof was the sole property of the pursuer.

Be that as it may, there was a much better argument for the pursuer which was not, in the event, made. In the course of his opinion the sheriff principal observed:[2]

> In passing, I might add that I am far from convinced that the common law any longer has anything to say on these matters at all in light of the Tenements (Scotland) Act 2004. But this issue was not explored in the parties' submissions, it being accepted, as I understood their respective positions, that the Act had no application in view of the express provisions in the titles.

The sheriff principal's doubt was justified. With the passing of the 2004 Act, the common law of the tenement is no more. And in principle, *all* tenements, whenever built, are subject to the division of ownership set out in ss 2 and 3 of the Act, and to the Tenement Management Scheme ('TMS') in schedule 1.[3] Now it is true that, as already mentioned, the Act does not apply to the extent that a particular topic is dealt with in the titles.[4] But so extensive is the new legislation that it will be a rare tenement indeed where the Act does not apply at least to some extent. Number 20 Summerfield Terrace is no exception.

In *Mehrabadi* the sheriff decided, and the pursuer accepted, that the dormer roof did not fall within the maintenance burden created in the 1960s. But from this the wrong conclusion was drawn. The effect of the absence of a title provision in respect of the dormer roof is not that its owner – the pursuer – must bear the cost of maintenance. Rather it is that the Tenement Management Scheme applies, and in particular rule 4 of the TMS which apportions liability in respect of the maintenance of the key parts of the building, known in the TMS as 'scheme property'. Naturally, the roof of a tenement is scheme property, and this includes a dormer roof (although not the window frame itself).[5]

On all of this the Act is perfectly clear. Section 4(6) says that:

> Rule 4 of the Scheme shall apply in relation to any scheme costs incurred in relation to any part of the tenement unless a tenement burden provides that the entire liability

---

1 Tenements (Scotland) Act 2004 s 1.
2 Paragraph 13.
3 Tenements (Scotland) Act 2004 ss 1 and 4. By s 4(2) the TMS does not apply in a case where the tenement is subject to the Development Management Scheme (which became available in 2009). For that Scheme see *Conveyancing 2009* pp 130–56.
4 The rule for the common law of the tenement was of course the same.
5 TMS r 1.3. The point is dealt with expressly in the report by Scottish Law Commission which led to the introduction of the legislation (Report on the *Law of the Tenement* (Scot Law Com No 162, 1998; available at www.scotlawcom.gov.uk) para 5.8: 'We … consider that the roof surrounding a dormer window ought, like the rest of the roof, to be scheme property.' The window frame is excluded by TMS r 1.3(b)(ii). It might be added that a new dormer is not excluded by r 1.3(a) ('any extension which forms part of only one flat') because, unlike the single-storey extension for which that exclusion is intended, a dormer is an integral part of the building.

for those scheme costs (in so far as liability for those costs is not to be met by someone other than an owner) is to be met by one or more of the owners.

In the present case there is indeed no 'tenement burden' (ie real burden) which covers the 'scheme cost'[1] incurred in the maintenance of the dormer roof. Accordingly rule 4 applies. This gives two alternatives: either the proprietor of each flat must contribute an equal share or, if any one flat in the building has a floor area which is more than one and a half times that of any other flat, liability is apportioned according to floor area.[2] Either way, the defender is liable for a share of maintaining the dormer roof.

Explaining pends

In *Hunter v Tindale*[3] the parties at least appreciated that matters were governed by the Tenements (Scotland) Act 2004. Unfortunately, however, they found the wrong part of the legislation.[4]

The case concerned the tenement at 121–125 Constitution Street in Leith. This comprises 10 flats with access to a rear courtyard being provided by an open pend. The pursuer owned a flat in the building, the defender the pend (only). When the pediment of the archway above the pend was repaired, the question arose as to whether the defender had any liability to contribute towards the cost. Perhaps unsurprisingly, the titles were silent on the matter. The pursuer's action was for payment of £677.

The pursuer's argument was that the pend was part of the tenement, that, more specifically, it was a 'close', and therefore that the defender was liable for a share of the cost. Assoilzying the defender, the sheriff[5] concluded that the pend was not part of the building, but without really explaining why. Even an open pend, of course, is covered both at the sides and at the top. If it also provides access to individual flats then it might plausibly be regarded as part of the building; if, in addition, it is made the common property of the owners of the flats in the titles, then its connection to the building is established beyond doubt. The present case was not like that. The pend gave direct access to only one of the flats, and its ownership was separated from ownership of the flats. In such a case a pend can seem more like an open passageway, uncovered at front and rear, than like an integral part of the building. That may have been the reasoning adopted by the sheriff.

---

1 The relevant head of 'scheme cost' is 'any costs arising from any maintenance or inspection of scheme property where the maintenance or inspection is in pursuance of, or authorised by, a scheme decision': TMS r 4.1(a). We do not know whether a proper 'scheme decision' (ie a decision by a majority of owners: see r 2.5) took place in *Mehrabadi*, but in any event where the owner of a roof maintains it, the act of maintenance is treated by the Act as if it was carried out as a result of a scheme decision: see Tenements (Scotland)Act 2004 ss 8(1) and 10.
2 TMS r 4.2.
3 2010 GWD 38-776.
4 In fairness it should be mentioned that the case was heard under the small claims procedure and that neither party was legally represented.
5 Sheriff N M P Morrison QC.

Suppose, however, that the pend at 121–125 Constitution Street was part of the building, as pends sometimes will be. What difference would that have made? The pursuer thought it important that the pend should be classified as a 'close'. But 'close' is defined in the Act as 'a connected passage, stairs and landings within a tenement building which together constitute a common access to two or more of the flats'[1] and, as the sheriff pointed out, these criteria are cumulative, so that it is necessary to show that there is 'a passage *and* stairs *and* landings',[2] which in the present case there was not. Why this was supposed to matter was, however, unclear. If the pend was not a close then it would at least be an innominate 'sector' (to use the language of the Act),[3] which means that it would include the side walls and ceiling as far as the mid-point.[4] But – and this is the important point – neither status, as close or sector, would create any liability for repairs. Liability under the Act is quite distinct from ownership. The pediment of the archway was part of the external wall of the building. That meant that it was 'scheme property' within the Tenement Management Scheme.[5] And, regardless of ownership, the repair of scheme property is to be paid for by the owners of all of the flats, usually in equal shares.[6] But the defender owned the pend, not a flat. There is nothing in the Act that could give rise to liability.

Redressing unfair maintenance allocations

Paying too much for the roof? Dissatisfied with the list of common parts to be maintained? If the title provisions seem unfair, can anything be done about them?

Maintenance burdens can of course always be changed by agreement, and in a tenement (or other community) this needs the consent of the owners of a mere majority of the flats.[7] But even a bare majority can be difficult to assemble, especially if the effect of the proposed variation is to benefit a small number of owners at the expense of the rest. In theory, however, there is also another way forward. The Lands Tribunal has extensive powers to vary or discharge title conditions. Traditionally, these powers have been used mainly in relation to use restrictions such as restrictions on building. Might they not also be used for maintenance obligations? That very question has now been tested in not just one case but two.

Benefit v burden

In *Kennedy v Abbey Lane Properties*,[8] Mr Kennedy owned commercial premises on the ground floor of what was otherwise a wholly residential building at Abbey

---

1 Tenements (Scotland) Act 2004 s 29(1) (definition of 'close').
2 Paragraph 13.
3 Tenements (Scotland)Act 2004 s 29(1) (definition of 'sector').
4 Tenements (Scotland)Act 2004 s 2(1). Beyond that point they would belong, respectively, to the flats on either side and to the flat above.
5 TMS r 1.2(c)(iii).
6 TMS r 4.2.
7 Title Conditions (Scotland) Act 2003 s 33, subject to a right to challenge the variation under s 37 For a discussion of the scope of s 33, see p 119 below.
8 29 March 2010, Lands Tribunal. The Tribunal comprised I M Darling FRICS.

Lane, Edinburgh. There were 32 units altogether and the building dated from 2004. In terms of the deed of conditions, Mr Kennedy was required to contribute 4.5% of the cost of maintaining the 'core common parts' of the building. As well as some exotica, these encompassed the usual sorts of thing – roof, external walls, foundations, and two separate common passageways and stairs. As Mr Kennedy did not have access to the common passageways and stairs, and objected to contributing towards their maintenance, he applied to the Lands Tribunal to vary the deed of conditions by removing this liability. His argument was a simple one. It was both unfair and contrary to common sense that he should have to pay for things which were of no benefit to his property. Evidence was produced to show that his position was not the normal arrangement in blocks of flats. Nor was it the default position under the Tenement Management Scheme. The application was opposed by only one of the proprietors (who, however, owned three flats).

In reaching a decision, the Tribunal is directed to have regard to the 10 factors set out in s 100 of the Title Conditions (Scotland) Act 2003, and in practice the Tribunal often proceeds by weighing factor (b) ('the extent to which the condition confers benefit on the benefited property') against factor (c) ('the extent to which the condition impedes enjoyment of the burdened property') and, if appropriate, factor (d) ('if the condition is an obligation to do something, how practicable or costly it is to comply with the condition').[1] Benefit, in other words, is measured against burden. If the benefit is small and the burden palpable, the variation is usually granted; otherwise it is usually refused. This approach, however, sits uneasily with an application in respect of maintenance provisions. For if the applicant is to be relieved of liability, then the working assumption[2] must be that the liability of the other proprietors in the tenement will meet with a corresponding increase. On a benefit-burden analysis the result is then equilibrium: for every £1 of which the applicant would be relieved, if the variation is allowed, the same £1 would be imposed on the other proprietors. And where burden and benefit are so precisely in balance, the case for variation is hard to make.

So it was in *Kennedy v Abbey Lane Properties*. As the Tribunal pointed out, the maintenance costs involved were relatively small, and, while their redistribution would have little impact on the 31 other proprietors, the retention of the status quo would not seriously harm the applicant. 'When viewed overall, we do not consider there is any material economic prejudice to the applicant and the impact on rental value is likely to be minimal.'[3] Wider considerations did not alter this conclusion:[4]

> In this situation there is undoubtedly an unusual arrangement where the commercial subjects are obliged to contribute to the maintenance of the common entrance and stair but just because it is unusual or possibly even unfair does not, by itself, mean the application is overall a reasonable one that justifies varying the deed of conditions. Indeed, without any information as to how the 4.5% figure was arrived at, it is

---

1 *Conveyancing 2007* pp 90–95.
2 Although, as we will see later, a questionable one.
3 Paragraph 45.
4 Paragraphs 42 and 43.

impossible to rule out the possibility that it fairly reflects the imposition of liability for these matters for which the ground floor commercial proprietor would not normally be liable – ie but for this liability, the figure might, for all we know, have been higher.

For whatever reason, the entrances and stairs have been included in the 'core common parts' which embraces a wide range of common features such as walls, roofs, services etc and might be seen as something of a catch-all category. ... [I]t would appear that a broadbrush approach has, not unreasonably and very probably intentionally, been adopted by the draftsman. For example, all flat proprietors share the stair maintenance costs, irrespective of which stair serves which flats. Indeed the failure, in an otherwise detailed set of conditions with a comprehensive interpretation section, to differentiate the position of the commercial property owner, or for that matter flat proprietors at different levels, suggests an intentional broadbrush approach to this particular title condition.

The application was accordingly refused.

Change in circumstances

One other statutory factor can sometimes be decisive in Tribunal applications. This is factor (a) ('any change of circumstances since the title condition was created'). For if time and change render a condition obsolete or harmful or unfair, the Tribunal will be disposed to alter it. The second case, *Patterson v Drouet*,[1] was fought mainly on the basis of factor (a).

Some background is needed here. When domestic rates were abolished in 1989, the legislation provided that all existing maintenance obligations apportioned by reference to rateable value (or assessed rental or annual value) should continue to stand. But as there would be no new valuations, the valuation would be frozen as at 1 April 1989.[2] Today, more than 20 years on, some of these valuations might perhaps be seen to have become unfair, because there may have been changes to the *relative* values of the properties. And, arguably, the unfairest case of all is where property that was in commercial use in 1989, and so had a high rateable value, has subsequently changed to domestic use and so should have a lower value. That was exactly the position in *Patterson*. On the basis of the 1989 valuations, the two flats on the ground floor of an eight-flat tenement in Holland Street, Glasgow were liable for around three-quarters of the maintenance costs. Yet the flats had since reverted to residential use. If the valuation roll had continued to be updated, the position would have righted itself in the course of time. As it was, the ground floor flats were subject to liability on a scale which had never been intended. The owners of the ground flats applied to have their liability reduced, and the application was opposed by the owners of three of the upper flats.

The Tribunal decided that, on the merits at least, the application ought to be granted:[3]

---

1 20 January 2011, Lands Tribunal. The Tribunal comprised J N Wright QC and I M Darling FRICS.
2 The relevant provision is now s 111 of the Local Government Finance Act 1992.
3 Paragraph 33.

Put shortly, the purpose of this title condition appears to us to have been to ensure that apportionment of common charges applicable to eight dwellinghouses would always be certain but would stay in line with current values. As we see it, three changes of circumstances in combination would make it reasonable in this particular case to vary the position which has now resulted: firstly, the change to commercial use of the applicants' properties; then the abolition of domestic rates and the resultant 'freezing' of values; and then the reversion back to residential use, resulting in frozen values bearing no relationship to current uses as intended by the deed of conditions. As a result of these changes in circumstances, the present apportionments produce gross disparities between two residential subjects and the other six residential subjects.

That is an important – perhaps even a ground-breaking – decision. But it was not enough to get the applicants home, for the Tribunal expressed reservations as to the competency of the application and continued the case for further consideration.

Competency

At this point it is helpful to revisit *Kennedy v Abbey Lane Properties*. Mr Kennedy's application was refused, but suppose that it had been granted. What would have happened then? Who would have picked up the 4.5% liability in respect of the passageways and stairs of which Mr Kennedy would now have been relieved? The working assumption both of the parties and of the Tribunal seems to have been that the liability would pass to the owners of the other 31 flats in the building. A moment's reflection, however, shows that this cannot be correct. Applications for variation must normally be brought under s 90(1)(a)(i) of the Title Conditions Act, and *Kennedy* was no exception. But in such an application the owner of a burdened property can only seek variation 'in relation to *that* property'. There is nothing surprising about this, for it would be a strange rule indeed which allowed an applicant to change the burdens on property belonging to other people. Consider, then, what would have happened if Mr Kennedy had been successful. His own title would be altered to relieve him of responsibility for the passage and stairs. But no corresponding increase in liability could have been imposed on the 31 other owners. The result would be a shortfall in respect of Mr Kennedy's now-missing share. As it happens, the Tenements (Scotland) Act 2004 has a solution for cases of this kind. Where the figures for maintenance of 'scheme property' do not add up, the titles are disregarded and the relevant rule of the Tenement Management Scheme – rule 4.2 – applies instead.[1] The result in most cases will be to impose equal liability on those who own the part in question – which, in the case of the passage and stairs at Abbey Lane, might (for all we know) include Mr Kennedy.

The same analysis applies to *Patterson v Drouet*. If the applicants ultimately succeed, the requested reduction in their liability – from 75% to 30% – will not in fact take effect. Instead there will be a shortfall, the title provisions will be overridden, and the Tenement Management Scheme will apply. But, unlike in

---

1   Tenements (Scotland) Act 2004 s 4(6).

Kennedy, the result will be highly favourable to the applicants, giving rise to an equal, or at least an equitable, liability all round. This result troubled the Tribunal. By s 90(5) of the Title Conditions Act a 'variation which would impose a new obligation' is not competent unless 'the owner of the burdened property consents',[1] and if the application in *Patterson* were to be granted, a new obligation would indeed be imposed, on the other flats in the building. Yet there was no question of the owners of those flats giving their consent. It was for this reason that the Tribunal continued the case for further submissions.

In fact we doubt whether there is a real difficulty here. It is true that to grant the application in *Patterson* will, in a sense, be to impose a 'new obligation' on the other flats. But there is no new real burden, the obligation in question being imposed by the Tenement Management Scheme and not by the Tribunal. The significance of this distinction is brought out by the language of s 90(5) itself. The 'new obligation' to which that provision refers is one which is imposed on a 'burdened property' (the owner of which can give his or her consent); and 'burdened property' is defined in s 122(1) of the Act as land which is subject to a real burden or title condition. But if a 'new obligation' must thus be a title condition, it is evident that a (statutory) liability under the Tenement Management Scheme does not qualify.[2]

This is not to say that the Tribunal should ignore the impact of the Tenement Management Scheme. On the contrary, it should be an important factor in deciding the application on its merits.[3] In *Kennedy* it would be a further reason for refusal, and with *Patterson* too the fact that bespoke title provisions would be replaced by a statutory formula would argue against the application being granted, although it may well be that that would be outweighed by other factors (and in particular by factor (a)).

The alternative of s 91

As the Tribunal acknowledged in *Patterson*, the Tenement Management Scheme can be avoided by bringing the application, not under s 90(1)(a)(i) of the Title Conditions Act (as is normal), but under s 91. This important provision allows applications by the owners of a quarter of the units in a tenement or other community for the variation or discharge of community burdens as they affect all or some of the units in the community. So a quarter of the owners can, by joining together, achieve a variation which affects all owners (and thus avoids any shortfall). The difficulty, of course, lies in persuading as many as a quarter of owners to co-operate, and much will depend on the size of the tenement. In a tenement of four flats or fewer, any one owner

---

1 This provision does not apply to applications under s 91, discussed below.
2 The official Explanatory Notes para 375 suggest that this provision (which was not in the Scottish Law Commission's draft bill) is intended to cover the case where the application is made by a tenant and will have the effect of imposing an obligation on the property in respect of which the application is made, with the result that it will affect the owner of that property and should require his consent.
3 See *Mrs Young and Others* 1978 SLT (Lands Tr) 28, decided under the predecessor legislation.

constitutes the required quarter and so can bring an application under s 91. For the applicants in *Patterson* to have done so, however, would have required the participation of the owner of another flat,[1] and for the applicant in *Kennedy* of a further seven.

Compensation

In the event that the applicants succeed in *Patterson*, the Tribunal has indicated that it will allow the respondents to pursue claims for compensation.[2] The relevant head in the compensation provisions is one to compensate the owners of the other flats 'for any substantial loss or disadvantage suffered … in consequence of the discharge'.[3] This would cover any decline in the value of the flats due to the increased liability but might also include a figure in respect of the increased maintenance payments that the respondents themselves might have to pay in the future. It will be interesting to see what kinds of sum turn out to be involved. If they are substantial, the applicants may yet conclude, as they are entitled to do,[4] that it would be better to drop the application and live with the unequal distribution of liability.

Altering common parts for the disabled

Common parts may not usually be altered without the agreement of all owners in the building,[5] and there is nothing in the Tenements (Scotland) Act 2004 to change the position.[6] This can create difficulties for the disabled who may, for example, need to install a ramp or handrail or make other changes to facilitate access to the building. A new statutory provision contains the basis for a future solution. Section 27 of the (UK) Equality Act 2010 empowers Scottish Ministers to make regulations allowing disabled persons[7] to make 'relevant adjustments' to common parts in buildings. Tenements are the main target here. 'Common parts' are defined as 'the structure and exterior of, and any common facilities within or used in connection with, the building or part of a building', while 'relevant adjustments' are 'alterations or additions which are likely to avoid a substantial disadvantage to which the disabled person is put in using the common parts in comparison with persons who are not disabled'.[8]

---

1 Between them the applicants owned two of the flats. But in addition to another six 'proper' flats, the basement beneath one of the applicant's flats was a separate unit, owned in conjunction with a flat in the next-door tenement.
2 Paragraph 35.
3 Title Conditions (Scotland) Act 2003 s 90(7)(a). For a recent case, see *G v A* 10 February 2010, Lands Tribunal (digested as Case (42) above).
4 Title Conditions (Scotland) Act 2003 s 90(9).
5 K G C Reid, *The Law of Property in Scotland* (1996) para 25.
6 While the TMS allows a majority to agree on 'maintenance' (r 3.1(a)), this word is defined in r 1.5 so as to exclude 'demolition, alteration or improvement unless reasonably incidental to the maintenance'.
7 By s 6(1) a person is disabled if he or she has a physical or mental impairment which has a substantial and long-term adverse effect on the ability to carry out normal day-to-day activities.
8 Equality Act 2010 s 27(5).

On 10 January 2011 the Scottish Government launched a consultation on the scope and content of the regulations.[1] Under the Government's proposals it would continue to be necessary to obtain the consent of all the owners for alterations, but that consent could not be unreasonably withheld, and the regulations would specify factors that owners should take into account when deciding whether it is reasonable to consent, for example:[2]

- The disabled person's disability
- Whether the work proposed is necessary to meet the disabled person's needs
- The safety of the people who live in the building
- Any cost to the owner
- Whether the adaptation would reduce the value of the owner's property
- Whether the adaptation would make it harder to rent or sell the owner's property
- Whether the building can be reinstated to its previous condition
- Whether consent would make the owner liable under any other rule or remedy
- Any Code of Practice issued by the Commission for Equality and Human Rights.

The work would be instructed by and paid for by the disabled person, but future maintenance would be a shared responsibility unless a written agreement was entered into providing otherwise. An owner could insist on such an agreement as a condition of giving consent. Incoming owners would be bound by the consent of their predecessors – contrary to the normal rule – provided that notice of the adaptation was registered in the Land Register or Register of Sasines. As this will cost £60, one imagines that registration will take place only in respect of major alterations. It is unclear whether registration is to be against the title of all the flats in the tenement or just the flat belonging to the disabled person. The latter would have little value in giving notice to potential purchasers.

MISSIVES OF SALE

Unusual or unduly onerous burdens

In the current recession, buyers sometimes find themselves casting around for grounds to extricate themselves from missives.[3] One such ground is that the real burdens and other title conditions are unusual or unduly onerous.

The background law is that the seller of land is taken to warrant that title conditions, unless known to the buyer at the time of missives, are neither unusual nor unduly onerous.[4] But in practice this is always a matter of express provision in missives. Typically the clause is in two parts: first, there is a warranty that there are no unusual or unduly onerous conditions; and second, that if there are,

---

1 *The Right to Adapt Common Parts in Scotland*, available at http://www.scotland.gov.uk/ Publications/2011/01/10092726/4. The proposals are modelled on s 52 of the Housing (Scotland) Act 2006, which allows the disabled to make alterations to privately rented housing.
2 Paragraph 2.4.
3 For previous examples, see *Conveyancing 2008* pp 81–85.
4 G L Gretton and K G C Reid, *Conveyancing* (3rd edn, 2004) para 6-05.

the buyer's only remedy is to rescind, which must be done within a stipulated period (such as ten working days) of receipt of the titles.[1] As there is relatively little authority on the meaning of 'unusual or unduly onerous', the decision in *Snowie v Museum Hall LLP*[2] is especially welcome.

Snowie concerned missives for the purchase of a number of apartments in the same new development. At the time of missives the deed of conditions had yet to be registered. The missives provided that:

> The title to be granted to the Subjects will take the form of a Disposition by the Sellers which shall contain such conditions as the Sellers think appropriate for the Development and the preservation thereof and which shall incorporate the prior conditions of title and the conditions contained in any Deed of Conditions relating to the Development which shall contain no unduly onerous or unusual conditions. The Deed of Conditions shall contain the allowance for the occupation of at least one dog, one cat and fish.

In due course the buyers sought to rescind the contract on the basis that one of the burdens in the deed of conditions – a prohibition of use (including ancillary use) for trade, business or profession – was unusual or unduly onerous. The argument, which has an air of desperation about it, was firmly rejected by Lord Glennie. The burden could not be said to be 'unusual' when it was present in the only styles book which was put before the court. And if it was 'usual' it was unlikely to be 'unduly onerous' – for why otherwise would people accept it? – especially as it would not in practice prevent business use of a kind which did not intrude upon neighbours.[3] The buyers could not, therefore, walk away from the contract.

Reasonable endeavours

Introduction

A developer (X) identifies a site with development potential. It enters into a contract with the owner (Y) to buy the site. But the development is likely to need one or more third-party consents. If those consents are unobtainable, the developer does not wish to proceed. So the obtaining of those consents is made a condition of the X/Y contract. But Y wants some assurance that X will indeed do its best to obtain those consents, for otherwise X could simply abandon the whole project if it so chose. So the X/Y contract will typically say that X must genuinely attempt to obtain the consents. Such expressions as 'reasonable endeavours', 'all reasonable endeavours' and 'best endeavours' are often encountered.

---

1 See eg cl 15 of the Combined Standard Clauses (available at http://www.lawscot.org.uk/members_information/convey_essens/stdmissives/).
2 [2010] CSOH 107, 2010 SLT 971. For a discussion see Robert Rennie, 'The ice cream man cometh' 2010 SLT (News) 165.
3 Paragraphs 14 and 15. Lord Glennie's view that business use was allowed if non-intrusive was founded on interpretation of the provision when it could much more readily have been founded on interest to enforce. See p 114 below.

The commonest type of consent that is needed is planning permission. But contracts also sometimes require one party to seek to enter into an agreement with another party, and there are examples of that from this year's crop of cases. And whilst it is usually the developer that is bound to seek a third-party consent, in some cases it is the seller, and two of this year's cases illustrate that situation.[1]

If things go wrong, and the developer decides not to go ahead with the project, the disappointed seller may argue that the developer failed to make reasonable attempts to secure the third-party consent. Another issue that can arise is whether what X has to do is expressed in such open-ended or indeterminate terms that no court could actually determine whether the result had been achieved. If that is so then the whole X/Y contract will be unenforceable.

A crop of four such cases arose in 2010, *Mactaggart & Mickel Homes Ltd v Hunter*,[2] *EDI Central Ltd v National Car Parks Ltd*,[3] *R & D Construction Group Ltd v Hallam Land Management Ltd*,[4] and *Scottish Coal Company Ltd v Danish Forestry Co Ltd*.[5] The first two are new cases, decided during 2010 at first instance; the others are cases on appeal to the Inner House, and in both the decision at first instance was affirmed.

Usually the X/Y contract says that the property transaction is not to take place until the result with the third party (Z) is in place. For example, X and Y enter missives that are subject to a suspensive condition about planning permission. But sometimes the contract provides for the property transaction to go ahead immediately, with a provision that if the result with Z is not achieved by a certain time then the property transaction will be put into reverse gear, ie by a re-conveyance. Two of this year's cases were of this 'reverse gear' type.[6]

Mactaggart & Mickel Homes Ltd v Hunter

In *Mactaggart & Mickel Homes Ltd v Hunter*,[7] the pursuer ('MML') concluded missives to buy a property near Balerno for £3.5 million. Of this price £1.5 million was payable at settlement and the balance of £2 million was payable when MML obtained planning permission for building 17 or more housing units on the site. MML was bound to use 'reasonable endeavours' to obtain such permission. If planning permission was not obtained, the property would be reconveyed to the sellers, and the sellers would be bound to repay the £1.5 million. The repayment would be due within 21 days of the service on the sellers of an 'unsatisfactory planning notice'. MML was to grant a standard security to the sellers, securing its obligation to reconvey. In the event that planning permission was not granted

---

1   *Scottish Coal Company Ltd v Danish Forestry Co Ltd* [2010] CSIH 56, 2010 SC 729 and *R & D Construction Group Ltd v Hallam Land Management Ltd* [2010] CSIH 96, 2011 GWD 2-85, discussed below.
2   [2010] CSOH 130, 2010 GWD 33-683.
3   [2010] CSOH 141, 2011 SLT 75.
4   [2010] CSIH 96, 2011 GWD 2-85.
5   [2010] CSIH 56, 2010 SC 729.
6   *Mactaggart & Mickel Homes Ltd v Hunter* [2010] CSOH 130, 2010 GWD 33-683 and *EDI Central Ltd v National Car Parks Ltd*. [2010] CSOH 141, 2010 GWD 37-754.
7   [2010] CSOH 130, 2011 SLT 75.

and the sellers failed to repay the £1.5 million ('the deposit') within the 21 days, the position was regulated by clause 13.6:

> The Purchaser is entitled at any time to rescind the missives without liability and to recover from the Seller:–
>
> (a) any shortfall between the price obtained on any re-sale of the Subjects and the Deposit;
> (b) damages calculated as the amount of interest which would have accrued at the rate specified in clause 13.4 on the Repayment Date from the Repayment Date until the earlier of:
>
> > (i) the date on which the price on any re-sale is received by the Purchaser; and
> > (ii) the date three months after the date upon which the Purchaser rescinds the Missives in accordance with this Clause;
>
> (c) ...
> (d) all expenses of advertising, all reasonable legal and other professional expenses and any other disbursements in connection with any re-sale; and
> (e) any other loss, damage and expense suffered by the Purchaser as a result of the Seller's failure to pay on time.

The missives also provided that the sellers would deliver to MML a power of attorney to grant a discharge of the standard security on behalf of the sellers – a curious situation in which the grantee of a standard security, at the time of granting, empowers the granter to discharge it. The transaction settled. MML was registered in the Land Register as proprietor, and the standard security in favour of the sellers was registered as well. The power of attorney was delivered. Needless to say, the wheels of the deal came off. MML served on the sellers an 'unsatisfactory planning notice'. The sellers did not repay the £1.5 million within 21 days. MML rescinded the missives. On the basis of the authority conferred by the missives, it executed a discharge of the standard security. It then raised the present action to recover the £1.5 million, minus the current value of the site.

The defence was, in substance, that MML was in breach of the contract by not having used 'reasonable endeavours' to obtain planning permission. After proof, it was held by the Lord Ordinary (Hodge) that MML had indeed used 'reasonable endeavours' and accordingly the defence failed. The Lord Ordinary made the following comment which will interest those drafting contracts of this type:[1]

> In my opinion the phrase 'reasonable endeavours' in its context imposes obligations on MML which are not as onerous as the phrase 'all reasonable endeavours', which was used in the contract in *Agroexport*,[2] and which required the court to consider whether there were reasonable steps which could have been taken but were not. The phrase is also less burdensome on the obligant than the phrase 'best endeavours', which appears to me ... to require something more than 'all reasonable endeavours'.

---

1 Paragraph 63.
2 *Agroexport State Enterprise for Foreign Trade v Compagnie Européenne de Céréales* [1974] 1 Lloyd's LR 499.

So there is a scale. 'Reasonable endeavours' is the weakest, 'all reasonable endeavours' is more demanding, and 'best endeavours' is the most demanding of all. But in *EDI Central Ltd v National Car Parks Ltd*, below, it was doubted whether 'best endeavours' really imposes more stringent obligations than 'all reasonable endeavours'. One may in fact wonder whether those who draft such contracts are always aware that judges may regard these differences in the words chosen as significant. Drafters beware.

But whilst the pursuer had won on the core issue, what was to happen? The missives provided for rescission, and MML did rescind. But rescission looks rather odd here, for two reasons. The first is that whilst rescission can make good sense where settlement has not taken place (eg a buyer fails to come up with the money, so the seller refuses to settle and subsequently rescinds), it is a more awkward concept where settlement has already taken place. In the second place, the missives in this case made provision for what was to happen on rescission. Hence the missives, though rescinded in one sense, were very definitely unrescinded in another sense. Moreover, the provision of the missives as to what was to happen if the missives were rescinded did not cover all possibilities. As the Lord Ordinary said:[1]

> Clause 13.6 envisaged that MML would re-sell the site to re-coup the £1.5 million, which it had paid out as the deposit. It provided that a claim for damages could include interest on the deposit, which had not been repaid, only for three months after the rescission, unless the re-sale of the site gave rise to a shortfall. The missives thus envisaged a prompt re-sale of the site after the rescission. The contract did not address the rights of the parties in at least two circumstances, namely (i) if MML did not sell but sought to retain the site and (ii) if the site on re-sale or on a proper valuation was worth more than the aggregate of the deposit and MML's contractual entitlement to interest as a component of its claim for damages.

As for the second of these points, whilst the action took the form of a claim for £1.5 million less the value of the site, the possibility existed, at this stage of the litigation, that the value of the site, notwithstanding the problems with planning permission, was greater than £1.5 million.

Given that the situation that had arisen was not provided for in the contract, the Lord Ordinary took the view that matters would have to be resolved by the application of the principles of the law of unjustified enrichment. He noted that this might be done either by allowing MML to retain ownership of the site, or by requiring MML to reconvey the site (which is what the defenders wished), in each case with an appropriate financial adjustment between the parties. The case was put out for further procedure.

EDI Central Ltd v National Car Parks Ltd

At issue in *EDI Central Ltd v National Car Parks Ltd*[2] was the Castle Terrace Car Park in Edinburgh, owned by Edinburgh City Council and leased to National

---

1 Paragraph 94.
2 [2010] CSOH 141, 2011 SLT 75.

Car Parks Ltd ('NCP') from 1995 to 2010. The lease required the property to be used as a car park. EDI Central Ltd, a company wholly owned by Edinburgh City Council, entered into a contract with NCP under which the site would be developed, to the profit of both parties. This project involved the assignation of the lease from NCP to EDI Central coupled with an immediate sublease from EDI Central to NCP. Clause 6 of the contract said that:

> The Developer [EDI Central] shall procure that the CT Project is pursued with all reasonable endeavours and as would be expected of a normal prudent commercial developer experienced in developments of that nature and in accordance with the Main Objectives. ...

Clause 13 added:

> The Developer and NCP shall use all reasonable endeavours to achieve the Main Objectives and shall act in good faith in respect of the same and in accordance with this Agreement.

The project foundered. The main problem was that the local authority would not agree to the redevelopment unless alternative parking facilities could be found nearby, and that proved too difficult to arrange. There was a provision in the contract whereby, if the project failed, EDI Central could require NCP to accept a re-assignation of the lease. When EDI Central sought to invoke this clause, NCP refused. EDI Central raised the present action to compel NCP to take back the lease. The defence was that EDI Central had failed to used 'all reasonable endeavours' to pursue the development plan. The Lord Ordinary (Glennie) agreed with the defender that 'all reasonable endeavours' imposes a higher standard than 'reasonable endeavours':[1]

> The obligation to use 'all reasonable endeavours' is a more onerous obligation than one simply to use 'reasonable endeavours'. I do not have to consider whether or not it is the same as one to use 'best endeavours', though I would have thought that any difference is likely to be metaphysical rather than practical. It is difficult to conceive that an obligation to use 'best endeavours' requires a party to take steps which are *ex hypothesi* unreasonable. ... It is not, I think, helpful to attempt to define more precisely what is encompassed by that obligation. It will, as Lord Hodge suggests,[2] require the Court to consider whether there were reasonable steps which could have been taken but were not taken. The party on whom the obligation is placed will be expected to explore all avenues reasonably open to him, and to explore them all to the extent reasonable. But unless the contract otherwise stipulates, he is not required to act against his own commercial interests. ... That point is, in any event, made clear here by the reference in clause 6 to the standards of 'a normal prudent commercial developer experienced in developments of that nature'. The word 'prudent' points to a legitimate consideration of his own financial and commercial interests. Nor is he required to persist where it is clear that further efforts will be fruitless. The reference to the developer being 'experienced in developments of that nature', shows that he

---

1 Paragraph 20.
2 The reference is to *Mactaggart & Mickel Homes Limited v Hunter* (discussed above).

is entitled to rely upon his judgement, informed by his experience, of what is and is not likely to bear fruit. If it is clear that he cannot succeed whatever further avenues he may take, he cannot be expected to continue wasting time, effort and expense. So also, if it becomes clear that one necessary hurdle cannot be overcome, he will not be expected to waste his time seeking to overcome other problems, since overcoming them would achieve nothing.

In the light of this approach it was held, after proof, that EDI Central had in fact used 'all reasonable endeavours' and accordingly decree was granted in favour of the pursuer. The Lord Ordinary also has a valuable discussion of the nature of good faith in a contractual context. He adds the remark: 'It is, of course, no part of Scots law that, in the absence of agreement, parties to a contract should act in good faith in carrying out their obligations to each other.'[1] That is orthodoxy. But heresy has never disappeared: compare, for example, *Howatson v Whyte*[2] where it was held that in pre-emption cases there is an implied duty of fair-dealing.

R & D Construction Group Ltd v Hallam Land Management Ltd

In *R & D Construction Group Ltd v Hallam Land Management Ltd*,[3] Hallam had an option on some land with development potential at Cleland, near Motherwell. The option period was five years and the exercise price was set at 75% of value, though the owner, Ms Kerr, also received an up-front grassum (£75,000) for granting the option. With that option in its pocket, Hallam then concluded missives to sell the land to R & D for a price of £571,314. The missives contained this clause (clause 4.1.10):

> The Missives shall be essentially conditional upon … the Seller [Hallam] agreeing a purchase price for the Subjects with the current proprietor [Ms Kerr] in terms wholly acceptable to the Seller (the Seller being required to use all reasonable endeavours in this regard).

The first part of this clause was to protect Hallam from the risk that the eventual price in the Kerr/Hallam contract might prove to be unacceptably high from Hallam's point of view. The second part (the part in brackets) was to protect R & D from the risk that Hallam might use the first part of the clause as a get-out-of-jail-free card in relation to the contract with R & D.

Problems arose with the Kerr/Hallam contract, chiefly because Ms Kerr and Hallam did not arrive at an agreement on the fair market value. The missives with R & D had a longstop date in them and eventually it passed without agreement between Hallam and Ms Kerr. R & D then sued to enforce its contract against Hallam. Hallam had two lines of defence. The first was that the 'wholly acceptable' provision made the contract too subjective to be enforceable in a court. How could a court or anyone else ever be able to say whether something was or was not 'wholly acceptable' to someone? The second was that (*esto* the contract

---

1 Paragraph 23.
2 14 July 1992, Forfar Sheriff Court, discussed at p 166 below.
3 [2010] CSIH 96, 2011 GWD 2-85.

was enforceable) Hallam had in fact used 'all reasonable endeavours' to reach agreement with Ms Kerr. At first instance the first defence was rejected, but the second upheld.[1] R & D reclaimed on the second point, and the defender, just to be safe, also reclaimed on the first point. Both reclaiming motions were refused. As to whether Hallam had used 'all reasonable endeavours', the three appeal judges were in agreement. The issue was essentially one of fact, and the view taken by a judge at first instance on a factual issue will not be set aside on appeal unless it is manifestly wrong.

On the other issue, Lord Reed put it thus: 'An obligation to use reasonable endeavours (or all reasonable endeavours) is generally enforceable, provided that the object of the endeavours is sufficiently definite.'[2] So the question was whether 'terms wholly acceptable to the Seller' could be considered sufficiently definite. All three appellate judges agreed with the Lord Ordinary that it was, albeit with what looks like a certain degree of hesitation on the part of one of them, Lord Drummond Young. Evidently this case lay fairly near the borderline between the enforceable and the unenforceable, and no doubt the court could reasonably have gone the other way. The next case, *Scottish Coal Company Ltd v Danish Forestry Co Ltd*, was also a borderline case, and here the court did go the other way.

Scottish Coal Company Ltd v Danish Forestry Co Ltd

In *Scottish Coal Company Ltd v Danish Forestry Co Ltd*[3] the word 'endeavours' was not used, but there was an agreement to agree with a third party on 'reasonable' terms. The issue was not the factual one as to whether enough 'endeavouring' had taken place, but rather the other issue, as to whether the objective aimed at (agreement with the bank on 'reasonable' terms) was sufficiently definite to enable a court to pronounce on what would count as meeting that objective.

Danish Forestry Co Ltd ('DFC') owned some land in Lanarkshire while Scottish Coal Company Ltd ('SCC') owned neighbouring land. Naturally enough, the former used its land for forestry and the latter for extracting coal. As it turned out that there was plenty of coal underneath the forestry land, the two companies entered a contract under which SCC took an option to buy DFC's land.[4] But whereas most options are structured so that, upon being exercised, the option holder pays a lump sum to the counterparty, in this case the option took a different form. Instead of a lump sum, SCC would make quarterly payments to DFC. But DFC wanted security for this, and so the option agreement provided that SCC would grant to DFC a standard security over the land being acquired. SCC's bank (Royal Bank of Scotland plc) would also be taking a security over the land. Here is what the contract said:

---

1 [2009] CSOH 128, digested as *Conveyancing 2009* Case (8).
2 Paragraph 66.
3 [2010] CSIH 56, 2010 SC 729. The Opinion of the First Division was delivered by the Lord President (Hamilton).
4 The coal was to be extracted by the open cast method, so that it would not have been enough for SCC to acquire the mineral rights. They needed the land itself.

10.1 The Company [SCC] shall grant in favour of Danish at the Settlement Date a Standard Security over the Option Area for (1) all sums due and which may become due by the Company to Danish in terms of this Agreement and (2) the performance of the Company's non-financial obligations in terms of this agreement. Danish agrees to enter into an agreement with the Company and/or the Company's bankers reasonably to regulate the relationship between the sums which will be recoverable under the Standard Security and the terms under which these sums will rank ahead of any other sums due by the Company to their bankers from time to time ('the Ranking Agreement') ...[1].

A notice exercising the option was sent and in due course RBS submitted its proposed ranking agreement. This said: '[DFC] shall not without the prior written consent of [RBS] exercise any of its powers of enforcement over [the land in question] or otherwise have recourse to the same.' DFC was (unsurprisingly) not happy with this. Impasse was reached. Eventually SCC raised this action to enforce the option contract. The defence was that the agreement to agree was unenforceable. The Lord Ordinary accepted this position.[2] SCC reclaimed, and the Inner House has now affirmed the Lord Ordinary's decision. We quote the Opinion:[3]

The word 'reasonable' (and perhaps also the word 'reasonably'), albeit itself imprecise, may in some circumstances require to be given a concrete meaning by a court of law (*Gloag on Contract* (2nd edn) at pages 11–12). Under section 8(2) of the Sale of Goods Act 1979 the court may be called upon to determine a 'reasonable' price for the purchase of goods; under a lease it may require to determine a 'fair' or 'reasonable' reviewed rental. But these will, at least ordinarily, arise in the context of there being a market or other context against which a reasonable price or a fair or reasonable rental can be determined. The present case is different. There is, so far as appears, no market or settled practice for ranking agreements. While some of the terms of such agreements may be conventional, others will depend crucially on what the relevant parties, having regard to their respective – possibly conflicting – interests, are able mutually to agree. These terms may include, as here, the maximum sum to be secured by the prior ranking security and whether the holder of that security is to be free at its own hand, without reference to the other security holders, to enforce its security. How is the court, without more definite contractual guidance, to determine what is in these respects reasonable?

This, like *R & D Construction Group Ltd v Hallam Land Management Ltd*, seems to us a borderline case. It is true that there is 'no market or settled practice for ranking

---

1 The Inner House noted (para 12) that 'the syntax of the second (critical) sentence is very odd. Read literally, the regulation envisaged is between "the sums which will be recoverable under the Standard Security" and "the terms under which these sums will rank ahead of any other sums due by [Scottish Coal] to their bankers from time to time". Regulation between such matters does not make sense.' The Court went on: 'Presumably this sentence was seeking to do two things: first, to provide in the body of the clause that the standard security was to be first ranking ... and, secondly, to regulate the (other) terms upon which the sums secured to Danish were to relate to sums otherwise secured to the Bank and Scottish Coal's other secured creditors. But no point was taken before the Lord Ordinary or before us about this infelicity. We proceed on the basis that the latter part of the sentence is to be read as we have explicated it.'
2 [2009] CSOH 171, 2010 GWD 5-79, digested as *Conveyancing 2009* Case (9).
3 Paragraph 17.

agreements'. But one might also say that there is 'no market or settled practice' as to what is 'wholly acceptable' to a party.

Supersession clauses and agreements to sign other agreements

Supersession clauses usually work well for straightforward transactions but often cause problems for more complex transactions. Equally, agreements to sign other agreements often cause problems, for obvious reasons. *Aziz v Whannel*[1] involved both. Another example from 2010 of an agreement between X and Y to enter into another agreement, also between X and Y, is *Smith v Stuart*,[2] discussed later.[3]

The owner of the Bathville Inn, Abdul Aziz, concluded missives, in August 2004, to sell it to Whitburn Trade Centre Ltd. The property was to be developed, and as part of the consideration there was to be conveyed back to the seller one of the new flats. Instead of this being a term of the missives themselves, the missives bound the buyer to 'enter into a Minute of Agreement with the Seller in terms of a draft thereof annexed and signed as relative hereto.'

Another clause of the missives was as follows:

> The Missives shall remain in full force and effect until implemented notwithstanding the delivery of a Disposition in favour of the Purchaser ... but that for a maximum period of two years or such longer period as may be necessary if founded upon in any proceedings raised prior to the expiry of the said two year period.

In November 2005 the missives were varied in a number of respects. James Whannel was substituted as buyer, and the seller was not only to receive one of the new flats but was to be entitled to buy two more at a total price of £50,000. As before, instead of this being a term of the missives themselves, the missives bound the parties to enter a separate 'minute of agreement'. No such minute of agreement was ever signed.

Although the Opinion does not say that the transaction settled, we think that it must have done so, immediately after the November 2005 missives. In October 2006 there was a further variation of the missives, saying that the buyer could, by paying the seller £150,000, cancel the seller's rights to the flats. But, said the variation, if the buyer did not do this by 30 April 2007, the seller could in turn serve notice cancelling the cancellation right. By 30 April 2007 the buyer had not exercised the cancellation right, and the seller served notice cancelling the cancellation right. In June 2007 the buyer died. It seems, though the point is not quite clear, that the development had not taken place. The seller claimed damages for the loss of his rights to the flats. He quantified his loss at £200,000 and sued the buyer's executrix for this sum. The defence was that the obligation about the

---

1 [2010] CSOH 136, 2010 GWD 33-682.
2 2010 SC 490, 2010 SLT 1249.
3 At p 182 below. Both these were cases where only two parties were involved. There can be cases – especially in commercial conveyancing – where X and Y agree that Y should seek to reach agreement with Z. For examples from 2010, see *Scottish Coal Company Ltd v Danish Forestry Co Ltd* [2010] CSIH 56, 2010 SC 729 and *R & D Construction Group Ltd v Hallam Land Management Ltd* [2010] CSIH 96, 2011 GWD 2-85, discussed above.

three flats was contained in a minute of agreement that had never been signed. There was, it was true, an obligation to sign it. But that obligation, argued the defender, had ceased to be enforceable two years after August 2004.

The Lord Ordinary (Glennie) took the view that, although the missives were written in such a way as not to incorporate the minute of agreement but merely to impose an obligation to enter into such a minute, it was clear from the whole circumstances of the case that they must have intended the minute of agreement to be directly binding, even without signature.

But that did not end the debate. The defender further argued that, even if the unsigned minute of agreement had binding effect, it could have such effect only as part of the missives themselves. And that would lead back to the same conclusion, for the missives had expired in August 2006. The Lord Ordinary rejected that argument thus:

> I find it difficult to see how the two year limitation could have applied to obligations under the Minute of Agreement. In terms it bites only upon the duration of the missives. When, subsequently, the parties reached agreement in terms of the 2005 Minute of Agreement, that too took effect as an agreement separate from the missives themselves. I see no basis upon which it can properly be said that the terms of clause 10 of the 2004 Missives have any impact on the obligations entered into in terms of the 2005 Minute of Agreement.

Thus in response to the defender's first argument (about lack of signature), the Lord Ordinary's view was that what the missives said about the minute of agreement – that the parties had to sign it – could be disregarded, ie that the minute of agreement was binding even without signature. The basis for this view of matters is not wholly clear to us. (For example, s 1(3) of the Requirements of Writing (Scotland) Act 1995, which might have been a basis for regarding the minute of agreement as binding despite the lack of signature, seems not to have been mentioned.) Our tentative interpretation of the decision is that the minute of agreement, as set out in a schedule to the missives, was deemed to be part of the missives themselves and hence directly binding.[1] But if that is so, a difficulty may arise. For the Lord Ordinary seems to dispose of the defender's second argument (about supersession) by saying that the minute of agreement was not subject to the supersession provision precisely because it was *not* part of the missives. A critic might remark that what is sauce for the goose is sauce for the gander.

The pursuer had also argued that the supersession clause was void. The basis for this argument was that it did not state when it was to begin to run, and in *Lonergan v W&P Food Service Ltd*[2] it had been held that supersession clauses that do not state their start date are void by reason of uncertainty. The Lord Ordinary said:[3]

> Standing the conclusion which I have reached on the main point, I do not need to decide this question. For my part, unaided by authority, I would have come to the

---

1 See for annexations s 8 of the Requirements of Writing (Scotland) Act 1995.
2 2002 SLT 908. See *Conveyancing 2002* p 57.
3 Paragraph 24.

conclusion that it was implicit in the terms of clause 10 that the period of two years commenced on the conclusion of the missives of which that clause formed part. But I note that Lord Clarke came to a different conclusion and I would, with respect, defer to his view on the matter.

Supersession clauses generally work satisfactorily in straightforward transactions. But in more complicated transactions they often cause problems, for the simple reason that it is very easy for two years to pass without matters having been fully settled.

A source of difficulty in this case was the device of one contract requiring the parties to enter into another contract. This device is quite often seen. But why not have just one contract? If at the time of the contract it is not clear whether certain obligations are to be activated, then conditions can be attached to those obligations.

REAL BURDENS

Interpretation

In *Snowie v Museum Hall LLP*[1] Lord Glennie was called on to interpret a real burden which, as so often in residential property, prohibited business use.[2] There were two related clauses in a deed of conditions.[3] First, it was provided that:

> No trade, business or profession may be carried out in the apartment (including the sale, making or manufacture of any beer, wine or liquors).

Then, in an attempt to eliminate the incidental or ancillary use which case law has tended to allow,[4] it was further provided that:

> Each apartment must be used as a private house only, and may not be used, even in an ancillary capacity, for any trade, business or profession.

It might be thought that these provisions are too clear to stand in need of interpretation. The matter seems perfectly simple: the apartment is not to be used for a trade, business or profession of any sort or to any extent. Full stop. Lord Glennie, however, held otherwise. In his view, business uses were permissible if they did not disturb the owners of other apartments, and it did not matter whether such uses were ancillary and occasional or a principal use carried out all day every day:[5]

---

1 [2010] CSOH 107, 2010 SLT 971. For a discussion see Robert Rennie, 'The ice cream man cometh' 2010 SLT (News) 165; Gillian Craig, 'Wriggle room?' (2010) 55 *Journal of the Law Society of Scotland* Sept/56.
2 The context was whether the burdens were unusual or unduly onerous, thus allowing the buyers to rescind the contract. It was held that they were not: see p 104 above.
3 At para 19 Lord Glennie lapses into English terminology, referring to the deed as a 'deed of covenants'.
4 *Colquhoun's CB v Glen's Tr* 1920 SC 737; *Low v Scottish Amicable Building Society* 1940 SLT 295.
5 Paragraph 15.

[T]he restrictions in the Rules contained in clause 2 of the Deed of Conditions, and indeed similar restrictions in other Deeds, must be given a sensible construction having regard to the nature of the scheme or Development to which they relate and the purpose for which they must be taken to have been included. ... The purpose of restrictions of this sort is to prevent the residential amenity of the Development being spoiled. The residential amenity of a Development is not spoiled by the fact that one or more of the owners of the apartments within it brings work home from the office. It may ultimately be a matter of degree. I do not need to decide whether it would be permissible ... for an owner of one of the apartments to carry on his business substantially or entirely from home, provided that he did not display any advertising and did not receive either deliveries or customers or clients. It is difficult to conceive that the artist who paints from home would be acting in breach of the Deed of Conditions, even if from time to time he was visited by his agent, a gallery owner or a potential buyer. So too, an advocate or solicitor who worked from home for most of the time, travelling only to attend court or meet clients, would not, in my opinion, be acting in breach of the restrictions. In both these cases, their activities would have no impact on the amenity of the residential Development. On the other hand, an estate agent who set up business in his own apartment, displaying advertising from the windows and perhaps from outside the main entrance door, and receiving prospective purchasers or tenants on a regular basis throughout the day, would very likely be found to be in breach. ... It is not easy to define where the line is to be drawn, but I suspect that in most cases, like the elephant of which lawyers are so fond, it will be easy to recognise cases falling either side of it.

Common sense is, however, an uncertain guide in matters of interpretation as in other areas of the law. It is, of course, not difficult to see why Lord Glennie was supportive of lawyers, artists and other professionals provided they work in a way which is considerate and unobtrusive. As he pointed out elsewhere in his judgment, it was precisely that sort of person who was likely to buy the up-market flats in this particular development.[1] But, however desirable this result might be, it could not be achieved by interpretation.[2] For there was nothing to interpret: the words were perfectly clear.

Now as it happens it is most unlikely that a neighbour could stop any of the uses of which Lord Glennie approves. But the reason is a quite different one. Although an owner who works from home is in clear breach of the deed of conditions, and although title to enforce such breaches lies with each and every neighbour – for the burdens were declared to be community burdens – it is doubtful that a neighbour could show interest to enforce in respect of a breach which was to all intents and purposes invisible. Interest to enforce requires

---

1 Paragraph 15.
2 In adopting this particular approach, Lord Glennie may have misunderstood a comment which he quotes (at para 12) by Sheriff J F Wheatley QC in *Wimpey Homes Holdings Ltd v Macari* (1985) *Unreported Property Cases from the Sheriff Courts* (eds R R M Paisley and D J Cusine, 2000) 208 at 210 to the effect that a no-business clause was not breached merely by 'taking a brief-case of papers home from work'. As the sheriff was drawing a parallel with transferring cigarettes from an ice-cream van to home for safekeeping, his supposition was presumably that the papers would not be worked on in the house.

material detriment to the value or enjoyment of the enforcer's (benefited) property.[1] If a bed-and-breakfast business next door does not give rise to sufficient disturbance to trigger interest to enforce, as been held,[2] the same must surely be true of silent or near-silent professional activity.

Community democracy

Majority rules

Democracy in 'communities' – in housing estates, blocks of flats and the like – was a key principle both of the Title Conditions (Scotland) Act 2003 and of the Tenements (Scotland) Act 2004. It is for a majority of owners, so the legislation provides, to decide who (if anyone) should manage the community, and what real burdens ('community burdens') should be in force. So a majority can appoint and dismiss a factor; a majority can decide to carry out repairs or not to carry them out; and a majority can vary the community burdens or even replace them with an entirely new deed of conditions setting out an entirely new set of burdens.[3] Of course, majorities can sometimes oppress, and for this reason the legislation allows certain of the majority decisions to be challengeable.[4] But, subject to that right of challenge, it is for a majority to decide how the community is to be run.

Application to sheltered housing

As applied to sheltered housing developments, this simple principle operates in a way which is altogether more complicated. First, in a number of cases – for example, in relation to the 'core' burdens which mark sheltered housing out from developments of other kinds – the majority required is two thirds rather than a simple majority.[5] And secondly, as a new case demonstrates, the ownership patterns found in sheltered housing can sometimes operate to defeat the will even of a two-thirds majority.

When the Title Conditions Bill was being debated in the Scottish Parliament, the public galleries were empty apart from a busload or two of elderly citizens, out for the day to impress on the legislators the problems facing the residents of sheltered housing. And of the powers sought by these citizens one was the power to dismiss existing management companies – believed, rightly or wrongly, to be charging too much and doing too little – and to replace them with more biddable and responsive alternatives. That appears to have been the background to *Sheltered Housing Management Ltd v Bon Accord Bonding Co Ltd*.[6]

---

1 Title Conditions (Scotland) Act 2003 s 8(3).
2 *Barker v Lewis* 2008 SLT (Sh Ct) 17, discussed in *Conveyancing 2008* pp 92–95.
3 Title Conditions (Scotland) Act 2003 ss 28, 29 and 33; Tenements (Scotland) Act 2004 sch 1 (Tenement Management Scheme) r 3.1.
4 Title Conditions (Scotland) Act 2003 s 90(1)(c); Tenements (Scotland) Act 2004 s 5.
5 Title Conditions (Scotland) Act 2003 s 54(5).
6 [2010] CSIH 42, 2010 SC 516, 2010 SLT 662. For a discussion from a different angle to the one taken here, see Ken Swinton, 'Varying community burdens' (2010) 78 *Scottish Law Gazette* 38.

The mystery of Dunmail Manor

The litigation concerned a sheltered housing development in Cults, Aberdeen, known as Dunmail Manor[1] and dating from 1986. There was a deed of conditions in the usual way, and the split-off writs had been grants in feu. When the appointed day came along a majority of the owners exercised their right under the Title Conditions Act to dismiss the manager and (former) feudal superior, Sheltered Housing Management Ltd (SHML), and to replace it with Peverel Ltd. But there was then a problem of a practical nature. Although it had ceased to be manager, SHML continued to own the warden's flat, the warden's office, guest bedrooms, and various other parts of the development used mainly for storage. Yet if Peverel was to provide a proper management service, it was essential that it could put an employee into the warden's flat and make use of the warden's office.

The response to this difficulty was commendably inventive. Section 33 of the Title Conditions Act allows a majority of owners to vary the burdens affecting a community, and 'vary' is expressly declared to include the imposition of new burdens.[2] So the decision was taken to replace the existing deed of conditions with a brand-new one. Many of the conditions in the new deed were similar or the same as before, but fresh burdens were introduced in respect of the parts of the development still owned by SHML. In particular the deed provided that:

3.1 The House Manager's Apartment and Office shall not be used otherwise than for occupation and use by the House Manager.

3.2 The Guest Rooms shall not be used otherwise than for occasional occupation by guests or visitors to the Proprietors or occupiers of Flats. Such occupation of the Guest Rooms shall be on such financial terms and subject to such conditions as the Factor shall from time to time determine having regard to the good estate management of the Development as a sheltered housing development.

Some thought was given as to payment to SHML for use of the warden's flat and office, for among the common charges to be paid by the owners was a new 'House Manager's Apartment Charge' fixed at £6,000 *per annum* subject to an annual adjustment in accordance with RPI.

It is worth pausing to see whether these amendments would have worked, even assuming they had been allowed. In fact it seems clear that their effect would have been confined to (considerable) nuisance value. It was not merely that no right to the £6,000 was conferred on SHML, meaning that if the owners, having collected the money together, had chosen to spend it in some other way there was nothing that SHML could do to stop them.[3] More importantly, there was also no obligation on SHML to lease the flat and office to the owners. Clause 3.1 comprised a prohibition, not a positive obligation. It stopped SHML using the

---

1 We do not know whether, as the name suggests, this was set up for retired employees of the Post Office.
2 Title Conditions (Scotland) Act 2003 ss 33(1), 122(1) (definition of 'variation').
3 Paragraph 14.

premises except for a house manager; it did not say that SHML had to make the premises available for this purpose. Indeed it could hardly have done so, for a real burden which requires the owner to lease property to a particular person at a particular rent is likely to fail as repugnant with ownership.[1] Thus, if it chose to do so, SHML could comply with the burden simply by leaving the premises unoccupied. The development would then be without a resident warden, with disastrous consequences for the residents.[2]

Be that as it may, the new deed of conditions, having been signed by the required majority, was then challenged by SHML in the Lands Tribunal under the minority-protection provisions of the Title Conditions Act which allow a disgruntled member of the community to apply for the preservation, unvaried, of the original burdens.[3]

The challenge in the Lands Tribunal

The challenge failed.[4] In terms of s 98 of the Act, the Tribunal can grant an application for preservation only if it is satisfied, having regard to the factors set out in s 100, that the proposed variation – in this case, the new deed of conditions – is either (i) 'not in the best interests of all the owners (taken as a group) of the units in the community', or (ii) 'unfairly prejudicial to one or more of those owners'. Naturally, the discussion in the present case focused mainly on (ii).

The Tribunal drew attention to what it saw as the broad thrust of certain provisions of the 2003 Act:[5]

> The 2003 Act goes some way beyond simply re-formulating and re-stating title conditions to enable them to work in a world without feudal superiors. It appears to us that there is a clear statutory intention to facilitate changes in the operation of property communities. The provisions of sections 52 to 54, particularly section 53, give new enforcement rights to proprietors within the community and able to demonstrate a real interest. Beyond that, however, there are provisions about management and there is this new right of majorities to impose additional burdens provided this is in the interest of the community as a whole and not unfair to the minority, particularly individual owners. This seems to involve recognition of a possible need to supplement or alter the titular arrangements entered into between developers and individual purchasers: a monopoly over management arrangements may have been created or title conditions may be seen as tilted in favour of the developer who either remains owner or is put in a position to deal in residual property. In the sheltered housing context, the evidence before us suggests that much current practice in the industry reflects a need to respond to such concerns.

---

1 Title Conditions (Scotland) Act 2003 s 3(6). The subject of 'repugnancy with ownership' is considered further below: see p 122.
2 It is to the credit of SHML that it did nothing of the sort but allowed Peverel to use the premises pending the outcome of the litigation. For the moment the litigation continues, because leave to appeal to the Supreme Court has been granted.
3 Title Conditions (Scotland) Act 2003 s 90(1)(c).
4 2007 GWD 32-533 (*Conveyancing 2006* Case (35)). The Tribunal comprised J N Wright QC and I M Darling FRICS.
5 At pp 35–36 of the transcript.

The Tribunal noted that it had hitherto been clear that SHML's premises were to be used for the purposes of the development. And indeed if a choice now had to be made between imposing a use restriction on SHML or forcing the owners to buy replacement accommodation elsewhere, fairness would point in favour of the former.

The Tribunal accepted that, in assessing whether the proposed changes were unfairly prejudicial within s 98, it was required to have regard to the statutory factors set out in s 100. These factors were designed with variation or discharge in mind and there was a certain artificiality in using them in the present context. But that was what s 98 required. The Tribunal found a number of the factors to be of particular assistance. In respect of factor (a) (change in circumstances) there had been significant changes since the original deed of conditions was registered in 1986, including (i) the abolition of superiorities, (ii) the replacement of SHML by Peverel, and (iii) the move within the sheltered housing sector generally from owning managers (such as SHML) to managers who were responsible to the owners.

Factor (c) (impeding of enjoyment of burdened property) also pointed in favour of allowing the new deed of conditions:[1]

> [O]n the applicants' approach that the residual property can now be viewed as available to be exploited separately, the individual sheltered flats are almost uninhabitable, and certainly not usable as sheltered housing, because there is no access to, for example, the main electrical equipment or the central alarm systems. The unreality of such a situation might seem of itself to justify the imposition of burdens restricting the use of the residential property to its present use, even although this is clearly a considerable fetter on the applicants' ownership.

Other of the statutory factors pointed in the same direction.

On the evidence, the Tribunal was satisfied that the proposed annual payment was reasonable and, taking the circumstances as a whole, concluded that the new deed of conditions was not unfairly prejudicial to SHML. It followed that the application for preservation of the old deed of conditions must be refused. In a subsequent hearing SHML was awarded £9,178 by way of compensation, being the difference between what the Tribunal took to be the market value of the property (£94,892) and the £6,000 annual payment capitalised at 7% (£85,714).[2] SHML appealed to the Inner House.[3]

The challenge in the Inner House

Before the Inner House the arguments advanced for SHML were quite different. Rather than attacking the merits of the new deed of conditions, SHML attacked its competency. Section 33 of the Title Conditions Act – the provision under

---

1 At p 38 of the transcript.
2 11 October 2007, Lands Tribunal (*Conveyancing 2007* Case (21)).
3 There was a preliminary dispute, resolved in SHML's favour, as to whether the appeal was out of time: see [2008] CSIH 58, 2008 SLT 1058 (*Conveyancing 2008* Case (36)).

which the new deed had been made – allowed community burdens to 'be varied ("varied" including imposed)'. But, said SHML, for a burden to be 'varied', it must exist in the first place. And, while the old deed of conditions did indeed burden the individual flats in the development, it placed no burdens on the premises retained by SHML. As those premises were unburdened, it must follow that no new burdens could be imposed on them under s 33. The court – an Extra Division of the Court of Session – agreed.[1] It was open to the owners to replace the real burdens in respect of those flats which were already subject to them. What they could not do was to impose burdens on premises which, at the moment, were wholly unburdened. The new deed of conditions was therefore invalid insofar as it purported to impose burdens on the property belonging to SHML. Leave to appeal to the Supreme Court has been granted.

The decision of the Extra Division is certainly defensible on the wording of the legislation. But it is so inconvenient for sheltered housing developments[2] that one might have expected the court to strive for a different answer. Admittedly, the position of sheltered housing under the Act is an unusual one and puts the legislation under strain. In an ordinary 'community' development, each unit is both a burdened and a benefited property, ie is both subject to the burdens and also carries a right to enforce the burdens against all other units. But many sheltered housing developments are lopsided: all units have enforcement rights,[3] but certain units – those, such as the warden's flat, which are reserved by the developer/manager – are often free from the burdens. Such units are benefited but not burdened. They are part of the development but only in a half-hearted sense. On the whole, the Act overlooks this half-heartedness. Although they do not affect all units, the burdens are, exceptionally, allowed to be community burdens, just as if they did.[4] Moreover – and this is important – even the unburdened units are declared members of the 'community'.[5] That means that when s 33 talks of variation by a majority of units, the unburdened units – the units belonging to SHML – count as part of the community and, potentially, as part of the majority. If, however, SHML could thus join in imposing new burdens on the other members of the community, it seems odd that, according to the Extra Division, those others could not join together to impose new burdens on SHML.

In our view it would have been open to the Extra Division to reach a different conclusion if it had been so minded. The whole emphasis of part 2 of the Act is on the community rather than the individual units of which the community is composed. And if s 33 is approached in this spirit, it can quite readily be interpreted as allowing a variation of a deed of conditions so as to affect any part of the community, whether that part is currently burdened (as must almost

1   [2010] CSIH 42, 2010 SC 516, 2010 SLT 662. The Opinion of the Court is given by Lord Eassie.
2   As counsel for the owners pointed out: see para 25.
3   The Act takes care of that: see s 54(1).
4   Title Conditions (Scotland) Act 2003 s 25(2).
5   Title Conditions (Scotland) Act 2003 s 26(2). It is possible that the court overlooked this, for otherwise it is hard to know why it thought (para 29) 'that the "community" whose majority is empowered to vary the community burdens' did not exist at the time of the second deed.

always be the case)[1] or unburdened (as in the exceptional case of units held back by a developer in sheltered housing). Not, of course, that this would have been of more than limited assistance to the residents of Dunmail Manor for, as already mentioned, even if the new deed of conditions had been allowed, it could not have forced SHML to release the warden's flat and office for occupation by the employee of a rival manager.

The meaning of variation

Thus far, the decision has been of importance only for sheltered housing. But there is one matter of more general importance. Section 33 allows the variation of community burdens, and variation includes the 'imposition of a new obligation'.[2] This leaves open the question of the type of new obligation that is allowed. Will any obligation do or does the reference back to 'varied' mean that a new burden must have some sort of relationship to that which it replaces? The Extra Division seems correct in deciding that a relationship is required. As the court points out, 'the scope of the exercise allowed by section 33 is that of varying or discharging exiting burdens rather than innovation by the creation of distinct new burdens'.[3] If that is right, it would also apply to the alternative method of varying community burdens in s 35 of the Act as well as to the provision for judicial variation made by s 91.

Appointing a factor

Finally, brief mention should be made of a different case but in the same general area of law. *Peverel Scotland Ltd v Giffen*,[4] a small claims case from Elgin Sheriff Court, concerned four blocks of flats at Findhorn all of which were subject to the same deed of conditions and thus part of the same 'community'. From 2000 onwards the development had been factored by Peverel on the basis of contracts entered into with the individual owners. On 12 December 2001 one of the owners, a Mr Giffen, cancelled his contract and refused to pay any more charges. In this action Peverel sought to recover charges for the period beginning on 28 November 2004, the date on which the Title Conditions Act came into force. By s 28 of that Act a majority of owners can appoint a factor and, where they do so, s 31 imposes equal liability on the owners for the factor's remuneration. Despite the ending of the contractual relationship, therefore, or so Peverel argued, Mr Giffen was liable for the charges on the basis of the Act.

The sheriff[5] disagreed. No decision had been taken by a majority of owners in the period after 2004. On the contrary, there was no interruption in the previous arrangements. Furthermore, s 28 was no more than a default provision which

---

1 Almost always because the defining feature of a community under s 26(2) is that the units within it are subject to community burdens.
2 Title Conditions (Scotland) Act 2003 s 122(1).
3 Paragraph 31.
4 April 2010, Elgin Sheriff Court.
5 Sheriff Noël McPartlin.

was 'subject to ... any provision made by community burden'. But in the present case there was such a provision, for clause 10 of the deed of conditions 'binds each flat owner in a tenement to share in the maintenance and cleansing of all common parts in it and binds them jointly to set up a rota for the sharing of work'.[1] The most that could be said was that a decision under s 28 might be permissible for the communal grounds of the development in respect of which there was no management provision.

The first ground of decision seems sound. Indeed in another case from 2010, *Strathclyde Business Park (Management) Ltd v BAE Systems Pension Funds Trustees Ltd*,[2] it was held that an appointment under s 28 cannot take place merely by implication. It is, however, impossible not to have doubts as to the second ground. A rota is not the same as a system of management, and a provision as to the former should not prevent a majority of owners from upgrading arrangements by switching to the latter.

Repugnancy with ownership

A real burden, says the Title Conditions Act, 'must not be repugnant with ownership'.[3] In *Sheltered Housing Management Ltd v Bon Accord Co Ltd*[4] the court expressed some puzzlement at this idea:

> So far as we can tell the notion of repugnancy with ownership appears to have evolved in the English law of easements. It presents difficulties, as is illustrated in the review of English authority conducted by Lord Scott and Lord Neuberger in *Moncrieff v Jamieson*.[5] The concept may be reflective of the particular features of the English law of easements. But, be that as it may, the legislature has chosen to deploy the phrase. ... Counsel on both sides appeared, in our view understandably, to struggle somewhat with the concept.

If the name is new, however, the concept is not.[6] And it does not derive from English law although there is a parallel concept in the English law of easements known as 'ouster'. In Scotland the doctrine of repugnancy with ownership applies to both real burdens and servitudes. It reflects two main policy principles. First, a merely subordinate or limited real right should not be so extensive in scope as to leave the owner with the shadow of a right but none of its substance. It is a burden on ownership, not ownership itself. Second, real rights are not and should not be the subject of party autonomy. Only certain such rights are recognised in our law and parties must make do with them as best they can. This principle of

---

1 Paragraph 14.
2 2010 GWD 39-791.
3 Title Conditions (Scotland) Act 2003 s 3(6).
4 [2010] CSIH 42, 2010 SC 516, 2010 SLT 662 at para 35 per Lord Eassie. Other aspects of this decision are discussed in the preceding section.
5 [2007] UKHL 42, 2008 SC (HL) 1.
6 K G C Reid, *The Law of Property in Scotland* (1996) para 391; Scottish Law Commission, Report on *Real Burdens* (Scot Law Com No 181, 2000) para 2.22. As the court recognised in *Sheltered Housing Management*, the actual expression or something like it is used by Lord Young in *Moir's Trs v McEwan* (1880) 7 R 1141 at 1145 and again in *Earl of Zetland v Hislop* (1881) 8 R 675 at 681.

numerus clausus, familiar in many legal systems, is not to be defeated by attempts to turn one sort of right into a right of a different character. Real burdens and servitudes should remain recognisably such.

The expression 'repugnant with ownership' – or at least the idea behind it – has been considered in recent years in the context of servitudes[1] but until now there was almost no modern authority in relation to real burdens. Roughly speaking, a burden is repugnant with ownership if the restrictions which it imposes are so severe as to remove most of ownership's content.

In *Snowie v Museum Hall LLP*[2] Lord Glennie was faced with a repugnancy argument in relation to (i) a prohibition of use of an apartment (including ancillary use) for any trade, business or profession, and (ii) a prohibition on leasing. In the event, Lord Glennie concluded that, properly construed, the burden did not prohibit leasing, but if it had he would have regarded this as repugnant with ownership and hence ineffectual. Conversely, the prohibition on business use was not, he decided, repugnant. These conclusions are plainly correct. Only the most severe restriction on *use* could be repugnant with ownership. But a restriction on the *performance of juridical acts*, such as leasing, is a different matter. Even so, some restrictions will be acceptable – for example, a right of pre-emption. But where a restriction turns into an absolute prohibition, it will not be allowed.

The issue arose again in *Sheltered Housing Management Ltd v Bon Accord Co Ltd* where a burden required that the house manager's flat and office in a sheltered housing development 'shall not be used otherwise than for occupation and use by the House Manager'. At one level this is no more than a restriction on use which, if it is unusual, is at any rate perfectly explicable in the context of sheltered housing. That was the view taken by the Lands Tribunal:[3]

> Real burdens are generally perpetual in nature and therefore liable to restrict to some degree, in perpetuity, the owner's right to exclusive occupation and use. Restrictions in the use of property which are conceived in the legitimate interests of other property owners are recognised and permitted. ... The extent of interference with the owner's exclusive enjoyment of his property will obviously vary with the terms of the restriction but will also vary with the nature of the property. Ancillary property is by its nature likely to be permanently shackled by a restriction, in the interests of the owners of the principal property, to ancillary use. It seems to us that the owners of the principal property, here the sheltered flats, have a proper and legitimate interest in establishing such a restriction, and we are not persuaded that there is anything in any way unusual or objectionable in these proposed burdens, which appear typical of modern provision in such property communities. The applicants as owners of the residual property will not be prevented from selling, or leasing, or granting security over, the residual property.

---

1 Usually in the context of parking. The most important case is *Moncrieff v Jamieson* [2007] UKHL 42, 2008 SC (HL) 1. Although s 76(2) of the Title Conditions Act expressly prohibits a servitude which is 'repugnant with ownership' the discussion of the issue has so far avoided that terminology. See *Conveyancing 2007* pp 108–11.

2 [2010] CSOH 107, 2010 SLT 97. Other aspects of this case are discussed at pp 104 and 114.

3 2007 GWD 32-533 (*Conveyancing 2006* Case (24)) at p 29 of the transcript. The Tribunal comprised J N Wright QC and I M Darling FRICS.

But that approach looks less convincing where, as had actually happened in the case, the owner of the flat and office had been removed as manager of the development and so was no longer in a position, other than through leasing, to use the property in the manner allowed by the burden. In effect, the restriction deprived – and was intended to deprive – the owner of the right to make personal use of its own property. Here one feels a line may have been crossed from a restriction which is permissible to one which is so severe that it infringes the rights of ownership itself. The issue was ventilated in argument on appeal to the Inner House but the case was decided on other grounds and the court declined to embark on an *obiter* discussion of what is a difficult matter'.[1]

Surviving feudal abolition: facility burdens

Where burdens survive feudal abolition this is usually because they fall within the 'common scheme' provisions in either s 52 or s 53 of the Title Conditions (Scotland) Act 2003. Typical examples of such community burdens are burdens affecting housing estates or tenements. But even where there is no element of a common scheme, burdens can sometimes survive. The most important example is where the burden is a facility burden.

What is a facility burden? The term was invented by the Abolition of Feudal Tenure etc (Scotland) Act 2000 and later found its way into the Title Conditions Act. It is defined in the latter Act as 'a real burden which regulates the maintenance, management, reinstatement or use of heritable property which constitutes, and is intended to constitute, a facility of benefit to other land'.[2] Examples of facilities, so the definition continues, include a common part of a tenement, a common area for recreation, a private road, private sewerage or a boundary wall. So a maintenance obligation in respect of the common areas in a housing estate or a private road or a boundary wall will usually be a facility burden. Section 56 of the Title Conditions Act explains the consequences. Where a burden imposed before the appointed day was a facility burden, it is enforceable after that day both by the owner of the facility and by the owner of any property 'to which the facility is (and is intended to be) of benefit'. So suppose for example that ten properties are served by the same private access road. In the titles of each a maintenance burden was imposed before the appointed day. The result is that the burdens are facility burdens, mutually enforceable among the ten owners.

Often facility burdens are *also* community burdens under either s 52 or s 53 and so part of a much larger burdens group. In that case it hardly matters that they are facility burdens, because they are already mutually enforceable within the development or other community. Much less commonly, however, a potential facility burden stands on its own, in which case it becomes of crucial importance whether it qualifies as a facility burden or not.

---

1 Paragraph 35.
2 Title Conditions (Scotland) Act 2003 s 122(1), (3).

That was the position in *Greenbelt Property Ltd v Riggens*,[1] the first decision in which facility burdens have been considered. The facts are of some interest. Back in 1997 Moss Homes Ltd acquired development land in Bellshill. Forty-seven houses were built and sold. Each house was given a right in common to the 'common parts' but it seems that, following *PMP Ltd v Keeper of the Registers of Scotland*,[2] the definition of these parts was too vague to carry any rights of ownership. As a result, Moss Homes was left with ownership of the common parts. In 2001 a section of the common parts was feued to Greenbelt and, in terms of the feu disposition, Greenbelt was to plant woodland and thereafter to manage and maintain it until 'such time as the Development Land[3] shall have ceased substantially to be used as a residential housing development'. In the event no trees were actually planted.

What happened next can readily be imagined. A new developer obtained planning permission to erect 12 houses on the land disponed to Greenbelt. Greenbelt, naturally enough, was disposed to sell. But the houses could not be built for as long as the land was subject to the 2001 real burden. Had the burden survived feudal abolition? It was imposed in a feu disposition and so was originally enforceable by the superior (Moss Homes). After the appointed day, however, there was no superior, and as the burdens were imposed on this property alone and not on other properties there could be no question of a common scheme and of ss 52 and 53 of the Title Conditions Act. The only plausible argument for survival was that the burden was a facility burden. If it was, it would be enforceable by the owners of the 47 houses as the parties benefited by the facility. If it was not, the burden was extinguished on the appointed day and the development could go ahead.

To test the issue, Greenbelt applied to the Lands Tribunal under its new jurisdiction to determine the validity and enforceability of burdens.[4] The application was opposed by the owners of one of the houses, who were not legally represented. It should be emphasised that the house owners had no rights in relation to the woodland area. They were not owners; they were not tenants; they had no servitude rights, and in any event there is no servitude recognised by Scots law which would allow them to wander in the property; and finally – and unusually in a case such as this – they had no obligation to pay for maintenance. Nonetheless, the Tribunal was willing to accept that, by providing amenity screening, the wood was a facility of benefit to the housing estate.[5]

The Tribunal was, however, far less sure that, as the definition of facility burden required, the wood was *intended* to constitute such a facility. In the end, and with some hesitation, the Tribunal concluded that it was not so intended. Partly this was because, as already mentioned, the house owners were not given

---

1 2010 GWD 28-586, a decision of the Lands Tribunal. The Tribunal comprised J N Wright QC and I M Darling FRICS.
2 2009 SLT (Lands Tr) 2. See further *Conveyancing 2008* pp 133–49.
3 Ie the land on which the 47 houses were built.
4 Title Conditions (Scotland) Act 2003 s 90(1)(a)(ii).
5 Paragraph 32.

any right of use or obligation of maintenance. But the main reason was that the superior had reserved a right of redemption in the feu disposition. Admittedly, that redemption had fallen with feudal abolition and could no longer be enforced,[1] but its terms were still relevant in order to show the parties' intentions. As the trigger for the redemption was the granting of planning permission for any use other than amenity woodland, this indicated an intention to take the land back and build more houses. In that connection it was important that the land was 'much larger than one would expect to be used just for amenity screening'.[2] Accordingly, the burden failed to qualify as a facility burden and so had failed to survive the appointed day. The development could go ahead.

Two further points seem worth making. First, despite the result, the Tribunal took a generally expansive view of the meaning of facility burdens. In considering whether a facility confers benefit, the Tribunal was willing to settle for passive or amenity benefit only and overlook the fact that the house owners had neither a right to use nor an obligation to maintain the land in question.[3] Although this burden failed, therefore, many others will qualify. Secondly, this approach has implications for maintenance obligations. In cases involving Greenbelt and similar organisations the arrangement is usually that Greenbelt owns and manages the woodland while the house owners are subject to a real burden to pay for the cost of that management. Doubts have sometimes been expressed as to the validity of the real burden on the basis that it may not be praedial or, in the language of the Act, 'relate in some way to the burdened property';[4] for it is not self-evident that a burden to maintain property which one is not allowed to use 'relates' in the required sense to the property which is being burdened. One effect of the decision in *Greenbelt Property* is to make these doubts less plausible.[5]

Clawback

Where land has development potential, a seller will sometimes seek clawback of a share of any development gain. Such clawback provisions are usually tied to the granting of planning permission: in the event that planning consent is given for development, the buyer must pay the seller a share of the uplift in value.

---

1 No notice apparently having been registered under s 18A of the Abolition of Feudal Tenure etc (Scotland) Act 2000 to preserve the redemption for the (former) superior. It could have been enforced against the original grantee as a matter of contract, but the current owner of the woodland (Greenbelt Property Ltd) was a different company from the original disponee (The Greenbelt Group of Companies Ltd).

2 Paragraph 43.

3 Paragraphs 32 and 46.

4 Title Conditions (Scotland) Act 2003 s 3(1). Section 3(2) adds that 'The relationship may be direct or indirect but shall not merely be that the obligated person is the owner of the burdened property.'

5 For the text of an Opinion commissioned by Consumer Focus Scotland on the broader question of the enforceability of Greenbelt burdens, see http://www.consumerfocus.org.uk/scotland/files/2010/11/legal-opinion-on-land-maintenance-companies.pdf. We are not able to agree with some of the reasoning in and conclusions of this Opinion.

The most efficient way of arranging clawback is usually by a minute of agreement secured by a standard security, and certain changes to the law of standard securities made by the Title Conditions (Scotland) Act 2003 were designed to make this method easier and more efficient.[1] The use of a real burden is less promising. It is true that a real burden can be used *indirectly* to prohibit the proposed development use and thus to force the buyer into seeking a minute of waiver. But real burdens like this have usually only a supporting role, and a standard security tends still to be necessary. Moreover, real burdens are only possible at all if the seller continues to own property in the neighbourhood which can be nominated as the benefited property.

But might a real burden be used *directly*? In other words, is it possible to have a real burden which states, plump and plain, that if planning consent is obtained, the buyer must pay part of the uplift to the seller? That was the question considered by the Lands Tribunal in *I & H Brown Ltd, Applicants*.[2] When Dotham Farm in Kirkcaldy was disponed in 2001, the disposition provided that:

> In the event of Planning Permission for development of the subjects or any part thereof being obtained other than for agricultural purposes for[3] opencast development, our said disponees and their foresaids shall pay to us and our successors and assignees whomsoever a sum equivalent to thirty per cent of the consequential net uplift in value of the subjects or part thereof over and above agricultural value, declaring that in the event of the parties failing to agree such value the same shall be ascertained by a Valuer nominated by agreement between the parties or in default of agreement by a Valuer nominated by the President for the time being of the Royal Institute of Chartered Surveyors in Scotland who shall act as an expert in this matter.

Later, the buyer applied to the Lands Tribunal for a determination as to the validity and enforceability of the provision as a real burden. The application was unopposed.

The Tribunal had no difficulty in finding that the provision was not valid or enforceable. Even if a benefited property existed – a matter on which there was no information – the provision plainly failed as a real burden:[4]

> [W]hatever the position might have been before the coming into force of the Act of 2003, we are satisfied, because of the nature of the burden, that even if there were some benefited property, it would not be possible for the 'benefited proprietor' to satisfy the test of interest to enforce under section 8(3) of the Act. Essentially, this is a monetary 'claw back' burden which does not come within any of the categories of 'personal real burden' recognised by the Act and, on the material before us, cannot satisfy the 'praedial' rule for validity as a real burden and cannot satisfy the test of interest to enforce.

---

1 Title Conditions (Scotland) Act 2003 s 111. For a discussion, see Scottish Law Commission, Report on *Real Burdens* (Scot Law Com No 181, 2000; available at www.scotlawcom.gov.uk) paras 9.30–9.37.
2 28 April 2010, Lands Tribunal. The Tribunal comprised J N Wright QC and I M Darling FRICS.
3 Presumably this should be 'or'.
4 Paragraph 6.

We would agree with the result[1] but think that the reasoning, in what is admittedly a very short judgment, may conflate the praedial rule with the rule for interest to enforce. Although there is some overlap of subject matter, the two are in truth quite different.[2] One is a rule of constitution, the other of enforcement. If a provision fails the test for interest to enforce, it cannot be enforced on this occasion and in respect of this breach but might possibly be enforceable on another occasion and in respect of a different breach; if it fails the praedial test, it is not a real burden at all and can never be enforced as such.

In the present case, the praedial test was not met. Section 3(3) of the Title Conditions Act requires that a real burden be for the benefit of the benefited property, whereas an obligation to pay money confers benefit only on the person to whom the money is paid. It follows that the provision was not a real burden at all and, that being the case, no question of enforcement – or therefore of interest to enforce – could arise. On the other hand, if the praedial test had been surmounted – if, in other words, the burden *was* capable of conferring benefit on a property – it would be a strong thing to say that there could never, under any circumstances (including those not within the contemplation of the court), be interest to enforce. The question of interest falls to be resolved on a case-by-case, breach-by-breach basis. Section 8(3)(a) talks of 'in the circumstances of any case'. It cannot sensibly be the subject of a universal finding.[3]

In fact there was at least one other ground on which the burden might have failed. By s 4(2)(a) of the Act the terms of a real burden must be 'set out' in the constitutive deed. In the case of an obligation to pay money, that is often taken to mean the specification of the actual sum due.[4] That requirement (if it is a requirement) is expressly waived by s 5(1) of the Act in respect of obligations to defray costs (such as maintenance costs) so long as the cost itself is properly identified. But the clawback provision in *I & H Brown Ltd* is neither an obligation to defray costs nor an obligation to pay a specified sum of money. It may not be sufficiently certain to qualify as a real burden.

Of course, as the Tribunal pointed out, failure as a real burden did not mean that the provision was wholly invalid. As the original buyer, the applicant was bound by the provision as a matter of contract. But any successor to whom the applicant conveyed the property would not be so bound.

Finally, it seems worth mentioning that direct clawback may be allowable in the case of two of the personal real burdens – the economic development burden and the healthcare burden. But if that is correct, it is due to express provision[5] and has no implications for the general law of real burdens.

---

1   For previous discussion, see Scottish Law Commission, Report on the *Abolition of the Feudal System* (Scot Law Com No 168, 1999; available at www.scotlawcom.gov.uk) para 5.23; K G C Reid, *The Abolition of Feudal Tenure in Scotland* (2003) para 4.12.

2   Report on *Real Burdens* para 4.16.

3   For another case in which the Tribunal sought to make a universal finding on interest, see *Clarke v Grantham* 2009 GWD 38-645 (*Conveyancing 2009* Case (26)) at para 39.

4   The point, however, is uncertain. For discussion, see K G C Reid, *The Law of Property in Scotland* (1996) para 418(4).

5   Title Conditions (Scotland) Act 2003 ss 45(3), 46(3). These provisions allow 'an obligation to pay a sum of money'.

ENFORCING STANDARD SECURITIES

Introduction

The year 2010 has turned upside down the law about the enforcement of standard securities.[1] There have been two major developments, and one minor. The two major developments have been (i) the Home Owner and Debtor Protection (Scotland) Act 2010, which requires new procedures in relation to residential property, and (ii) *Royal Bank of Scotland plc v Wilson*,[2] in which the Supreme Court held that a view about how standard securities can be enforced – a view held for the last 40 years, backed up by all conveyancing writers and also by Inner House authority – is simply wrong. (iii) The third development was about what happens if it turns out that there is a tenant in the property, the change having been made by the Housing (Scotland) Act 2010. Although the Home Owner and Debtor Protection (Scotland) Act 2010 was chronologically the first, we will deal with *Wilson* first, since it is about the Conveyancing and Feudal Reform (Scotland) Act 1970 as it was before the 2010 amendments.

A preliminary point is that none of these changes affects the operation of the Consumer Credit Act 1974. Not many standard securities are subject to that Act, but some are. So, for example, where a standard security is subject to the 1974 Act, enforcement continues to require the service of a default notice,[3] and that requirement is additional to the requirements of the 1970 Act, as now amended.

The Supreme Court lays down the law

Introduction

The statutory provisions for enforcing standard securities are complex and hard to understand[4] – indeed, it may well be that they really do not make sense. That was so even when the Conveyancing and Feudal Reform (Scotland) Act 1970 was in its original form. A further layer of complexity was added by the Mortgage Rights (Scotland) Act 2001,[5] and the process has continued with the Home Owner and Debtor Protection (Scotland) Act 2010. The Scottish Law Commission has

---

1 2010 also saw the publication of Mark Higgins, *The Enforcement of Heritable Securities*. By bad luck, this was before the *Wilson* decision, and moreover the Housing (Scotland) Act 2010 had not yet been passed, though the Bill is mentioned at para 11.2. Despite the unlucky timing, the book is invaluable, and anyone seeking to enforce a standard security, and anyone opposing an enforcement procedure, should have this book to hand.

2 [2010] UKSC 50, 2010 SLT 1227, 2010 Hous LR 88. The case raises difficult issues, and what follows is unlikely to be the last word. No doubt views will differ.

3 Consumer Credit Act 1974 s 87. This is not to be confused with a notice of default under the 1970 Act.

4 At para 15 Lord Rodger comments that 'even Professor Gretton and Professor Reid have felt moved to warn that "The law about the enforcement of standard securities is a subject of great and unnecessary complexity: it is a veritable maze"' (citing G L Gretton and K G C Reid *Conveyancing* (3rd edn 2004) para 19-32). And at para 70 Lord Hope quotes *Conveyancing 2009* p 179 for the view that the law is of 'labyrinthine complexity'.

5 For which see *Conveyancing 2001* pp 75–85.

announced that it will be looking at the law of heritable security,[1] and one of the aims will be to rationalise the provisions about enforcement so that readers of the legislation will in future have at least a sporting chance of grasping what the law is.

Royal Bank of Scotland v Wilson: an overview

Royal Bank of Scotland plc v Wilson, in court for 12 years,[2] has now culminated in a bombshell decision from the Supreme Court. First, a few words about the case's history. The action began in 1998, and the first reported decision, in the sheriff court, was dated 2001.[3] The decision was against the defenders, who then appealed to the Inner House. The Inner House decision[4] was a key case on the 'cautionary spouses' doctrine, originally established by the House of Lords in *Smith v Bank of Scotland*.[5] Whilst *Smith* has never been overruled, it has suffered so much sniping and snipping in subsequent case law that it may be wondered whether much is left, and this phase of the *Royal Bank of Scotland plc v Wilson* litigation was the most important of these snipping decisions. But although the defenders were unsuccessful on this plea, they had other pleas, and back the case went to the sheriff court. Here begins the current phase of the litigation.

Francis and John Wilson were brothers. Francis was married to Annette. John was married to Norma. In 1991 Francis and Annette borrowed from the Royal Bank of Scotland plc (RBS) to buy a house. About the same time John and Norma borrowed from the RBS to build a conservatory. The loans were secured on their respective houses, which were next to each other in Loanhead, Midlothian, each of which was co-owned by the respective spouses. The securities were drafted in such a way as to secure anything imaginable, including debts that the two wives had nothing to do with:

> We ... and ... spouses ... (hereinafter referred to as 'the Obligant') hereby undertake to pay to The Royal Bank of Scotland plc (hereinafter referred to as 'the Bank', which expression includes its successors and assignees whomsoever) on demand all sums of principal, interest and charges which are now and which may at any time hereafter become due to the Bank by the Obligant whether solely or jointly with any other person, corporation, firm or other body and whether as principal or surety; declaring that ... in the event of the foregoing personal obligation being granted by more than one person the expression 'the Obligant' means all such persons together and/or any one or more of them; and in all cases the obligations hereby undertaken by the Obligant shall bind all person(s) included in the expression 'the Obligant' and his, her or their executors and representatives whomsoever all jointly and severally without the necessity of discussing them in their order.

---

1 Scottish Law Commission, *Eighth Programme of Law Reform* (Scot Law Com No 220 (2010), available at www.scotlawcom.gov.uk) para 9.34.
2 We repeat what we have so often said, that it is extraordinary how long some cases take.
3 *Royal Bank of Scotland plc v Wilson* 2001 SLT (Sh Ct) 2, digested as *Conveyancing 2000* Case (53). The sheriff was R G Craik.
4 *Royal Bank of Scotland plc v Wilson* 2004 SC 153, digested as *Conveyancing 2003* Case (40).
5 1997 SC (HL) 111.

The brothers were in partnership together, and in fact they had two firms, F J Wilson Associates and Wilson Brothers. After the two loans just mentioned were taken out, these firms also borrowed from the same bank, RBS. The result was that the securities covered the partnership debts. One must wonder to what extent the wives were aware of this.[1]

Both firms eventually defaulted. The contract (drafted by the bank) provided that the interest rate would be *whatever the bank wanted*,[2] and when default happened the bank decided it wanted 25% *per annum*. We do not propose to discuss the ethics of the bank's conduct.[3]

On 20 June 1995 the bank sent this letter to each of the brothers:

Our Penicuik Branch

I regret to learn that your indebtedness to the Bank as undernoted at our above Branch is not being repaid in accordance with arrangements and I have therefore to advise that unless within ten days from the date of this letter you effect repayment of the whole sums due to the Bank or, alternatively, make a substantial payment to account within that period coupled with acceptable proposals to take care of the remaining indebtedness I shall have no alternative[4] but to institute proceedings against you for recovery. Such proceedings will involve expense for which you will be liable and it is therefore in your own interest to give this matter your immediate attention.

No letter was sent to the two Mrs Wilsons. The money was not paid and the bank then made an application to the sheriff court:

(1) To grant warrant to the pursuers in terms of section 24(1) of the Conveyancing and Feudal Reform (Scotland) Act 1970 to enter into possession of ... being the subjects described in the Standard Security by Francis John Wilson and Mrs Annette Wilson for all sums of money due and that may become due to The Royal Bank of Scotland plc ... and to exercise in relation to the said subjects all powers competent to a creditor in lawful possession of the security subjects including the power of sale of the said security subjects.

(2) To grant warrant to officers of court summarily to eject[5] the defenders, and their family, goods, gear, and effects, from the said subjects, and to make the same void and redd, that the pursuers, or others in their name, may enter thereto and peaceably possess and enjoy the same.

---

1 The two Mrs Wilsons in fact averred that they had *not* understood what was happening. For example, each pled that she 'would not have signed the standard security had she been aware that it extended to borrowings relating to the first defender's business': see *Royal Bank of Scotland plc v Wilson* 2004 SC 153 at 156. It seems that no final finding was made as to whether this was true.

2 See para 52 of the opinion issued by the Inner House.

3 In the Supreme Court Lady Hale commented (para 80) that 'the Bank, of course, has every interest in allowing the debt to mount up until it gets close to the value of the home'. Presumably she was referring to the case where, as here, the interest rate was very high. She noted (same para) that in this case 'the debt had escalated to astronomical proportions'.

4 Phrases of this sort are often found in letters from banks. 'We shall have no alternative ...' Or 'we are unable to comply with your request ...' What is in reality a decision by the bank in its own financial interests is represented as something that is mysteriously outwith its sphere of choice.

5 As originally drafted, this was phrased as a crave for removing. Later it was amended to a crave for ejection, as given above. The removing/ejection distinction is a troublesome one.

Thus there was neither a calling-up notice nor a notice of default. The creditor had proceeded direct to a s 24 application.

The Wilsons' main line of defence was about the second crave, the warrant to eject. They argued that the sole basis for warrant to eject in such cases is a warrant granted under s 5 of the Heritable Securities (Scotland) Act 1894. Although passed long before 1970, this provision applies to standard securities.[1] Section 5(1) provides:

> Where a creditor desires to enter into possession of the lands disponed in security, and the proprietor thereof is in personal occupation of the same, or any part thereof, such proprietor shall be deemed to be an occupant without a title, and the creditor may take proceedings to eject him in all respects in the same way as if he were such occupant: Provided that this section shall not apply in any case unless such proprietor has made default in the punctual payment of the interest due under the security, or in due payment of the principal after formal requisition.

The bank, argued the defenders, had not made 'formal requisition' and so was not entitled to a warrant to eject. This argument was upheld by the sheriff.[2] The Wilsons also argued that the bank had failed to establish default.[3]

The bank appealed to the Inner House, which reversed the sheriff's decision, holding that the bank had proved default[4] and that the s 24 procedure satisfied the 'formal requisition' requirement of the 1894 Act.[5] The Wilsons appealed to the Supreme Court, which has now reversed the decision of the Inner House, holding that the requirements of the 1894 Act had not been satisfied.[6] But when the case was being heard in London, a new issue arose that had not been one of the grounds of appeal and which had hardly been considered in the courts below. It was that, quite apart from the issue about warrant to eject, the bank's case was undermined more fundamentally by the fact that it had not served a calling-up notice. It is this aspect of the case – the need for a calling-up notice – that is the real bombshell. The two issues (warrant to eject and calling-up notice) are to some extent interlinked, but for the sake of clarity we set them out separately.

We begin with a preliminary point: was this a form A or a form B security? After setting out the three roads to sale established by the 1970 Act, we then deal with the two major issues in the case, taking the more important one (calling-up notices) first.

---

1 Because of s 32 of the Conveyancing and Feudal Reform (Scotland) Act 1970.
2 This decision has not been reported and is not available on the Scottish Courts website, though to some extent it can be reconstructed, in part from a note at 2008 GWD 2-35 and in part from the quotations from the sheriff's decision given in the Inner House case (*Royal Bank of Scotland plc v Wilson* 2009 SLT 729). We are grateful to the sheriff, Charles Stoddart, for giving us a copy.
3 Sheriff Stoddart's first finding in fact and law was that 'the pursuers have failed to prove that the defenders are in default of their obligations'.
4 This issue seems not to have been pursued in the Supreme Court. At first instance the bank was unable to satisfy the sheriff as to the sum claimed. The Wilsons called at the proof an expert on banking practice, Malcolm Platt, who said that the documentation produced by the bank did not sufficiently confirm its claim. The Inner House dismissed Mr Platt's evidence (para 52).
5 [2009] CSIH 36, 2009 SLT 729. The Opinion of the Court was delivered by Lord Nimmo Smith. For a discussion, see *Conveyancing 2009* pp 177–79.
6 [2010] UKSC 50, 2010 SLT 1227, 2010 Hous LR 88.

Form A or form B?

Were the securities in the *Wilson* case form A securities or form B securities? It may not matter, but then again, it may, because on one theory the method of enforcing a standard security depends on whether it adopts form A or form B.[1] The 1970 Act says that form A is 'to be used where the personal obligation is included in the deed' and that form B is 'to be used where the personal obligation is constituted in a separate instrument or instruments'.[2] Why the 1970 Act thought it necessary to make this distinction we do not know. Much of the 1970 Act is fussy and over-prescriptive. Be that as it may, were the standard securities in the *Wilson* case form A or form B? Ken Swinton has expressed the view that they were form A.[3] That may well be right, because the standard securities did contain an obligation to pay. But it is also arguable, we think, that they were form B standard securities. Consider the wording. The borrowers bound themselves to pay ... what? Answer: money that they were bound to pay. The security deeds identified no debt. Instead, in the words of the Act, 'the personal obligation is constituted in a separate instrument or instruments'. Hence the security deeds apparently met the definition of a form B security. It might be argued that even if the debts owed by the Wilsons were constituted by other instruments, they were *also* constituted by the security deeds, because they contained the words 'we ... undertake to pay to The Royal Bank of Scotland plc ... on demand ...'. That argument perhaps leads to the conclusion that the securities were *both* form A *and* form B. The issue seems to us to border on the insoluble.[4]

It may be added that it is not easy to rescue the wording of the security deeds[5] from either vacuity or incoherence or both: vacuity, because it is vacuous to bind yourself to do what you are bound to do; incoherence, because of the words 'on demand'. The day when repayment of a loan falls due is determined by the provisions of the loan contract.[6] For example, suppose that there is a loan repayable on the third anniversary of the date of the advance. Does the expression 'on demand' mean that the loan is magically converted into an on-demand loan? Or does it mean that, even after maturity at the end of the three years, it is still not payable, notwithstanding the terms of the loan contract, unless there is a 'demand'. Either view seems absurd, which is why the phrase seems incoherent.

---

1 This is the view expressed in Ken Swinton, 'Enforcing standard securities: *Royal Bank v Wilson (No 2)*' (2010) 78 *Scottish Law Gazette* 87.
2 Conveyancing and Feudal Reform (Scotland) Act 1970 sch 2.
3 Swinton (2010) 78 *Scottish Law Gazette* 87.
4 A parallel problem arises with one of the commonest forms of security, where the security deed is itself the instrument constituting the personal obligation, so that it looks like a form A security. The deed then adds that it also secures all other debts due by the debtor to the creditor – so that it secures, or potentially secures, a 'personal obligation ... constituted in a separate instrument or instruments'. Does that make it a form B security?
5 Which is standard wording used by banks in countless transactions.
6 This is so regardless of whether the loan is repayable in a lump sum (as in so-called 'interest-only' loans) or whether it is repayable in instalments (as in so-called 'repayment' loans). In the former there is a single maturity date and in the latter there are numerous partial maturity dates.

The three roads to sale

A debtor defaults on a secured loan. The bank decides to enforce the security by sale. Is a calling-up notice necessary? The question is straightforward. The answer ought to be straightforward too. It is not. The 1970 Act offers three roads to sale, ie three ways whereby a standard security holder can obtain power of sale. The first is the calling-up notice. The second is the notice of default. The third is an order under s 24. As will be seen later, the Home Owner and Debtor Protection (Scotland) Act 2010 now says that for residential property, but only for residential property, road 1 will in future join up with road 3.

Road 1: calling-up notices

Section 19(1) says:

> Where a creditor in a standard security intends to require discharge of the debt thereby secured and, failing that discharge, to exercise any power conferred by the security to sell any subjects of the security or any other power which he may appropriately exercise on the default of the debtor within the meaning of standard condition 9(1)(a),[1] he shall serve a notice calling-up the security. ...

A calling-up notice is not relevant to the question of *when* payment becomes due. That is a matter for the loan contract itself. If the loan is an on-demand one, a calling-up notice could be used to demand payment, but it would be hard to imagine a rational creditor using it in that way, because such notices are subject to a two-month interval.[2] If the loan contract is an on-demand one, the creditor can demand payment of the whole sum immediately, and the creditor will in practice already have sent a demand for payment. Thus the real function of a calling-up notice is not – appearances notwithstanding – to demand payment. Rather, it is a formal notice saying that if payment is not made within two months then the right to sell will emerge. The notice starts the sale clock ticking.

Calling-up notices have hitherto been used in a substantial minority of cases.[3] Commonly they are then backed up by a court action that seeks declarator of the creditor's right to sell, plus a crave for ejection. The *Wilson* case does not call any of this into question. It is about whether a creditor can go down one of the *other* roads.

Roads 2 and 3: the meaning of 'other requirement'

Standard condition 9(1) says:

---

1 Which is to say, sale, plus ancillary remedies. Standard condition 9 is set out below.
2 There is a parallel argument: if financial default can be met instantly by a s 24 application, why bother to serve a two-month calling-up notice? This argument suggests that s 24 was not intended for cases of financial default.
3 According to Peter Nicholson, 'Default Position' (2010) 55 *Journal of the Law Society of Scotland* Dec/56, about 20% of cases have (hitherto) proceeded by calling-up notice. We do not know how many have proceeded purely by notice of default, but we would imagine that the number must be vanishingly small, so that almost all of the remaining 80% must have involved a s 24 application.

The debtor shall be held to be in default in any of the following circumstances, that is to say –

(a) where a calling-up notice in respect of the security has been served and has not been complied with;
(b) where there has been a failure to comply with any other requirement arising out of the security;
(c) where the proprietor of the security subjects has become insolvent.

Under the Act, breach of standard condition 9(1)(b) opens the gate to the other two roads to sale, namely notice of default and s 24 order.[1] So if default under standard condition 9(1)(b) covers monetary default, the unpaid creditor has the choice of all three roads. But if standard condition 9(1)(b) does not cover monetary breach, then, in the event of monetary breach the creditor does not have the option, but can achieve power of sale *only* by a calling-up notice.[2]

Standard condition 9(1)(b) applies 'where there has been a failure to comply with any other requirement arising out of the security'. It is doubtful whether this provision can be understood simply by studying the statutory text. For one thing, the word 'other' presupposes that compliance with a calling-up notice, in standard condition 9(1)(a), is itself a 'requirement arising out of the security'. But it is hard to see how that could be so. The debtor's obligation to pay is not a requirement of the security but of the loan contract which the security secures. One could read 'security' non-literally, to mean the *deed* that creates the security, but again this hardly helps because no such deed makes compliance with a calling-up notice[3] a 'requirement', and, more fundamentally, a standard security need not contain any obligations, as the secured obligations can be set out in a separate document. Or one could read 'security' non-literally to mean the whole set of 'requirements' under the 1970 Act, but this too would not help because the Act does not require compliance with a calling-up notice, for such a notice is merely notice that if payment is not forthcoming then certain consequences may follow. Once more, it is necessary to emphasise that the obligation to pay, and the time when the obligation to pay becomes due and resting owing, are matters for the loan contract.

It seems to be accepted that standard condition 9(1)(b) covers the case where there is a *non-monetary* breach, such as a failure to maintain the property. The big question is whether it covers *monetary* breach as well. The word 'other' might suggest not. But, as already noted, standard condition 9(1)(a) is only about non-compliance with a calling-up notice, and breach of the obligation to pay the secured debt is something that happens – as we have noted above – separately from the issue of a calling-up notice. Suppose that at Whitsunday Macbeth borrows £100,000 from Ophelia repayable at Martinmas. He fails to pay on that day. He is immediately in contractual default, whether or not Ophelia serves

---

1 Conveyancing and Feudal Reform (Scotland) Act 1970 ss 21(1), 24(1).
2 But because of the provisions of the Home Owner and Debtor Protection (Scotland) Act 2010, in future it will in most cases be necessary to have a s 24 application *in addition to* a calling-up notice.
3 As opposed to compliance with the payment requirements of the loan contract.

a calling-up notice. So perhaps the word 'other' does not in itself exclude the possibility that standard condition 9(1)(b) can cover failure to pay.

A further possibility is that it all depends on whether the security is a form A security or a form B security. In the latter, the deed does not contain the obligation to pay, so that 'other requirement' could not refer to monetary breach. On this argument, a s 24 application in relation to monetary breach is incompetent for form B standard securities but not for form A standard securities.[1]

Until the Supreme Court's decision, the accepted view was that standard condition 9(1)(b) covered monetary as well as non-monetary breach, with the result that the unpaid creditor had all three options open: calling-up notice, notice of default, and s 24 order. This opinion had prevailed ever since the 1970 Act was passed, no doubt because it was the view of Professor Halliday.[2] In 1998 it was confirmed by the Inner House, in *Bank of Scotland v Millward*.[3] That case was about road 2 (notice of default) rather than road 3 (s 24 application), but if a notice of default is competent then a s 24 application is competent as well. The established view was confirmed once again by the Inner House in the *Wilson* case.

The need for calling-up: what the Supreme Court decided

The Supreme Court took a different view. It read s 19(1) literally: 'Where a creditor … intends to require discharge of the debt thereby secured and, failing that discharge, to [sell], *he shall serve a notice calling-up the security …* '. Here the bank did require the discharge of the debt, which failing it would sell. Therefore, said the Justices, it was mandatory to serve a calling-up notice. No such notice had been served. Hence the decision of the Inner House fell to be reversed, and *Bank of Scotland v Millward* overruled.

One of the Justices, Lord Rodger, offered an additional argument:[4]

Where the debtor fails to comply with a personal obligation constituted by a separate instrument,[5] he fails to comply with a requirement under that instrument. But it is hard to see how he can properly be said to have failed to comply with a requirement 'arising out of the security'.

On this view, standard condition 9(1)(b) is unavailable for monetary breaches in form B cases. And whilst that argument does not apply to form A cases, Lord Hope goes on to say that 'it is hard to see why Parliament would have intended to distinguish between Form A and Form B standard securities in this respect'.[6] Ken Swinton accepts the first part of this (about form B cases) but not the second, and

---

1   This is the approach taken by Ken Swinton, 'Enforcing standard securities: *Royal Bank v Wilson (No 2)*' (2010) 78 *Scottish Law Gazette* 87.
2   Professor Halliday's views are discussed in the *Wilson* case. See in particular Lord Hope at para 68. But Lords Hope and Rodger do not see eye-to-eye on the question of what Halliday thought: see Lord Rodger's comments at para 47.
3   1999 SLT 901.
4   Paragraph 41.
5   That is to say, a form B security.
6   Paragraph 43.

concludes that 'where the security is in Form A, ie contains a personal obligation *in gremio* then a default notice and a section 24 application are competent'.[1] Since in his view the securities in the *Wilson* case were form A securities, for Ken Swinton Lord Hope's comments were *obiter dicta*. Indeed, for him the actual *ratio* of the case is limited to the ejection issue (discussed below).

He may be right. Our impression is that the Wilsons appealed solely on the ejection issue. If that is so, then everything that was said about s 19 being mandatory may have been *obiter dicta*,[2] unless it is competent for the Supreme Court to make a formal ruling on a point not appealed, or unless an appellant can add grounds of appeal at the oral hearing in London.[3] But whether or not the 'calling up is mandatory' point is part of the *ratio* of the decision, there can be no doubt that the decision will be accepted as authoritative on the point. Moreover, in our view the Supreme Court took that view in relation to *all* standard securities, without reference to the distinction between form A and form B. The reason for this lies in the mandatory language of s 19. We see Lord Hope's comments on form A and form B as interesting musings that are not central to the decision.

In the case much is said about the late Jack Halliday. Whilst the Halliday Report of 1966,[4] which led to the 1970 Act, is mentioned, the discussion focuses on Halliday's post-1970 writings. We think it worth quoting from the 1966 report the passage which was later to form the basis for standard condition 9(1):[5]

Default means:

(a) failure by the Borrower after a demand in writing by the Lender to make any payment of principal or interest payable to the Lender in terms of the deed, standard conditions or Schedule[6]

(b) failure by the Borrower to observe or perform any of the other conditions or obligations imposed on him by the standard conditions or Schedule

(c) the Borrower entering into any composition or arrangement with or for the benefit of his creditors or becoming insolvent. ...

1 Ken Swinton: 'Enforcing standard securities: *Royal Bank v Wilson (No 2)*' (2010) 78 *Scottish Law Gazette* 87, 90.

2 However, the absence of a 'formal requisition', such as a calling-up notice, was crucial to the ejection issue, discussed below. Thus the bank's decision not to serve a calling-up notice was fatal *both* to its power of sale (because of s 19 of the 1970 Act) *and* to its power to eject (because of the lack of a 'formal requisition' in terms of s 5 of the 1894 Act).

3 According to Bryan Heaney: '[O]nly minutes into the argument in the Supreme Court, Lord Walker asked a question that introduced a new argument for the appellants' to wit, that s 19 appeared to be in mandatory terms: See http://ukscblog.com/case-comment-royal-bank-of-scotland-plc-v-wilson-anor-2010-uksc-50.

4 *Conveyancing Legislation and Practice* (Cmnd 3118, 1966).

5 At p 109. The provisions about enforcement are passed over by the body of the Halliday Report in silence, being tucked away in Appendix F. The impression given is that enforcement was regarded as a mere detail. Jack Halliday was juggling two jobs (partner in a busy law firm, and professor at the University of Glasgow) and half-way through the committee's deliberations he picked up a third, Scottish Law Commissioner. The other committee members were also busy professionals. Perhaps some of the details in the appendices were left to the committee's secretary, A J ('Sandy') Sim, a distinguished civil service lawyer who probably had more time than the members of the committee to sit down and work through (and write up) some of the details.

6 The reference to 'the Schedule' seems to be a reference to the schedule that the deed could, optionally, have. See p 106 of the Report. The idea seems to have been that of a schedule of variations of the standard conditions.

Since the 1966 report had the distinction between form A and form B, the words 'in terms of the deed' are awkward. Still, the impression we form from the quoted text is that the intention was that calling-up would be the sole road to sale in cases of monetary breach. What became standard condition 9(1)(b) was, we incline to think, intended for non-monetary breach, such as failure to maintain.

Assessment

Is the decision correct in requiring a calling-up notice for monetary breaches? The enforcement provisions of the 1970 Act are not well drafted, and so the search for the 'true' meaning may be in vain. That said, the approach taken by the Supreme Court is probably a more coherent reading of the statutory provisions than the approach traditionally taken. But nevertheless one must have reservations, for *error communis facit jus*, that is to say, an interpretation of the law that is universally shared is itself law even if it ought not to have been adopted in the first place. Like most such tags, it is less a rule than a thought for the day, but like other thoughts for the day it has some force. The availability of a s 24 application had been accepted from the very outset in 1970. Almost no one had questioned it. Over the years countless standard securities have been enforced in that way. It is not clear that there was any strong policy-based objection to this way of proceeding. Might there not have been a case for saying that the entrenched view, even if originally wrong, must now be considered right? An argument of that kind succeeded in, for example, *Rhone v Stephens*,[1] an English conveyancing case where the House of Lords decided not to overturn a long-established view of the law. We express no view on this issue but merely regret that it was not explored by the Supreme Court.[2]

Implications for notices of default

In *Wilson* there was no notice of default. Nevertheless the logic of the decision is clear: notices of default are almost never competent.

Procedure in future

Since virtually every case where a creditor seeks to enforce a standard security is a case where the 'creditor ... intends to require discharge of the debt thereby secured', henceforth a calling-up notice is going to be necessary in virtually every case. Had the Home Owner and Debtor Protection (Scotland) Act 2010 not been passed, the effect of the *Wilson* decision would have been that s 24 applications would have become almost unknown. But that Act requires a s 24 application even where there has been a calling-up notice in cases where the property in question is residential property.[3] So s 24 applications will continue to flourish,

---

1 [1994] 2 AC 310. We thank Scott Wortley for drawing our attention to this example.
2 As noted above, it is unfortunate that counsel for the respondents seem not to have enjoyed much opportunity to marshal arguments and authorities in relation to the 's 19 is mandatory' issue.
3 Subject to one exception, discussed below.

except in non-residential cases. Notices of default, however, are likely to become even rarer.

Obtaining vacant possession

'There has to be power actually to get the occupiers out of the premises. Without this the other remedies, such as the power of sale, will not work.' So says Lady Hale in *Wilson*.[1] There is much truth in this, but as a legal proposition it would not be quite accurate. There are two qualifications. A creditor could competently sell with the occupiers still in the premises, leaving it to the buyer to decide what to do about them. Further, if the lease pre-dates the security, it will normally have the status of a prior real right, and so the creditor would have no legal basis for seeking vacant possession against the occupiers – the security has effect subject to the lease. That would not prevent enforcement by sale, but such a sale could not prejudice the position of the tenant or lessee. If the lease post-dates the security it will be trumped by the security,[2] though even in such a case, if the tenancy is a profitable one, the creditor might decide to sell the property with a sitting tenant.

But in most cases there is no tenant, and the creditor does wish to obtain vacant possession. Often the debtor flits voluntarily. But if that does not happen, how is vacant possession to be obtained? On this simple question the legislation is a mess. As previously mentioned, s 5(1) of the Heritable Securities (Scotland) Act 1894 says:

> Where a creditor desires to enter into possession of the lands disponed in security, and the proprietor thereof is in personal occupation of the same, or any part thereof, such proprietor shall be deemed to be an occupant without a title, and the creditor may take proceedings to eject him in all respects in the same way as if he were such occupant: Provided that this section shall not apply in any case unless such proprietor has made default in the punctual payment of the interest due under the security, or in due payment of the principal after formal requisition.

How does this relate to the 1970 Act? Standard condition 10 says that 'where the debtor is in default, the creditor may … enter into possession of the security subjects'. That refers to the three kinds of 'default' set out in standard condition 9(1) (quoted above). Although in all three cases the creditor is empowered to 'enter into possession', this statement turns out not to be entirely true. It is true (or sort of true) in case (a) (non-compliance with calling-up notice) but not in cases (b) and (c), in respect of which the Act says that the right to take possession does *not* arise merely because of default. Rather, default gives the creditor the right to ask the court to be given the right to take possession.[3] Section 24 empowers the court to grant warrant to the creditor to exercise various remedies including the power to enter into possession.

---

1 Paragraph 81.
2 For changes to the *procedure* for removing such a tenant, see the discussion of the Housing (Scotland) Act 2010 at p 155 below.
3 See s 23(2) of the 1970 Act. Lord Rodger notes the anomaly at para 24 of the Supreme Court case.

Tensions between the 1970 Act and the 1894 Act

Between the 1970 Act and the 1894 Act there are two tensions. The first is procedural. Does a creditor proceeding under the 1970 Act, who has obtained a right to possession under that Act, and has perhaps even obtained a warrant from the court authorising possession to be taken, need to obtain a warrant to eject under the 1894 Act if the debtor does not flit?

In *Wilson* the sheriff held that 'section 24(1) of the 1970 Act makes no provision for ejection as a remedy for default: such a remedy only arises under section 5 of the 1894 Act'.[1] Similar remarks have been made before. Thus Sheriff-Principal Caplan in a 1989 case said:[2]

> Standard Condition 10(3) gives the creditor the remedy of entering into possession of the security subjects but proceedings necessary to enforce that remedy are part of the normal array of common law procedural remedies available to a creditor in a right and are not applications to the court defined by the 1970 Act. Put another way the 1970 Act nowhere provides for a creditor applying to the court for the remedies of declarator and ejection.

There can be no doubt that this is correct. The provisions of the 1970 Act are only about the *right* to take possession and do not touch on *ejection*. For if X has possession but Y has the right to possession, that fact does not of itself give Y a power to eject X. Y's mere right to possession has to be made effective by obtaining a warrant to eject.[3] It is perhaps odd that under the 1970 Act the court can (under s 24) expressly authorise the creditor to take possession, and yet that authorisation still needs to be backed up by a distinct warrant. Yet that is the position. If the procedure is happening through s 24 of the 1970 Act, the warrants can be combined in a single action, that is to say, the creditor can seek warrant to take possession and at the same time seek warrant to eject.

The second tension is more substantive. The 1970 Act has detailed rules as to when and how the creditor becomes entitled to possession. But the 1894 Act has its own rules. Must the creditor satisfy *both* sets of requirements? This question was the focus of the litigation in *Wilson* all the way up to the Supreme Court, at which point it was joined by the other – and ultimately more important – issue, namely the 'calling up is mandatory' issue.

None of the three types of default set out in standard condition 9(1) matches up perfectly with s 5 of the 1894 Act. If there is a calling-up notice then there is indeed 'formal requisition'. But the converse may not be true, for there are various requirements about calling-up notices, and it might be that a formal requisition could fail to comply with those requirements.[4] 'Default in the punctual payment of the interest' might partially match up with standard condition 9(1)(b) ('where there has been a failure to comply with any other

---

1 As quoted in the Inner House at para 43.
2 *Hill Samuel & Co Ltd v Haas* 1989 SLT (Sh Ct) 68.
3 Or to remove, but the ejection/removing distinction does not need be discussed here.
4 In *Wilson* Lord Hope says that a notice of default could satisfy the requirements of the 1894 Act: see para 59.

requirement arising out of the security'). But at all events it is apparent that some types of 'default' under the 1970 Act simply do not match up with the 1894 Act. That is so for standard condition 9(1)(c) ('where the proprietor of the security subjects has become insolvent') and is also so for at least some of the possibilities under standard condition 9(1)(b) (eg failure to maintain the property).

So how do the provisions of the 1894 Act and the 1970 Act relate to each other? The 1970 Act says that the right to possession arises in certain specific circumstances. Section 5 of the 1894 Act gives a *separate* basis for obtaining a warrant to eject. Does a creditor who wishes to eject a debtor have to establish a right under *both* statutes? Or only one? Either answer seems odd. It is difficult to suppress the suspicion that the issue was not considered when the 1970 Act was on the stocks.[1]

In *Wilson* the sheriff agreed with the debtors that the requirement of the 1894 Act for a 'formal requisition' is not in itself satisfied by the s 24 procedure, so that it must be separately satisfied if warrant to eject is to be granted. And he held that in fact it had not been separately satisfied. The Inner House disagreed, taking the view that if the right to possession emerges under the 1970 Act, then that fact automatically satisfied the preconditions for a warrant to eject under the 1894 Act:[2]

> The 1970 Act equiparates the position of a creditor whose debtor is in default under standard condition 9(1)(b) with the position of a creditor who has served a calling up notice which has not been complied with, resulting in a default under standard condition 9(1)(a). Where the court holds it to be established that there is default within the meaning of standard condition 9(1)(b), the creditor may apply to the court for warrant to exercise any of the remedies which he is entitled to exercise on a default within the meaning of standard condition 9(1)(a). A creditor who serves a calling up notice is making a formal requisition for the purposes of the 1894 Act. This places the creditor whose debtor is in default in the same position. Such a creditor is entitled to exercise all the remedies which would be open to a creditor who has served a formal requisition in terms of s 5 of the 1894 Act. Section 5 of the 1894 Act expressly confers the right to take proceedings for ejection. Just as the creditor cannot enter into possession when there is a default under standard condition 9(1)(b) unless he obtains the court's authority under s 24(1), so he cannot operate his remedy of ejection without an application under the same section. The two remedies are intrinsically interrelated. In most cases the issues affecting the exercise of the remedies of entering into possession and ejection of the debtor are the same. If the debtor is in occupation of the subjects, the remedy of possession of the subjects alone will be of little avail to the creditor, since without free occupation there will be no rent to recover.[3]

Thus, says the Inner House, s 24 procedure of itself satisfies the pre-conditions of the 1894 Act so that a warrant to eject can simply be included in the crave and no separate 'formal requisition' has to be averred or proved.

---

1 The issue is not mentioned in the Halliday Report (*Conveyancing Legislation and Practice* (Cmnd 3118, 1966)).
2 Paragraph 42.
3 We do not entirely follow these last few words. If there is free occupation there is no tenant and so no rent.

The Supreme Court in turn disagreed with the Inner House, taking the view that a creditor seeking a warrant to eject must aver, and if need be prove, 'formal requisition', and that a s 24 application does not in itself suffice for this purpose.[1] Thus whilst a creditor may obtain the right to possession under the 1970 Act, that right does not in itself justify the court in granting warrant to eject. The 'formal requisition' requirement of the 1894 Act must be separately satisfied.

Theoretically one point remains open: whether a creditor could obtain warrant to eject *solely* by satisfying the requirements of the 1894 Act? The Supreme Court does not address the point. It held only that the creditor, to obtain a warrant to eject, must satisfy the requirements of the 1894 Act. It did not specifically hold that the requirements of the 1970 Act must *also* be satisfied. But that must, we think, be the law: any other rule would be absurd.

On the facts of *Wilson*, might the letters posted in 1995 count as 'formal requisition'? The Supreme Court considered this possibility but rejected it. Lord Hope said that 'the word "formal" is not defined in the 1894 Act, but it should be understood as requiring the creditor to provide full details of the security to the proprietor so that the basis for the demand is made clear'.[2]

The issue about what counts as 'formal requisition' becomes a very minor one as a result of the 'calling up is mandatory' aspect of the decision. If a calling-up notice is served, that counts not only as a calling-up notice for the purposes of obtaining power of sale under the 1970 Act but also as a formal requisition for the purposes of obtaining a warrant to eject under the 1894 Act. The question 'does a s 24 application in itself satisfy the requirements of the 1894 Act?' will in future be relevant only to the vanishingly small number of cases where no calling-up notice is needed.

This approach – that a creditor cannot obtain a warrant to eject without satisfying *both* the 'right to possession' requirements of the 1970 Act *and* the 'right to eject' requirements of the 1894 Act – could occasionally run into problems. Suppose, for example, that an owner is paying the bank regularly but not maintaining the property. In such a situation the bank could obtain a s 24 order authorising it to take possession and to sell. This is one of the rare cases where a calling-up notice would not, under the *Wilson* decision, be required. Yet since the debtor is not in financial default, could the creditor satisfy the requirements of the 1894 Act? Seemingly not. The result would be that the creditor would be entitled to take possession (s 24 order) but at the same time would not be entitled to take possession (1894 Act). That is a strange conclusion, but the poor quality of the legislation may make strange conclusions unavoidable.[3]

---

1 See eg Lord Hope at paras 71 and 75 and Lady Hale at para 81.
2 Paragraph 60. And see paras 13, 22 and 81. The Supreme Court clearly was unhappy with the fact that the 1995 letters had been sent only to the husbands but do not seem to have made this a ground, in itself, for holding them not to have been 'formal requisitions', perhaps because of the point made in the Inner House case at para 47. A further problem about regarding the 1995 letters as 'formal requisition' is that they did not actually demand payment of the whole sum but only 'a substantial payment to account … coupled with acceptable proposals to take care of the remaining indebtedness'.
3 The same issue would arise for standard condition 9(1)(c).

Finally, s 5(1) of the 1894 Act says: 'this section shall not apply in any case unless such proprietor has made default in the punctual payment of the interest due under the security, or in due payment of the principal after formal requisition'. Is formal requisition needed only in the case where the principal is demanded? Or is it also needed where unpaid interest is demanded? The issue is perhaps not important because in practice banks seek payment of the whole caboodle. But for what it is worth, the sheriff and the Inner House disagreed on this point, the sheriff holding that 'formal requisition' is needed in both cases, and the Inner House that it is needed only in the case of the principal. As the Supreme Court seems not to have commented on this point, the view of the Inner House presumably remains good law. If so, and since in practice any default involves at least some element of interest default, banks could circumvent the need for 'formal requisition'. But that would be true only for the purposes of obtaining a warrant to eject, and they would still need to serve a calling-up notice (which counts as 'formal requisition') if they wish to sell.[1] In theory they could decide to enforce by letting out the property, and in that case a calling-up notice would not be needed, though warrant to eject would be.[2]

When will standard conditions 9(1)(b) and (c) be relevant in future?

As we read the case, *Wilson* says that where a creditor in a standard security seeks to sell, a calling-up notice is necessary. As we have indicated, that may in fact have been the original intention of the Halliday Committee. But that leaves a puzzle as to the purpose of standard conditions 9(1)(b) and (c). The former covers non-monetary breach, such as a failure to maintain, the latter where the debtor is sequestrated. Yet it is hard to imagine any case where a creditor would need to invoke these provisions. In the case of an on-demand loan, the creditor can demand full payment at any time, and does not need to justify the demand by reason of, for example, failure to maintain the property. If the loan is a term loan, in practice the loan contract will have an 'acceleration' clause whereby the creditor can, in defined circumstances, demand repayment of the whole loan immediately. Those circumstances will include any material breach, and will also include the debtor's insolvency. Hence if a debtor fails to maintain the property, or is sequestrated, a creditor does not need to make use of standard conditions 9(1)(b) or (c), for calling-up will be possible. Pursuing this line of thinking, one wonders why standard conditions 9(1)(b) and (c) were included in the legislation in the first place.

---

1 One of the puzzles of both the 1970 Act and the 1894 Act is that taking possession is dealt with in a way that is not clearly connected with other remedies, especially sale. For example, does the 1894 Act mean that, on default, the bank could eject the debtor but then twiddle its thumbs, happily contemplating the rising interest bill? Is there not an obligation, after taking possession, to sell, or at least to let out the property, which is a lawful alternative, albeit one seldom used? Taking possession must be for some purpose.

2 Unless the property was already let out, in which case the creditor could simply take the rent. One thing a creditor cannot do, we suggest, is take possession and then occupy the property for its own benefit, though in the past that occasionally happened with private lenders.

So on the *Wilson* approach, standard conditions 9(1)(b) and (c) seem redundant. That point might be used as an argument against the Supreme Court's decision. But as we have already suggested, it is difficult to come up with *any* interpretation of the enforcement provisions of the 1970 Act that does not lead to odd conclusions. For example, on the approach taken until the Supreme Court decision, the overlap between standard conditions 9(1)(a) and (b) was puzzling.

Default

In the sheriff court and in the Inner House much of the debate was about whether there had been 'default' for the purposes of standard condition 9(1)(b). The sheriff held that the bank had not proved default, but the Inner House reversed. This issue is closely connected with the issue of 'formal requisition' because, if there was a failure to require payment, then that might mean both (i) that there had been no default for the purposes of the 1970 Act and (ii) that the requirements of the 1894 Act had not been met. Since the Supreme Court held that the creditor should have served a calling-up notice, the whole issue of default as discussed in the lower courts seems to have become irrelevant.

Existing titles: a risk of challenge?

Suppose that there is now an ordinary transaction – ie a transaction with an ordinary seller, but where at some earlier stage there had been a sale by a heritable creditor carried out in a way that, applying *Wilson* retrospectively, is now known to have been erroneous. And assume that the current seller is a GRS proprietor.

Actually, in most counties this can hardly happen. Take Renfrewshire, which became operational for the Land Register in 1981. Any sale by a heritable creditor since then will have triggered first registration, even if the property was previously unregistered. So the seller today (2011) can be expected to be someone who has a title in the Land Register that is fully indemnified. And even if the current seller of property in Renfrewshire is a GRS proprietor (not very likely), any sale of the property by a heritable creditor would have had to have happened so long ago that prescription should have run. But in some counties, the position could be different. The last counties to become operational became so in 2003. Suppose that in 2002 someone bought a property in Ross and Cromarty from a standard security holder. If that person is now (2011) selling, the title will still be a GRS title, and positive prescription would not have run its course until 2012.

There are three possibilities in relation to this hypothetical Ross and Cromarty property. The first is where there was a calling-up notice. Such cases are unaffected by the *Wilson* decision.

The second is where the sale happened solely on the basis of a notice of default. Such cases are, we think, rare, but there may be a few. Here the possibility of a challenge to the GRS title is, no doubt, small in practice, but there probably does exist a theoretical risk. The procedure was not valid[1] and, in the absence of prescription or of a Land Register title, the main line of defence would seem to be s 41(2) of the Conveyancing (Scotland) Act 1924,[2] which protects those who have bought in good faith from a heritable creditor. In such cases good faith will no doubt exist. But the section also requires the sale procedure to have been *'ex facie regular'*. It could be argued that, in the light of *Wilson*, a sale that happened solely on the basis of a notice of default was not *ex facie* regular. But if *ex facie* regularity is judged at the time of the sale, as surely it ought to be if the provision is to do the job for which it was enacted, then a sale that took place in a way blessed by Inner House authority and that every conveyancer in Scotland would have certified as valid seems likely to be a sale that was *ex facie* regular.[3]

The third possibility is that the sale was on the basis of a s 24 decree. Here the s 41 argument would seem even stronger. But there is another argument too. If the s 24 decree was *in foro*, the case will be *res judicata*. But even if it was *in absentia*, reponing would now be impossible, because once a decree *in absentia* has been 'implemented' it cannot be opened up by reponing, and a s 24 decree is implemented by sale.

So in our view the theoretical risk to a GRS title where there is a s 24 sale by a heritable creditor within the prescriptive progress – our hypothetical Ross and Cromarty case – is so slight as to be negligible. Where the sale was solely on the basis of a notice of default the theoretical risk is more substantial. And in either case the *practical* risk is likely to be very small indeed: few debtors would be interested in trying to challenge an old sale.

With a s 24 sale the doubt is so small that we do not think it need be mentioned when applying for first registration. But if the sale within the prescriptive progress was solely on the basis of a notice of default (which in practice would be uncommon) then there would seem to be enough doubt to call for disclosure of the issue to the Keeper. And in such cases a title insurance policy might be advisable.

Buying from a heritable creditor

The other type of case is where a heritable creditor obtained its (apparent) power of sale before the Supreme Court's decision was announced,[4] but had not sold by that time. In some of these cases the creditor has gone back to square one and served a calling-up notice. That has also been happening, we understand, in cases where the bank had already raised a s 24 action before the Supreme Court

---

1 In this and the following paragraphs we are assuming that all s 24 cases and all notice of default cases were in themselves wrong in the light of *Wilson*. Actually that is not quite true, because even on the basis of the *Wilson* decision a few such cases will have been right.
2 Though this section speaks only of the old forms of heritable security, it is applied to standard securities by s 32 of the 1970 Act.
3 That is our view. Robert Rennie takes a narrower view of s 41(2): see 'Law v practice: Royal Bank of Scotland plc v Wilson' 2010 SLT (News) 219. A possible difficulty with using s 41(2) is that, on one reading, it distinguishes between (i) the acquisition of the power of sale and (ii) its exercise, and that the protection applies only in respect of (ii).
4 24 November 2010.

decision was announced but had not yet obtained decree. But take those cases where the creditor obtained decree before the announcement, had not yet sold the property, and has now decided to press ahead with the sale. Here it makes no difference whether the defaulting owner held on a Land Register title or on a GRS title, for the question is not the validity of the current owner's title but of the creditor's power of sale. We understand that in such cases creditors are offering to buyers a title insurance policy, though we have also heard that the terms of some of these policies are unusual in that the sum claimable is limited to the current sale figure, rather than the value of the property at the time of a future successful challenge. Of course, the possibility always exists of the buyers taking out top-up cover.

How big is the risk? If the creditor is selling solely on the basis of a notice of default, there is a problem. But there can be few such cases. The more important question is whether a s 24 decree granted before the appearance of the *Wilson* decision can be relied on by the buyer. This has already been discussed. Once the sale has happened, the decree has been implemented and so reponing would cease to be a possibility. On this view of matters, title insurance is not actually necessary. But it may be prudential.

It is worth reflecting that reponing is *always* a possibility for decrees *in absentia* of *any* type.[1] Yet conveyancing and other legal business are not paralysed by that fact. Consider, for example, the provision of the Home Owner and Debtor Protection (Scotland) Act 2010, discussed below, which says that in future most cases where standard securities are enforced will need a s 24 decree. No doubt in practice many such cases will be undefended so that the resulting decree will be *in absentia*. But will that make such properties unsellable? The question answers itself.

Might s 24 decrees be wholly void?

It might be argued that s 24 decrees are simply void and that, in the absence of a calling-up notice, no power of sale could exist.[2] We do not see it that way. The 1970 Act empowers the sheriff to grant to a creditor the power of sale. This is not like, say, a justice of the peace purporting to grant decree of divorce. The sheriff in granting power of sale has acted *intra vires*. It is true that the decree should not in fact have been granted, but that is a systemic issue in civil procedure, and the general principle is that a decree is not invalid merely because, if the parties had all advanced the right legal arguments and placed before the court all the facts, and the sheriff or other judge had been informed by a helpful archangel as to where the truth lay, the decision would have been a different one. The statute has given the sheriff a power and the sheriff has exercised that power. So where a s 24 warrant has been granted, the result is to confer power of sale. Given the decision in *Wilson*, we now know that the debtor could have successfully opposed

---

1 Subject to certain qualifications such as OCR 7.5.
2 Under the *Wilson* doctrine, there could be a very few cases where s 24 procedure would indeed be appropriate. But this rather theoretical point is ignored in this section of the discussion.

a s 24 application.[1] But if that has not happened, and the decree is granted and extracted, the brute fact is that a power of sale does exist.

Advice from the Keeper and the Law Society

Soon after the decision, the Keeper put the following (understandably rather non-committal) notice on the Registers of Scotland website:[2]

> A number of practitioners have contacted RoS seeking clarity on the position of the Keeper and pending applications following the Supreme Court judgment on the case of the *Royal Bank of Scotland plc v John Patrick McCormack Wilson*. We understand that the Law Society of Scotland is currently considering the matter. The Keeper is, of course, unable to provide legal advice to solicitors and practitioners on the effect of judicial decisions. The onus remains with solicitors to determine the effect, if any, of the judgment on the particular transaction they are involved in. If the solicitor is content that the statutory procedures have been complied with, then an affirmative response to the power of sale compliance question in the relevant Land Registration application form should be provided. If the solicitor feels unable to supply an affirmative response, then, as in any other case where no affirmative response can be given, the Keeper will feel bound to exclude indemnity. This does not necessarily mean that the title is challengeable, although it does open up the potential for the register to be rectified if the Disposition granted by the creditor was subsequently reduced.

Land Register application forms have a specific question about whether, if the transaction is a purchase from a heritable creditor, the statutory requirements have been satisfied. We think that the Keeper's statement simply means that if this box is ticked, and nothing else is said on the application form, the Keeper will normally issue a land certificate with no exclusion of indemnity. On the other hand, if the application does say that there may be doubt about the title, the Keeper is likely to respond by adding an exclusion of indemnity.

On 1 December 2010 the Law Society of Scotland put this on its website:[3]

> Solicitors involved in repossession transactions should be aware of a recent decision from the UK Supreme Court which has overruled long-established procedures by holding that the creditor must proceed by way of a calling-up notice. *Royal Bank of Scotland plc v Wilson* [2010] UKSC 50 overturns the standard practice of most secured lenders in Scottish repossession proceedings of raising a writ founding on a 'default' in terms of standard condition 9(1)(b) of Schedule 3 to the Conveyancing and Feudal Reform (Scotland) Act 1970 and seeking recovery in terms of s 24 of the Act.
>
> The decision has thrown into doubt numerous ongoing transactions relating to repossessed homes. While it is essentially a matter of law, the Society's initial advice to solicitors acting for purchasers (and their mortgage lenders) is not to settle until selling creditors either produce evidence that they have followed the correct procedure or offer

---

1 For clarity, we are not here referring to those (very rare) cases where, under *Wilson*, s 24 is in fact appropriate. Nor are we referring to future cases that are routed through s 24 by virtue of the Home Owner and Debtor Protection (Scotland) Act 2010, discussed below.

2 http://www.ros.gov.uk/public/news/royalbank.html.

3 http://www.lawscot.org.uk/members/member-services/professional-practice/professional-practice-updates-.

adequate Title Indemnity Insurance. The Keeper's position is that it is for solicitors to determine what effect, if any, the judgment has on particular transactions. If the solicitor is not satisfied that the correct statutory procedures have been followed then this will have to be disclosed on the land registration application form and the Keeper will almost certainly exclude indemnity when issuing the Land Certificate.

Bruce Ritchie, Director of Professional Practice at the Society, said: 'The Society's Conveyancing and Civil Justice Committees will be looking at this in detail, but our preliminary view on current sale transactions that have not yet settled is that buyers' solicitors should be firm about declining to settle the transaction until they are satisfied their clients' position (including lenders for whom they are acting) is properly protected from challenge.'

Warrandice and missives

The traditional practice has been, and continues to be, that a disposition on sale by a heritable creditor has a clause binding the debtor in absolute warrandice and, as far as the heritable creditor is concerned, granting fact and deed warrandice only. The warrandice flowing from the debtor is likely to be of little or no value. Whether fact and deed warrandice constitutes a guarantee of the validity of the creditor's power of sale is a question on which there is no authority, but if it does not provide that guarantee then it would be difficult to see what content it could have. It may be added that there is an argument that heritable creditors ought to be granting absolute warrandice. A buyer is expected to pay a full market price in this as in ordinary cases, so why should the warrandice be of a lower grade? There is a link between the question of warrandice and the question of title insurance, for the financial standing of a selling heritable creditor is commonly comparable with the standing of an insurance company. Thus for example a disposition with absolute warrandice from a major bank is presumably just as good as a title insurance policy from an insurer.

We understand that, in the light of *Wilson*, some selling creditors are seeking agreement in missives that there is no guarantee that the enforcement process has been valid and that the warrandice clause will be qualified accordingly. The reasonableness of this seems to us questionable.

Filling in the Land Register application forms

We read the Keeper's statement, quoted above, as meaning that if question 6 on the application form[1] is ticked 'yes' then indemnity is unlikely to be excluded, but if it is ticked 'no' then indemnity is likely to be excluded. Of course, no one wishes to see an exclusion of indemnity, but it must be borne in mind that failure to fill in the application form properly may subvert the Keeper's indemnity.[2] Can the applicant tick 'yes'? If the analysis suggested above is right then the answer will usually be in the affirmative.

---

1 'Have the statutory procedures necessary for the proper exercise of the power been exercised?' On form 1 (first registrations) this is Q 10.
2 See the word 'carelessness' in s 9(3)(a)(iii) of the Land Registration (Scotland) Act 1979 and the word 'careless' in s 12(3)(n) of that Act.

There is one benefit of having a land certificate with exclusion of indemnity. Because of a mistake in the Land Registration (Scotland) Act 1979, positive prescription does not run on a fully indemnified land certificate. But it can run where there is an exclusion of indemnity.[1] So to the extent that any risk is perceived to exist, there is a certain logic to going down this route – ie answering 'no' in the application form and then applying to the Keeper, after 10 years, for deletion of the exclusion. That is presumably the expectation of creditors who are offering title insurance. But of course if the risk of a challenge to the title is slight now, it would be yet slighter after 10 years anyway, prescription or no prescription.

Effect on postponed securities

Where there is a sale based on a s 24 decree (alone), what are the implications for postponed standard securities when the buyer's title is registered? If the analysis above is right, there are no particular implications, for such a sale is effective and the postponed securities are extinguished in the usual way.[2]

Legislation?

We understand that the Scottish Government plans to consult on whether legislation is needed as a result of the decision. It is rumoured that creditor interests have been pressing for the decision to be reversed. We would agree that there is a need for the whole system of enforcing standard securities to be reviewed, but we doubt whether the Supreme Court's decision makes special legislation necessary. As for the enforcement cases that were active just as the decision came out, many of which were capsized by the decision, they will have been resolved well before any special legislation could come into force. Already-settled cases are, we have suggested above, not usually rendered challengeable by the decision. As for future cases, the only change for banks is that they will always have to serve calling-up notices – something that they often did anyway. This is hardly a major burden.

Snakes and ladders

The battle between Royal Bank of Scotland plc and the Wilsons has been going on for 12 years. Is it over now? Presumably not. The bank has been trying to enforce its two securities, and so far has been unsuccessful, but the securities seem to be valid, and they seem to secure sums of money that have not in fact been paid, though there may be dispute about the exact amount due. The result of the Supreme Court's decision is that the bank has slipped down the snake all the way back to square one – where it was back in 1998 (except that it must have paid large sums in legal fees). But square one is not only the tail of the snake but the foot of the ladder. So presumably the bank can start all over again.

---

1 See s 1 of the Prescription and Limitation (Scotland) Act 1973 as amended by the Land Registration (Scotland) Act 1979 s 10.
2 Conveyancing and Feudal Reform (Scotland) Act 1970 s 26(1).

Home Owner and Debtor Protection (Scotland) Act 2010

Introduction

The changes wrought to the enforcement of standard securities by the Home Owner and Debtor Protection (Scotland) Act 2010[1] are at least as important as the *Wilson* decision. The Act implements, though with variations, the recommendations of the *Debt Action Forum Final Report* (2009).[2] One of the underlying motives of the Act is to 'keep people in their homes' as far as possible. Part 1 is aimed at doing this where there has been default on a standard security, part 2 where there is a bankruptcy, whether by way of sequestration or by way of trust deed.

The Act is already in force: see the Home Owner and Debtor Protection (Scotland) Act 2010 (Commencement) Order 2010[3] and the Home Owner and Debtor Protection (Scotland) Act 2010 (Transitional and Saving Provisions) Order 2010.[4] These are two of a raft of six statutory instruments generated by the Act.[5] The others are (i) the Act of Sederunt (Sheriff Court Rules) (Enforcement of Securities over Heritable Property) 2010[6] which makes consequential amendments to the Act of Sederunt (Summary Applications, Statutory Applications and Appeals etc Rules) 1999[7] and to the Ordinary Cause Rules in schedule 1 to the Sheriff Courts (Scotland) Act 1907, (ii) the Home Owner and Debtor Protection (Scotland) Act 2010 (Consequential Provisions) Order 2010[8] which amends the styles of notices in schedule 6 to the Conveyancing and Feudal Reform (Scotland) Act 1970, (iii) the Applications by Creditors (Pre-Action Requirements) (Scotland) Order 2010,[9] and (iv) the Lay Representation in Proceedings Relating to Residential Property (Scotland) Order 2010.[10]

Residential cases to go through the s 24 procedure

Part 1 of the Act is about the enforcement of 'residential standard securities'. There are two main changes to the law. In the first place, under current law it is possible for a standard security to be enforced without any court action, except to remove a debtor who refuses to leave. The creditor can attain a power of sale through a calling-up notice or notice of default, and both are extra-judicial processes. The Conveyancing and Feudal Reform (Scotland) Act 1970 does, however, provide a judicial route in the shape of a s 24 application. The 2010 Act says that, for residential cases, the creditor will in future always have to use a s 24 application – with one important exception, discussed below.

---

1 For a note of scepticism about the legislation, see a letter by J W S Macfie in (2010) 55 *Journal of the Law Society of Scotland* Feb/10.
2 Noted in *Conveyancing 2009* p 179.
3 SSI 2010/314.
4 SSI 2010/316.
5 For an overview, see Mark Higgins, 'An orchestra of instruments' (2010) 55 *Journal of the Law Society of Scotland* Oct/22.
6 SSI 2010/324.
7 SI 1999/929.
8 SSI 2010/318.
9 SSI 2010/317.
10 SSI 2010/264.

That, however, does not mean that calling-up notices will be superseded. The effect of the *Wilson* case[1] is that calling-up notices are needed in virtually every case where the creditor wishes to enforce a standard security. Thus the net result of *Wilson* and the new legislation is that, in enforcing a standard security over residential property, the creditor will need both to serve a calling-up notice[2] and also (unless the exception applies) to make a s 24 application. The Act was drafted before the Wilson decision, and so does not list 'service of a calling-up notice' as one of the boxes to be ticked before the sheriff will grant decree. But we presume that, in the light of *Wilson*, decree will not be granted unless the sheriff is satisfied about the calling-up notice.

The exception: 'voluntary surrender'

The exception, ie residential cases where a s 24 application is not needed, is where there has been a 'voluntary surrender' of the property. The test is:[3]

    (a) the security subjects are unoccupied; and
    (b) each of the persons specified in subsection (2) below has, in writing –
        (i) certified that that person does not occupy the security subjects and is not aware of the security subjects being occupied by any other person;
        (ii) consented to the exercise by the creditor of the creditor's rights on default; and
        (iii) certified that the consent is given freely and without coercion of any kind.

Who are 'the persons specified in subsection (2) below'? They are:[4]

    (a) the debtor;
    (b) the proprietor of the security subjects (where the proprietor is not the debtor);
    (c) the non-entitled spouse of the debtor or the proprietor of security subjects which are (in whole or in part) a matrimonial home;
    (d) the non-entitled civil partner of the debtor or the proprietor of security subjects which are (in whole or in part) a family home; and
    (e) a person who has occupancy rights in the security subjects by virtue of an order under section 18(1) (occupancy rights of cohabiting couples) of the Matrimonial Homes (Family Protection) (Scotland) Act 1981.

'Pre-action requirements'

Part 1 further provides that, before seeking a s 24 order, the creditor must satisfy certain 'pre-action requirements'. These are set out in a new s 24A of the 1970 Act which is inserted by s 4(1) of the 2010 Act:[5]

---

1 *Royal Bank of Scotland plc v Wilson* [2010] UKSC 50, 2010 SLT 1227, 2010 Hous LR 88, discussed in the previous section.
2 With rare exceptions.
3 Conveyancing and Feudal Reform (Scotland) Act 1970 s 23A(1), inserted by the Home Owner and Debtor Protection (Scotland) Act 2010 s 1(3).
4 Conveyancing and Feudal Reform (Scotland) Act 1970 s 23A(2).
5 They bear some resemblance to another set of pre-action requirements enacted in 2010. These are the requirements where possession is sought under a Scottish secure tenancy: see Housing (Scotland) Act 2001 s 14A, inserted by the Housing (Scotland) Act 2010 s 155.

(2) The creditor must provide the debtor with clear information about –

(a) the terms of the standard security;

(b) the amount due to the creditor under the standard security, including any arrears and any charges in respect of late payment or redemption; and

(c) any other obligation under the standard security in respect of which the debtor is in default.

(3) The creditor must make reasonable efforts to agree with the debtor proposals in respect of future payments to the creditor under the standard security and the fulfilment of any other obligation under the standard security in respect of which the debtor is in default.

(4) The creditor must not make an application under section 24(1B) of this Act if the debtor is taking steps which are likely to result in –

(a) the payment to the creditor within a reasonable time of any arrears, or the whole amount, due to the creditor under the standard security; and

(b) fulfilment by the debtor within a reasonable time of any other obligation under the standard security in respect of which the debtor is in default.

(5) The creditor must provide the debtor with information about sources of advice and assistance in relation to management of debt.

(6) The creditor must encourage the debtor to contact the local authority in whose area the security subjects are situated.

(7) In complying with the pre-action requirements the creditor must have regard to any guidance issued by the Scottish Ministers.

(8) The Scottish Ministers may by order made by statutory instrument make further provision about the pre-action requirements, including provision –

(a) specifying particular steps to be taken, or not to be taken, by a creditor in complying with any requirement;

(b) modifying or removing any requirement;

(c) making different provision for different circumstances.

The statutory instrument contemplated by subsection (8) has been issued: the Applications by Creditors (Pre-Action Requirements) (Scotland) Order 2010.[1] Article 2 is about the information that must be provided to the debtor about the default. Article 3(1) says:

(1) In complying with the pre-action requirement ... the creditor must –

(a) make reasonable attempts to contact the debtor to discuss the default;

(b) provide the debtor with details of any proposal made by the creditor, set out in such a way as to allow the debtor to consider the proposal;

(c) allow the debtor reasonable time to consider any proposal made by the creditor;

(d) notify the debtor within a reasonable time of any decision taken by the creditor to accept or reject a proposal made by the debtor; and

(e) consider the affordability of any proposal for the debtor taking into account, where known to the creditor, the debtor's personal and financial circumstances.

Article 4(1) supplements s 24A(4)(a) of the 1970 Act (quoted above):

---

1 SSI 2010/317.

(1) Steps taken by the debtor which are steps within the meaning of section ... 24A(4)(a) of the 1970 Act include providing documentary evidence to the creditor –

(a) of submission of a claim to an insurer under a payment protection policy currently held by the debtor in respect of the security or the contract to which the security relates, where the evidence demonstrates a reasonable expectation of eligibility for payment from the insurer, unless paragraph (3) applies;

(b) of submission of an application by the debtor to a support scheme run by Scottish Ministers or the United Kingdom Government, where the evidence demonstrates a reasonable expectation of being eligible for support in respect of the security or the contract to which the security relates, unless the creditor does not participate in, does not agree with any term of, or does not agree to the sale of the property in accordance with such a scheme or unless paragraph (3) applies; and

(c) demonstrating that the debtor or a person acting as agent for the debtor is actively marketing the property for sale at an appropriate price in accordance with professional advice, unless paragraph (4) applies.

In relation to (c) the debtor has to provide the lender with a copy of the Home Report.[1]

The Scottish Government has issued 'guidance' about the pre-action requirements.[2] One recommendation is that 'creditors should ... make an effort to ensure that information is communicated to the debtor in a language he or she can readily understand'.[3]

The reform may be less radical than at first appears, for two reasons. In the first place, mortgage lenders are in any event subject to the Financial Services Authority's *Mortgage Conduct of Business Rules*. The second is that the Mortgage Rights (Scotland) Act 2001 already gave the court discretionary powers. It may be added that where 'the payment to the creditor within a reasonable time of any arrears, or the whole amount' is in prospect most lenders would not be raising an action anyway.

Lay representation

A third reform effected by part 1 of the Act is to allow for lay representation in enforcement proceedings.[4]

Relationship to 2001 Act: opt out and opt in

How does the new legislation relate to the Mortgage Rights (Scotland) Act 2001? In broad terms it supersedes it and indeed much of the 2001 Act is repealed.

---

1 See Article 4(2).
2 http://www.scotland.gov.uk/Publications/2010/08/03135325/4.
3 At the same time 'it is recommended that creditors should ensure that standard correspondence is written in "plain *English*"'. (Emphasis added but quotation marks as in the original.)
4 Home Owner and Debtor Protection (Scotland) Act 2010 s 7, inserting a new s 24E into the Conveyancing and Feudal Reform (Scotland) Act 1970 and a new s 5F into the Heritable Securities (Scotland) Act 1894.

Of course this does not mean less protection for debtors: rather the opposite. In brief, whereas the 2001 Act required debtors to make an application to the court in order to invoke their rights, the new legislation turns things round and says that in all cases (subject to the exception) the creditor must take the case to court.[1] Thus whereas the 2001 Act worked on an opt-in basis, the new Act works on an opt-out basis. Those parts of the 2001 Act that require the service of notices remain in force.[2]

Some conveyancing implications

Those taking title from a standard security holder should in future check that the requirements of the 2010 Act have been complied with. The first question is whether the case is one governed by the 2010 Act. The Act covers any 'standard security ... over land or a real right in land used to any extent for residential purposes'. That does not mean that the debtor has to have been the occupier. Suppose that a person owns a flat as an investment, and, having a 'buy-to-let mortgage', defaults on the loan. It appears that such a case would be covered by the new legislation. And while a standard security over, say, commercial property would not be covered by the 2010 Act, a standard security over a farm normally would be covered, because a farm is likely to have on it a place of residence.[3]

If the new legislation does apply, the selling lender will have to produce to the buyer either (i) a s 24 warrant or (ii) evidence to show why a s 24 warrant was not needed. The latter may not be straightforward, as a glance at the statutory requirements makes plain.[4] The lender is going to have to produce a signed waiver from at least one person and in some cases more than one. Even the lender may be unsure who the relevant people are – for example, the lender may not know whether the debtor is married – and the buyer, at one remove, is even less likely to know whether the right people have signed. The legislation does not provide for an affidavit that the debtor does not have a non-entitled spouse.

How picky should a buyer be? This is often an issue when buying from a heritable creditor. Perhaps it would be sensible if lenders, when preparing their *pro forma* waiver forms, inserted a box in which the debtor could insert the names of those others (if any) whose signature is also necessary. Most debtors can manage to remember whether they are married. That would provide at least some assurance to the buyer. It would also provide some assurance to the heritable creditor, which needs to be sure that its decision not to seek a s 24 order is lawful.

---

1   But for 'entitled residents' there is still an application procedure: Conveyancing and Feudal Reform (Scotland) Act 1970 s 24B, inserted by s 5 of the Home Owner and Debtor Protection (Scotland) Act 2010.
2   Mortgage Rights (Scotland) Act 2001 s 4, although parts of this provision are repealed by s 8(4) of the 2010 Act.
3   On this issue, see Mark Higgins, *The Enforcement of Heritable Securities* (2010) para 6.7.
4   See Conveyancing and Feudal Reform (Scotland) Act 1970 s 23A, discussed above.

Tenants in occupation

Suppose that when a bank seeks to enforce a standard security, it discovers that the property is occupied not by the owner but by a tenant. What happens now?

If it pre-dates the security, the tenancy has priority. That does not mean that the bank cannot enforce the security by sale, but, rather, that any sale will be subject to the tenancy. That will be the position whether or not the lender knew of the existence of the tenancy when the security was granted.

The alternative possibility is that the tenancy post-dates the security. In that case the tenancy, though valid as between the tenant and the owner, is trumped by the security, which is the prior real right.[1] In cases of this sort the tenant deserves some sympathy, because in practice the tenant is highly unlikely to be aware that the tenancy is a defeasible one. The tenant may be a good citizen, duly paying the rent, and yet suddenly be facing homelessness. But equally the creditor's plight must be recognised. The security pre-dates the tenancy, the creditor has not consented to the tenancy, and yet its existence is a problem for the enforcement of the security. There is no perfect solution here to a problem caused by the owner's insolvency, but the law has to make a decision, and the law sides with the creditor.[2] The tenant then has a damages claim against the owner, or ex-owner, for breach of the contract of tenancy, but in practice the owner is unlikely to be worth suing.

In this situation a practical issue arises. The creditor has a warrant for ejection. The sheriff officers arrive and knock at the front door. The door is opened by a surprised tenant who knows nothing at all about what is happening and who must now leave, despite holding a valid tenancy and despite having been a regular payer of the rent. The issue was litigated in a sheriff court case in 1997, *Tamroui v Clydesdale Bank plc*,[3] in which it was held that a warrant to eject the owner is not in itself a good warrant to eject a tenant. The decision effectively ensured that the tenant had a breathing space in which to look for alternative accommodation. This rule was, however, rather a precarious one, being based only on sheriff court authority.

We mentioned the Debt Action Forum earlier. About the beginning of 2010 a sub-group was set up to look at the question of tenants, and its report, *Repossessions Group: Protection of Tenants: Final Report*, appeared in 2010.[4] A number of recommendations emerged from this report, one of which was that the *Tamroui* decision should be given a statutory basis, and ss 152 and 153 of the Housing (Scotland) Act 2010 have now done this.[5] What will happen to the other recommendations remains to be seen.

---

1 This result may follow from the general principles of property law, though in practice is usually attributed to standard condition 6, which forbids the owner to let out the property without the creditor's consent. Standard condition 6 was the basis of the leading case in this area, *Trade Development Bank v Warriner & Mason (Scotland) Ltd* 1980 SC 74.

2 As already pointed out, where the tenancy pre-dates the security, the law sides with the tenant, even if this is unfair to the creditor, who granted the loan unaware of the tenancy.

3 1997 SLT (Sh Ct) 20. Some sources give the name as 'Tamouri'.

4 http://www.scotland.gov.uk/Resource/Doc/315546/0100344.pdf.

5 The same issue has caused concern south of the border, and in 2010 an entire Act of Parliament was devoted to the question: Mortgage Repossessions (Protection of Tenants etc) Act 2010.

TRUST DEEDS FOR CREDITORS AND THE FAMILY HOME

Part 1 of the Home Owner and Debtor Protection (Scotland) Act 2010 is discussed above. Part 2 (ss 9–13) is about the treatment of residential property where there is sequestration or a trust deed for behoof of creditors.[1] Section 40 of the Bankruptcy (Scotland) Act 1985 provides that in certain cases the court has the power to refuse the sale of the home by the trustee in sequestration or to delay it for up to one year. Section 11 extends this period from one year to three.

Perhaps more importantly, section 10 allows a trust deed for creditors to exclude the debtor's dwellinghouse. Previously, that was effectively impossible, for a trust deed that excluded the dwellinghouse could never become a protected trust deed. Now it can. Of course, the creditors can veto this, for a trust deed cannot become a protected trust deed if the creditors vote against it. In theory creditors could choose always to veto such trust deeds, and if so the reform would have achieved nothing, though equally it would have caused no harm. But it seems likely that in practice, where the equity in the house is small, creditors will accept the exclusion. The reform in effect brings Scots law into line with English law, for a comparable exclusion of the home has long been possible in the English equivalent of the trust deed, the IVA (individual voluntary arrangement).[2]

INTERPRETATION OF DEEDS AND BOUNDARY DISPUTES

Invoking the 'matrix of facts'

The 'Hoffmann approach'

Contracts, in Lord Wilberforce's celebrated phrase, must be interpreted by reference to the 'matrix of facts' in which they are set.[3] And, more recently, in *Investors Compensation Scheme Ltd v West Bromwich Building Society*, Lord Hoffmann built on this approach by setting out five rules of interpretation.[4] The first two are that:

(1) Interpretation is the ascertainment of the meaning which the document would convey to a reasonable person having all the background knowledge which would reasonably have been available to the parties in the situation in which they were at the time of the contract.

(2) The background was famously referred to by Lord Wilberforce as the 'matrix of fact', but this phrase is, if anything, an understated description of what the background may include. Subject to the requirement that it should have been reasonably available to the parties and to the exception to be mentioned next, it includes absolutely anything which would have affected the way in which the language of the document would have been understood by a reasonable man.

---

1 See further the Bankruptcy (Scotland) Amendment Regulations 2010, SSI 2010/367.
2 For some discussion see Alistair Burrow, 'Trust rewritten' (2011) 56 *Journal of the Law Society of Scotland* Jan/44.
3 *Prenn v Simmonds* [1971] 1 WLR 1381 at 1384.
4 [1998] 1 WLR 896 at 912–13.

The idea that writing can only be understood fully by looking at all the background circumstances – at 'absolutely anything' – has not been universally welcomed, at least in Scotland. And there has been a particular reluctance to extend this principle from ordinary contracts to leases. Thus in *Multi-link Leisure Developments Ltd v North Lanarkshire Council*,[1] a decision on leases from 2009, an Extra Division of the Court of Session struck a cautious note:[2]

> We should say at the outset that we do not see the relevance for the present case of the observations of Lord Hoffmann in *Investors Compensation Scheme Ltd v West Bromwich Building Society* and *Bank of Credit and Commerce International SA v Ali*, which seem to be invoked – almost as a matter of ritual – in all cases involving construction of contracts. For our part, we have considerable sympathy with Prof McBryde's discussion of the problems that 'the Hoffmann approach' (in so far as it truly innovates on the previous law) may create for lawyers and clients (see McBryde, *The Law of Contract in Scotland*, paras 8.25–8.27).
>
> In any event, Lord Hoffmann's observations were made in the context of commercial contracts, whereas this case is about a Scottish lease of heritable property. The man on the Jubilee line on his way to Canary Wharf has less to say to us in this context than the Scots conveyancer with whose mindset we are more familiar.

A lease, of course, is a type of contract, albeit one that may bind third parties. And if the 'Hoffmann approach' is thought awkward for leases, it is likely to be a good deal more awkward for dispositions or other conveyancing deeds. For one thing, many deeds which fall to be interpreted are of considerable antiquity, so that the 'matrix of facts' may have occurred in a virtually irretrievable past. For another, conveyances being concerned with real rights and not merely with personal, disputes, when they arise, often involve successors who have no insight into, or wish to be bound by, the mindset of the original parties. This is not, of course, to say that conveyances must be interpreted in a literalist manner and without regard to background circumstances. It is well settled that extrinsic evidence is available to explain the meaning of provisions in deeds. But, if only for practical reasons, it seems necessary that the use of such evidence should be subject to greater restraint than is suggested by Lord Hoffmann's formulation.

This issue was touched on twice in 2010. In upholding the decision of the Inner House in the *Multi-link Leisure Developments* case, albeit for different reasons, the Supreme Court avoided direct comment on the *dictum* quoted above, although Lord Clarke did say that:[3]

> I detect no difference between the principles applicable to the construction of a lease in Scotland and in England. The true construction of clause 18.2 of the lease depends upon the language of the clause construed in the context of the lease as a whole, which must in turn be considered having regard to its surrounding circumstances or factual matrix.

---

1 2010 SC 302.
2 Paragraphs 23 and 24 per Temporary Judge Sir David Edward QC giving the Opinion of the Court.
3 [2010] UKSC 47, 2011 SLT 184 at para 45. See also Lord Hope's view, at para 21, that the Hoffmann approach was an expression of 'common sense principles'.

Of greater significance, at least for conveyancers, was the decision of the Lands Tribunal in *Welsh v Keeper of the Registers*.[1]

The decision in *Welsh*

With the onward march of registration of title, boundary disputes today are, increasingly, disputes as to the meaning of plans on land certificates. And, as we saw last year, such disputes can be difficult to resolve, particularly if the disputed area is too small to be properly captured by the title plan.[2] Just occasionally, however, one of the combatants argues that the title plan is inaccurate and falls to be rectified. In this way a Land Register dispute may be turned into what is in substance a Sasine dispute, because to resolve a question as to inaccuracy may require a consideration of the prior Sasine titles.

That was the position in *Welsh v Keeper of the Registers of Scotland*.[3] Dissatisfied with the plan in his land certificate, Mr Welsh asked the Keeper to rectify it. When the Keeper refused, Mr Welsh appealed to the Lands Tribunal. The application was opposed by his neighbour.

The location of the boundary in question depended on the split-off writ in favour of the neighbour, a disposition granted in 1962. The description of the relevant area was as follows:

> fields and enclosures marked Numbers ... fifty nine (part) (59 part) [and] fifty eight a (part) (58a part) ... on the Ordnance Survey Map (Scale Twenty five inches and three hundred and forty four decimal or one thousandth parts of an inch to one mile) Edition 1911 Lanarkshire Sheet XXIV, 8; all as the said plot or area of ground hereby disponed is shown coloured ... blue ... and outlined within the boundaries coloured red on the Plan thereof being an Excerpt from said Ordnance Survey Sheet annexed and subscribed as relative hereto.

The plan was no more helpful. Despite being described as an 'excerpt' from the 1911 OS map, it was merely an approximate copy on a much smaller scale. Having regard to that scale, and to the thickness of the boundary lines, it was not possible to decide whether the disputed area lay inside or outside the land conveyed. How, then, was the boundary to be correctly plotted? It was accepted that the boundary followed the line of a track, but the track had itself changed course over the years, a change which could be demonstrated by comparing the 1911 OS map with its 1965 equivalent. The difficulty was obvious: if the track was the boundary, should this be taken as the track in 1911 or in 1962, at the time the disposition was actually granted?

In seeking to answer this question, both parties had recourse to the factual matrix – to the background circumstances surrounding the granting of the deed. As the Tribunal explained:[4]

---

1 2010 GWD 23-443.
2 *Conveyancing 2009* pp 173–77.
3 2010 GWD 23-443. The Tribunal comprised J N Wright QC and I M Darling FRICS.
4 Paragraph 41.

[B]oth parties recognised the need for a so-called 'Hoffmann' approach (*Investors Compensation Scheme Ltd v West Bromwich Building Society*) of taking the 'matrix of fact' into account, ie considering the background or surrounding circumstances as known to the parties in order to assist in determining the intention of the deed. We should perhaps mention that there did at times appear to be a concentration on the intention of the person who drew up the deed plan, but we think it is the intention of the granter of the deed, or perhaps the parties to the underlying contract, that has to be determined on an application of the rules of construction.

The case, however, shows the difficulties of such an approach as applied to elderly deeds. As the 1911 route of the track favoured Mr Welsh and the 1962 route his neighbour, each sought to fortify his position by reference to what they claimed to be background circumstances. For Mr Welsh it was argued that the description in the 1962 disposition mentioned, if obliquely, the 1911 OS map. For his neighbour it was argued that a person in 1962 was hardly likely to convey land by reference to a line of track which had long since been departed from. In evaluating these arguments, the Lands Tribunal gave greater prominence to the parties' supposed (if objective) intention than the meagre evidence might seem to warrant. The line of the track was only relevant – only part of the matrix – the Tribunal said, if we can 'establish that the granter, or the parties, knew of its existence at the time'.[1] On the other hand, the 1962 line could be established as paramount without proving a site visit by the person who drew up the map, for '[i]n our view ... the granter of the deed, and the parties to the contract, need only have known the approximate position of the barn ... and the track running beside it, to have decided that the boundary would be fixed under reference to these'.[2]

The Tribunal's eventual decision, in favour of the 1962 line, is one with which we have no difficulty. But the reasoning seems over-Hoffmanned. To attempt to trace nuances of intention more than 50 years after the event is to move from evidence to speculation. If parties convey by reference to a track,[3] then it is certainly reasonable to take the line of the track as it existed at the time of the conveyance unless there is compelling evidence to the contrary. Further than this it seems neither necessary nor wise to go.

Rectification and proprietors in possession

As has just been seen, it may be no easy matter to demonstrate that the Register is inaccurate. But even if it can be done, there is still no guarantee that the applicant will get 'his' property back. For the inaccuracy cannot be rectified, and the land restored, if possession is with the neighbour and not the applicant: there can be no rectification against a proprietor in possession.[4] And in the absence of rectification, the applicant's claim resolves into one for indemnity from the Keeper.[5]

---

1 Paragraph 51.
2 Paragraph 62.
3 In the present case the reference was implicit rather than explicit.
4 Land Registration (Scotland) Act 1979 s 9(3)(a). Four exceptions are listed, including rectification by consent.
5 Land Registration (Scotland) Act 1979 s 12(1)(b).

The difficulty is illustrated by a significant new case, *Burr v Keeper of the Registers*.[1] The Burrs had acquired their land in 2003 at around the same time as their neighbour to the west, a Mr Anderson, acquired his. Both grants were split-offs from the same estate, and the title to each was registered in the Land Register. Almost from the beginning there was disagreement as to the precise boundary between the two grants, and matters came to a head when, in June 2006, Mr Anderson employed a surveyor to mark out the boundary on the ground by means of marking posts. When the Burrs disputed the boundary and moved the posts, Mr Anderson reinstated them – a sequence of events which seems to have been repeated more than once. By this time the Burrs had examined the plan in their land certificate and concluded that it was wrong in respect that it omitted a strip of land, part of which was the subject of the dispute with Mr Anderson. The Keeper was persuaded of the error, but when the Burrs applied for rectification, on 15 February 2007, the application was refused on the basis that Mr Anderson claimed to be a proprietor in possession. Rectification could not therefore proceed.

The Keeper's attitude here should be noted. Where possession is disputed, the Keeper lacks the information to adopt a view of her own. This, however, is less neutral as to its practical effects than might at first appear, for in acknowledging the possibility that someone other than the applicant is in possession, the Keeper is almost bound under the legislation to find against him and to refuse rectification.[2] It is then for the applicant, if he has the means and the determination, to fight it out in the Lands Tribunal. Although the form of proceedings there is an appeal against the Keeper's decision,[3] the Keeper is not usually represented, and the litigation is in substance one between the applicant and, if he should choose to take part, the applicant's rival.

So it was in *Burr v Keeper of the Registers*. Rectification having been refused, the Burrs appealed against the Keeper's decision. The appeal was opposed by Mr Anderson. Meanwhile, events had moved on, for in recent months Mr Anderson had removed part of the original fence and taken up possession of the disputed strip. As at the date of the hearing, therefore, there could be no doubt that he was a 'proprietor in possession'. This raised rather sharply a question which has not previously been determined: what is the relevant date at which one must be in possession in order to claim the status of 'proprietor in possession'? The difficulty was noticed by the Scottish Law Commission in its recent review of the law of land registration. 'Potential dates', said the Commission, 'include the date (i) of application for rectification, (ii) that litigation on the issue is initiated, (iii) of decree in that litigation, or (iv) of rectification being effected by an appropriate change in the Register.' But, so far at least, no choice had been made between them.[4]

---

1 12 November 2010, Lands Tribunal. The Tribunal comprised J N Wright QC and K M Barclay FRICS.
2 This is because the Keeper cannot rectify to the prejudice of a proprietor in possession unless one of four exceptions applies: see Land Registration (Scotland) Act 1979 s 9(3)(a).
3 Under Land Registration (Scotland) Act 1979 s 25.
4 Scottish Law Commission, Discussion Paper on *Land Registration: Void and Voidable Titles* (Scot Law Com DP No 125, 1994; available at www.scotlawcom.gov.uk) para 4.24.

In *Burr* a choice could not be avoided. The Tribunal put matters in this way:[1]

> There is also an important consideration as to the appropriate time at which the issue
> of in possession falls to be determined. This is not the date of either party's acquisition
> of their property. Nor is it the date of the hearing. Rather, it is the date of the application
> to rectify – 15 February 2007 – or perhaps the decision, apparently shortly after the
> letter of 13 April 2007 from which it was clear that there was a dispute about possession
> and that it would not be possible for the Keeper to proceed to rectification without
> that dispute being resolved by the court or Tribunal.

The Tribunal thus offered not one date but two: the date of application to
rectify or, perhaps, the date of the Keeper's decision in relation to the application.
Either would have the effect of excluding evidence of Mr Anderson's subsequent
possession. Indeed such exclusion seems to have been accepted by Mr Anderson's
solicitor,[2] so that the Tribunal's decision on this point appears to have proceeded
on a concession. On the other hand, the tying of possession to rectification,
whether the date of application or of decision, seems supported by the 1979 Act,
the relevant provision of which states that 'if rectification under subsection (1)
above would prejudice a proprietor in possession, the Keeper may exercise his
power to rectify only where ... '.[3]

Who, then, was in possession on 15 February 2007 when the Burrs applied for
rectification, or in the weeks that followed, as the Keeper came to a decision? Had
the question been asked in respect of a year earlier, the answer would have been
plain. Following a proof the Tribunal concluded that the line of the relevant fence
was such that the disputed strip was originally in the possession of the Burrs. The
only possessory acts attributable to Mr Anderson, the depositing of cuttings from
his garden, did nothing to alter the position: 'we would not regard throwing grass
or other garden cuttings over into a field which was being grazed by someone
else's cattle as sufficient to establish possession'.[4] But in the months leading up
to the application for rectification Mr Anderson had been busy placing, and then
replacing, marking posts which were designed to incorporate the disputed strip.
Did that mean that Mr Anderson was in possession at the time of the application?
The Tribunal thought not:[5]

> The position at the beginning of this phase appears to us important: if there had
> up until then been no possessory acts in the disputed area by anyone, as was the
> position in *Safeway*,[6] the act of 'staking' the boundary might be very significant.
> If one party has actually been possessing and using the disputed area before the
> assertion of possession, 'staking' by that party may serve to reinforce his claim, but
> 'staking' by the other party may be of little significance, particularly if it is promptly
> challenged.

---

1 Paragraph 27.
2 Paragraph 22.
3 Land Registration (Scotland) Act 1979 s 9(3)(a).
4 Paragraph 39.
5 Paragraph 28.
6 *Safeway Stores plc v Tesco Stores Ltd* 2004 SC 29, discussed in *Conveyancing 2003* pp 91–96.

As possession had originally been with the Burrs and not with Mr Anderson, the 'staking' activities of the latter must be seen as 'assertions referable to the dispute'[1] rather than as autonomous acts of possession.

In the context in which they were made, these remarks seem justifiable as well as leading to an apparently just result. Furthermore, they derive a certain amount of support from two passages in the *Safeway* case.[2] But it is not clear how far they can be regarded as a general rule, applicable to all cases, or whether such a rule, if established, would be either coherent or meritorious. Take, for instance, the facts of *Kaur v Singh*.[3] A flat was acquired under a forged disposition at a time when the 'true' owner was out of the country. The acquirer was duly registered as owner, and took possession, in March 1996. In May 1996, on her return to Scotland, the 'true' owner recovered possession by the simple expedient of changing the locks. In December 1997 the acquirer broke into the flat and changed the locks in turn. Who, on the Lands Tribunal test, was in possession in December 1997? Was it the 'true' owner, on the basis that she had previously been in possession for 19 months and that the most recent break-in was simply an 'assertion referable to the dispute' on the part of the acquirer? Or could the acquirer appeal to the events of May 1996 to argue that he was the only proper possessor since that date? It is doubtful whether the Tribunal's test contributes anything useful to the answer.

We mention this example not to question the Tribunal's test but to suggest that there are limits to its usefulness. Probably it is not of much help where the fact patterns are complex and the rival possessory acts prolonged, as was the case in *Kaur v Singh*. And arguably, too, it is of little help where a possessory act is complete in itself, ie where it results in the unequivocable dispossession of one party by another party. Where the test is likely to be of assistance is in a case like *Safeway*, or *Burr* itself, where a reasonably settled state of possession is disturbed by last-minute acts of disruption by a rival. For there is much to be said for discouraging such acts, and obvious merit in taking a longer-term view of the state of possession.

SOLICITORS

Bird v Bank of Scotland plc[4] is a horror story. Those of a nervous temperament should not read on.

In the autumn of 2000 Mr Bird wished to buy a property in Aberdeen from Mr and Mrs Townsley. He instructed Russell Taylor to act for him in the purchase. The price was to be £200,000. He was obtaining a loan from the Bank of Scotland and the latter instructed Mr Taylor to act for it in relation to the secured loan. Thus far,

---

1   Paragraph 28.
2   *Tesco Stores Ltd v Keeper of the Registers of Scotland* 2001 SLT (Lands Tr) 23 at 37; *Safeway Stores plc v Tesco Stores Ltd* 2003 GWD 20-610 at para 80 per Lord Hamilton ('It is clear, however, that the issue of possession should not be looked at only as at October 1999 [the time of the application for rectification] but over an appropriate tract of time preceding that month.')
3   1999 SC 180.
4   [2010] CSOH 162, 2011 GWD 1-34.

thus ordinary. Mr Taylor concluded missives, but the buyer named in the missives was not Mr Bird. It was Yearcom Ltd, a company of which Mr Taylor was the sole director. Mr Bird and the bank were unaware of what was happening. Mr Taylor then drew down the loan and used it to pay the sellers, who granted in exchange a disposition – in favour of Yearcom Ltd.[1] The standard security was granted by Mr Bird, not by Yearcom Ltd. The disposition was never registered.[2] Whether the standard security was registered or not does not appear from the Opinion of the Lord Ordinary (Lord Menzies) but we assume that it was not. 'Mr Taylor was subsequently sequestrated, found guilty of professional misconduct and struck off the roll of solicitors. The firm of which he was a partner was dissolved and its business was taken over by a judicial factor.'[3] After settlement, Mr Bird took possession of the property, and remains in possession. It seems that title remained and remains vested in Mr and Mrs Townsley, the sellers.

For some time Mr Bird made the ordinary monthly payments to the bank. But eventually he stopped paying and demanded repayment of what he had so far paid. He then raised an action against the Bank of Scotland in which he sought:[4]

> (1) Reduction of the standard security granted by him in favour of the defenders on the ground that he was induced to execute it by the fraudulent misrepresentations of the defenders' agent Mr Taylor, (2) repetition of the monies paid by him to the defenders in error, or in the alternative (3) damages of £300,000 in respect of the fraudulent misrepresentations of the defenders' agent Mr Taylor.

The defender counterclaimed for the balance of the loan, £317,961.62. We do not know the basis for this seemingly high figure. The original loan seems to have been in the sum of £209,077 – itself a slightly surprising figure since it was greater than the purchase price. Moreover, given that Mr Bird had for some time at least been making monthly payments, it is not easy to see how the total debt could have been so high.[5]

The Lord Ordinary agreed that Mr Bird's signature on the standard security had been obtained by Mr Taylor by fraud. He also agreed that when Mr Taylor obtained Mr Bird's signature on the standard security he was acting as the bank's agent. And as he observed, 'the general rule is that a principal cannot take advantage of the fraud of his agent'.[6] On that basis he held that the standard security fell to be reduced. But of course that was of little real assistance to Mr Bird and of little real disadvantage to the bank, for the security was invalid anyway, for the granter had no title, and it had never been registered. The main

---

1 Another odd aspect of the case is that the missives seem to have stated the price not at £200,000 but at £170,000, and presumably that was the figure that Mr and Mrs Townsley thought they had sold the property for, and, when settlement happened, presumably that was the sum they were paid. However, these points are not explored in the Lord Ordinary's Opinion.
2 We do not know why. Presumably Mr Taylor's intention was to register it.
3 Paragraph 2.
4 Paragraph 3.
5 Cf *Royal Bank of Scotland plc v Wilson* 2010 SLT 1227 where the bank seems to have charged 25% interest. Was Bank of Scotland charging Mr Bird that sort of rate?
6 Paragraph 42.

issue in the case was whether Mr Bird owed to the bank the money that it had advanced. The bank had indeed given the money to Mr Taylor. But did the money reach Mr Bird?

The question was whether, at the time when Mr Taylor misappropriated the money, he held the money as agent for the bank or as agent for Mr Bird.[1] If he held it as agent for the bank, then the money had never reached Mr Bird, and accordingly Mr Bird was not the bank's debtor, from which it would follow not only that he was not bound to pay anything more, but also that he was entitled to recover what he had already paid. That would leave the bank with the right to recover the money from Mr Taylor or perhaps from Yearcom Ltd (likewise problematic, since that company was, according to the Companies House website, dissolved on 5 April 2002). But if at the time of misappropriation Mr Taylor held the money as agent for Mr Bird, then matters would be otherwise: Mr Bird would have received the loan and would be bound, therefore, to repay it.[2]

The Lord Ordinary decided that the money was held by Mr Taylor as agent for Mr Bird:[3]

I agree with the argument advanced for the defenders that the money was transferred to Mr Taylor in his capacity as agent for the pursuer. This is the point which is described as 'the time of drawdown' of the Loan in the defenders' general mortgage terms and conditions, clause 7.6 of which provides for the loan funds to be 'remitted to the Borrower's solicitor'. At the time of this transfer the bank lost control and possession of the money. Although Mr Taylor gave undertakings to the bank in the certificate of title about what would happen to the money, once transfer had occurred the money ceased to be the bank's. If Mr Taylor acted in breach of his undertakings (as it appears that he did), the bank might have remedies against him, or against the pursuer, but they could not simply instruct Mr Taylor as their agent to return the monies to them. The monies had passed outwith their control. In holding the monies in a client account, Mr Taylor was holding them on behalf of the pursuer rather than the defenders.

As a result, Mr Bird has to pay off a mortgage on a property he does not own. Of course, the unfairness to Mr Bird does not mean that the decision is wrong. As the Lord Ordinary says, this is a case of two innocent victims – Mr Bird and the bank. Mr Taylor was sequestrated, making any recovery from him – whether by Mr Bird or by the bank – problematic. It may be that the Scottish Solicitors' Guarantee Fund intervened, but we have no information about this.

What about the position of Mr and Mrs Townsley, the sellers? It seems that they acted in good faith throughout. They entered into missives to sell to Yearcom Ltd. They disponed to Yearcom Ltd. They were paid in full. Perhaps they had never even heard of Mr Bird, at least until the balloon went up. They now find themselves having both (i) the money and (ii) the title to the property. It might be asked why, now that everything has come to light, they have not granted a corrective disposition, ie a disposition to Mr Bird. We do not know the answer,

1 Possibly at some stage he held it for Yearcom Ltd.
2 Of course, Mr Bird would still have his rights against Mr Taylor.
3 Paragraph 41.

but we can see that the case is difficult. Their deal was with Yearcom Ltd. So why should they now be disponing to someone else?

It seems likely that the missives with Yearcom Ltd have long since been superseded. But if the disposition is still in existence, presumably the rights it confers are now vested in the Crown, since Yearcom's dissolution.[1] So perhaps the Queen's and Lord Treasurer's Remembrancer could deal with the title to the property. But that would still leave open the basic question of who *ought* to have the property. Mr Bird? But he was not the buyer in the missives and he was not the grantee in the disposition. Mr and Mrs Townsley? But they sold the property and were paid the price. Yearcom Ltd? That might be the right answer, though because that company is dissolved, it would be represented by the Queen's and Lord Treasurer's Remembrancer. If Yearcom was in cahoots with Mr Taylor, it is likely that it would be under an obligation to convey to Mr Bird – though that would have to be done by the Queen's and Lord Treasurer's Remembrancer. But all this is highly speculative.

Was the decision, namely that Mr Taylor held the loan funds on behalf of Mr Bird, right? This seems to us a difficult question. The Lord Ordinary says that 'the bank lost control and possession of the money'. But that perhaps presupposes the conclusion. If X hands money to an agent, Y, then X has not lost control and possession[2] of the money, so long as Y behaves properly. Control will be lost if Y misappropriates the money, but that loss of control does not negate the agency. Again, 'once transfer had occurred the money ceased to be the bank's'. That is true, but it would be equally true for a transfer to an agent. If X transfers money to Y, as agent, and Y deposits that money in a bank account, the money is Y's, though Y holds it as agent for X. 'If Mr Taylor acted in breach of his undertakings (as it appears that he did), the bank might have remedies against him, or against the pursuer, but they could not simply instruct Mr Taylor as their agent to return the monies to them.' That depends on whether Mr Taylor held the money as agent. An agent who holds money can always be instructed to return the money. 'In holding the monies in a client account, Mr Taylor was holding them on behalf of the pursuer rather than the defenders.' Again we have reservations. The client account is for funds held for clients. But the bank was a client. (And presumably Yearcom Ltd was a client as well.) The fact that the loan money entered the client account seems, in itself, neutral as to *which* client it was being held for. It is not the case that when a bank hands money over to a law firm, whose client it is, the money is not held for the bank. Whether it is held for the bank or for another client depends on the facts and circumstances of the case. It may be that the law firm receives the loan on behalf of the borrower as from the very outset. But it is equally possible, it seems to us, for the law firm to receive the loan as agent for the lender, holding it as such until the conditions for the release of the loan to the borrowing client are satisfied. In these reflections, we do not wish to say that the

---

1 Under what is now s 1012 of the Companies Act 2006 and was formerly s 654 of the Companies Act 1985.

2 The conventional view is that only corporeal property is susceptible of possession, but the issue does not need to be pursued here.

Lord Ordinary's decision was wrong, merely that it seems to us that this was a case that perhaps could have gone either way.

FAIR DEALING IN PRE-EMPTIONS

Selling more

A standard problem in pre-emptions is of the person burdened wishing to sell an area which does not correspond exactly to the subject matter of the pre-emption (the 'pre-emption land'). Where, as is typically the case, the property being sold is *less* extensive than the pre-emption land – where, in other words, only part of that land is being sold – matters are straightforward, if only because pre-emption clauses standardly refer to the sale of the land 'or any part thereof'.[1] So on the one hand, the part that is being sold must be offered back to the pre-emption holder; and on the other, the part that remains continues to be affected by the pre-emption.[2]

The position seems less clear if what is being sold is *more* extensive – if, in other words, the sale is for the pre-emption land plus some adjoining land belonging to the same person. The difficulty is perhaps more practical than legal. A pre-emption cannot be circumvented simply by bundling up the pre-emption land with other land. The sale, therefore, triggers the pre-emption, and the land must be offered back in the usual way. But at what price and on what terms? If the subjects are marketed and sold as a single unit, how is the pre-emption holder to know what to offer in order to acquire the land?

This issue has never been the subject of a reported case, but in the last year an unreported case from 1992 has come to light.[3] This is *Howatson v Whyte*, decided in Forfar Sheriff Court on 14 July 1992.[4] The story it discloses is complex and the facts disputed, but its essential features are as follows. In 1980 Mr Arbuckle feued land in Angus to Mr and Mrs Howatson. The feu disposition contained a clause of pre-emption. At the same time the parties entered into a minute of agreement in terms of which Mr Arbuckle agreed to give the Howatsons first refusal in respect of certain other land ('the option ground') which he still retained. Not being contained in a conveyance, this second pre-emption was contractual in nature and not a real burden, but nothing turns on the point.

Some years later, in 1988, Mr Arbuckle decided to sell some of his land including the option ground. The property was marketed as a single lot and without mention of the pre-emption. When a buyer expressed interest, the existence of the pre-emption was disclosed and negotiations took place, the upshot of which was that the buyer offered separately – and through two different companies in which he had an interest – for (i) the option ground and (ii) the rest

---

1 See eg the style in J M Halliday, *Conveyancing Law and Practice* vol 2 (2nd edn 1997) para 32-80.
2 See C Waelde (ed), *Professor McDonald's Conveyancing Opinions* (1998) 261–64.
3 As usual, the person responsible for its excavation is Professor Roddy Paisley of Aberdeen University. We are most grateful to him for sharing it with us.
4 The signature on the judgment is indecipherable. The resident sheriff at Forfar in 1992 was S O Kermack.

of the subjects. The combined price was as previously agreed, but the amount attributed to the option ground was disproportionately high. More precisely, whereas the price of (ii) worked out at £827 per acre, the price of (i) was almost double, at £1,637 per acre. As this was beyond the Howatsons' means, they were unable to exercise the pre-emption, and the sale went ahead.

The Howatsons were aggrieved, and suspected collusion between Mr Arbuckle's executors (for Mr Arbuckle had died during the negotiations) and the end-purchaser. One possibility might have been to seek reduction of the disposition.[1] Ultimately, however, they settled for an action of damages for breach of contract. Their argument was based on an implied term of what might be called fair dealing or good faith. In agreeing a pre-emption, they argued, the parties must be taken to have agreed that the offer back of the property, when it came to be made, must be in response to an offer from a third party which was (i) acceptable in content, (ii) at arm's length and in good faith, and (iii) unconnected with any other offer. It was thus a breach of contract for parties to collude in the manner which was alleged to have occurred in the present case.

The implied obligation of good faith asserted by the pursuers is one that not everyone might accept.[2] But the sheriff accepted it. And following a proof, the sheriff also accepted that there had in fact been collusion designed to prevent the exercise of the pre-emption. Damages were therefore awarded.

Wider implications

Howatson v Whyte is a decision of some importance for cases where more than the pre-emption land is being sold. It means that if the land is sold in a separate lot, it must be fairly priced by reference to any other land which the same person is also seeking to sell. A different approach, not discussed in *Howatson*, would be for both properties to be sold as a single lot, with the result that both (ie including the land *not* subject to the pre-emption) would be offered back to the pre-emption holder. This seems permissible provided the seller can demonstrate that, unless he could sell both properties, he was unwilling to sell either.[3]

There are also wider implications. If the decision is correct and is followed – neither of which can be taken for granted – it seems to mean that fair dealing is needed, not only in a case like the present, but in all cases involving pre-emptions. It is easy to think of examples where this might be relevant.

One is where the pre-emption land is bought at above market value – thus discouraging the exercise of the pre-emption – but where there is also a concealed agreement by which the seller is to 'pay back' the excess in some way, whether in cash or by some other, less direct means. Such arrangements, surely, fall foul of *Howatson v Whyte*.

---

1 *Matheson v Tinney* 1989 SLT 535; *Roebuck v Edmunds* 1992 SLT 1055. Of course this would be successful only in the event that the pre-emption was found to have been breached.
2 Cf the comments of Lord Glennie in *EDI Central Ltd v National Car Parks Ltd* [2010] CSOH 141, 2010 GWD 37-754 at para 23 quoted at p 109 above.
3 We are grateful to Bruce Merchant both for the example and for the line of argument.

Another concerns contractual pre-emptions. At one time these were un-common (although the facts of *Howatson v Whyte* provide an example), but they have become very common indeed in the form of cut-down real burdens. Thus, no pre-emption imposed in a grant of feu is enforceable today other than as a contractual term between the original parties, and hence is not enforceable at all where the first feuar has conveyed the property on.[1] And, following the recent decision in *Braes v Keeper of the Registers of Scotland*,[2] the same is true of pre-emptions imposed in (ordinary) dispositions unless a benefited property was expressly nominated. Avoiding such contractual pre-emptions may seem invitingly straightforward. Suppose, for example, that Alan has a contractual pre-emption in respect of land belonging to Barbara. If Barbara sells to Claire, she must offer the land back to Alan; and if Alan decides to buy, Claire will not get the land. Suppose, however, that Barbara and Claire seek to avoid the pre-emption in the following way. Barbara will convey the land, as a gift, to her husband, Duncan. In principle, the pre-emption is then at an end: it did not affect Barbara because the transfer to Duncan was a gift and not a sale, and it cannot affect Duncan because he is not a party to any contract with Alan. So it seems that Duncan is now free to sell the land to Claire. So Claire gets the land, Duncan (and presumably Barbara) the money, and Alan gets nothing.

We suspect that arrangements of this kind are sometimes used. But, following *Howatson v Whyte*, can this really be said to be fair dealing on the part of Barbara? The facts, admittedly, are quite different from those in *Howatson*. In giving the property to Duncan, Barbara is doing something which she is perfectly entitled to do and which does not, of itself, engage the pre-emption. There was no offer to purchase, and so no requirement of good faith in respect of such an offer. Yet if the only or main purpose of the sequence of events is to defeat the pre-emption, there seems room for doubt as to whether Barbara is fulfilling her contractual obligations to Alan.

BREAKING UP IS HARD TO DO

Two people are in a relationship. They own a house or flat. They break up. The property will provide a rich source of possibilities for the ex-lovers to pursue their disagreements with each other. This year has produced a further crop of such cases. These battles are handled by litigation lawyers. But conveyancers need to keep an eye on such cases, because they show where the dangers lie. The job of conveyancers is, as far as possible, to keep their litigation partners unemployed, by ensuring that the scope for dispute is minimised from the outset.

---

1 An exception is the small number of cases where the pre-emption was preserved as a personal real burden by registration of the appropriate notice before the appointed day under s 18A of the Abolition of Feudal Tenure etc (Scotland) Act 2000.

2 [2009] CSOH 176, 2010 SLT 689, discussed in *Conveyancing 2009* pp 113–16.

Divorce: one party buying out the other

Under s 8 of the Family Law (Scotland) Act 1985, the court can order that, where the house is co-owned, one party must convey his or her share to the other, the value of that share being taken into account in the overall settlement. In effect this is a power to order one party to sell his or her share to the other party. But such an order can be made only as part of the divorce itself. It cannot be made while the action is still depending and it is as yet unknown whether decree of divorce will be granted. In other words, it cannot be deployed as an interim measure.

The 1985 Act does indeed give the court extensive interim powers, including, under s 14, the power to order the sale of the family home.[1] But hitherto it has been assumed that that means ordering the property to be put on the market and sold to a third party. The novelty in *Adams v Adams*[2] was that the pursuer (the wife) asked for the court to order the defender to sell his half share of the property to her. The request was granted.

The pursuer in fact asked for vacant possession, but the court refused to include that in the order, because until such time as decree of divorce was granted, the parties were still married, and hence the husband had the right to be in the matrimonial home in terms of the Matrimonial Homes (Family Protection) (Scotland) Act 1981. But in fact it seemed that the defender was prepared to move out. And of course his rights would come to an end as and when decree of divorce was finally pronounced.

How strong a precedent this case is, may be arguable. The defender might have tried to persuade the court that the order requested by the pursuer was incompetent, because it was in substance a *pre-divorce* property transfer order – in other words, the case would be that the pursuer was seeking to circumvent the intentions of the legislation. But that line of reasoning seems not to have been advanced.

Unmarried co-owners: division and sale

For spouses (and civil partners), s 19 of the Matrimonial Homes (Family Protection) (Scotland) Act 1981 gives the court a discretion to delay or even refuse an application of division and sale in respect of the matrimonial home.[3] Section 19 does not, however, apply to cohabitants. So whilst cohabitants, not being married, cannot take the *Adams* route (discussed above), they can take the route of division and sale. In such an action, does the property have to be put on the market and sold to a third party, or can one party insist on buying out the other at a fair market value? In *Scrimgeour v Scrimgeour*[4] it was held that this is competent but the law on this issue is in fact unsettled. In *Berry v Berry (No 2)*[5] the

---

1 This is one of the 'incidental orders' governed by s 14. Section 14(2)(a) allows the court to order the sale of any property, not just the family home.
2 2010 SLT (Sh Ct) 2, 2010 Fam LR 30.
3 For such a case this year see *B v B* 2010 GWD 24-454 (Case (13)).
4 1988 SLT 590.
5 1989 SLT 292.

soundness of *Scrimgeour* was doubted. In *Gray v Kerner*[1] the *Scrimgeour* decision was followed, but the court's attention was not drawn to *Berry*. *Ploetner v Ploetner*[2] was a somewhat unclear case which seems to follow *Berry*. *Wilson v Hervey*[3] did not decide the point but contained *dicta* leaning towards *Berry*. We incline to think that *Scrimgeour* was sound.[4] In the case the action was undefended. If each party wished to buy out the other, then whoever made the higher offer would presumably win.[5]

Dividing up the proceeds of sale

If the family home is sold on the market, it is a good plan to get the parties to agree in writing what is to happen to the proceeds of sale. But what happens if there is no such agreement, or no clear agreement? That will often be the case in an action of division and sale, for if the parties were on good terms, the action would not have been needed in the first place. The answer in general terms is straightforward: the net proceeds are divided according to the share of the title. So if Jack and Jill are equal co-owners, the net proceeds are divided between them equally. If Lesly, Lesley and Leslie are cohabiting co-owners and their respective shares of the title are 30%, 30% and 40%, that is how the net proceeds should be divided. But whilst that is the general principle, in practice complications can arise.

In the first place, the courts have shown a certain willingness to use the division of the proceeds of sale as a convenient way of settling debts between the parties. So if a house belonging to Jack and Jill is sold, and the net proceeds are £200,000, and Jack happens to owe Jill £10,000, the court may say that the division is not to be £100,000 each, but rather than Jill should be paid £100,000 plus £10,000 from Jack's share, ie a total of £110,000, and that Jack accordingly should receive only £90,000. This was the approach taken in *Gray v Kerner*[6] and confirmed in *McMahon's Tr v McMahon*[7] although with the qualification that only such debts as have some connection with the property can be dealt with in this way. The qualification may have been imposed because the debtor in *McMahon's Tr* was insolvent, so that there was a danger of upsetting the priority rules in bankruptcy. We incline to think that this area of law is unclear.

---

1 1996 SCLR 331.
2 1997 SCLR 998.
3 2004 SCLR 313.
4 See Bankton 1.8.40; Bell, *Commentaries* I, 62; *Milligan v Barnhill* (1782) Mor 2486. Roman law also so provided.
5 See a case decided in the Imperial Court on 1 March 214, involving a dispute between co-owners who were brothers, having inherited the property in question: *Codex* 3.37.1 (see *Conveyancing CCXIV* for further discussion). There is useful material in G MacCormack, 'The *actio communi dividundo* in Roman and Scots Law', in A D E Lewis and D J Ibbetson (eds), *The Roman Law Tradition* (1993), and in the chapter by Duard Kleyn and Scott Wortley on Co-ownership in R Zimmermann, D Visser and K Reid (eds), *Mixed Legal Systems in Comparative Perspective: Property and Obligations in Scotland and South Africa* (2004).
6 1996 SCLR 331.
7 1997 SLT 1090.

In the second place, consider *McKenzie v Nutter*, decided in 2006.[1] Here X and Y bought a house together for £105,000. X contributed £73,000 from his own resources. The balance of £29,000 they borrowed jointly. Title was taken in both names equally between them. They split up even before Y moved in and there was an action of division and sale. The question for the court was how the proceeds of sale should be divided. It was held that the whole net proceeds should go to X. The court took the view that Y had contributed nothing and so the 50% of the title she had acquired had constituted an unjustified enrichment. This decision comes close to tearing up the terms of the title. We will need to return to it later.

The *Esposito* case

And now comes *Esposito v Barile*.[2] X and Y bought a house together, in Monifieth in Angus. They were not married. The price was £153,000. X contributed £35,000 from his own resources. The balance of £118,000 they borrowed jointly. Thus far the story is comparable to *McKenzie v Nutter* (discussed above). But whereas in that case the title shares had been equal, in the new case the title was divided 94/153 to X and 59/153 to Y. The logic of this is easy to see. X was contributing £35,000 plus half the loan (ie £59,000) = £94,000. Y was contributing £59,000. Thus the title share exactly tracked their contribution to the price.

They split up and there was an action of division and sale. But (unlike *McKenzie v Nutter*) no attempt was made to argue that the division of the proceeds should not track the share of title. Accordingly the court ordered: 'the subjects should be sold and the proceeds divided between the pursuer and the defender in accordance with their respective *pro indiviso* share therein'. So far, so good. The sale went ahead. The price achieved was £173,000. By this stage the balance due to the lender was £105,279.82. The expenses came to £3,194.45.

How the proceeds were distributed

The law agents who had carried out the sale now proceeded as follows.

   (i) They deducted the expenses. This was agreed by both parties. So: £173,000 minus £3,194.45 = £169,805.55.
   (ii) They deducted the secured loan. So: £169,805.55 minus £105,279.82 = £64,525.73.
   (iii) This latter sum, £64,525.73, they divided according to the title shares, bringing out a balance due to X of £39,639.29[3] and £24,886.44[4] to Y.

---

1 2007 SLT (Sh Ct) 17. For a discussion, see *Conveyancing 2006* pp 117–21.
2 2010 GWD 23-447.
3 On our (no doubt fallible) arithmetic this figure should in fact be £39,643.26. The difference is trivial.
4 On our (no doubt fallible) arithmetic this figure should in fact be £24,882.47. The difference is trivial.

In tabular form:

Gross sale price	£173,000.00
Take off expenses of £3,194.45	£169,805.55
Take off secured loan of £105,279.82	£64,525.73
X's share (94/153 of £64,525.73)	£39,639.29[1]
Y's share (59/153 of £64,525.73)	£24,886.44
Total distributed to X and Y	£64,525.73

The alternative proposal

X was unhappy. He argued that the agents had gone about it the wrong way. He argued that the secured loan was deducted at the wrong stage in the calculation. Instead of the division into two pots happening at the end of the calculation, it should have happened at the beginning, thus:

(a) The first step should have been that the £173,000 should have been divided into the two pots according to their respective title shares. Thus £106,287.57 to X's pot and £66,712.43 to Y's pot.

(b) The expenses (£3,194.45) should have been recouped equally from each pot, ie each pot contributing £1,597.22. That would have left £104,690.35 in X's pot and £65,115.21 in Y's.

(c) The secured loan (£105,279.82) should have been recouped equally from each pot, ie each pot contributing £52,639.96. That would have left £52,050.44 in X's pot and £12,475.30 in Y's.

In tabular form:

	X's pot	Y's pot
£173,000 divided by title share	£106,287.57	£66,712.43
Take off expenses (£3,194.45), equally	£104,690.35	£65,115.21
Take off secured loan (£105,279.82), equally	£52,050.44	£12,475.30
Final figure for distribution to owners	£52,050.44	£12,475.30

Thus on the method actually adopted by the agents (which we will dub method A), X was paid £39,639.29, whereas on the other method (which we will dub method B) he would have been entitled to £52,050.44. The discrepancy arises from the fact that in a case of this sort it makes a difference at what point in the calculation the secured loan is taken off.

According to X, Y had been unjustifiably enriched at his expense, and was therefore due to pay him £12,411.14 to balance the account. He raised an action accordingly.

---

1 For this and the line below, see the previous footnotes.

The court's decision

In this action X called on Y to pay him the balance due to him, being the difference between (i) what he actually received under method A and (ii) what he should have received under method B. On method A, he argued, the return on his investment was barely £5,000 and yet the defender, who had made no capital investment at all, received almost £25,000.

He could, instead, have tried to sue the agents who had, on his view, divided the proceeds wrongly, but he preferred the more direct approach of claiming from Y, on the basis of the law of unjustified enrichment, and the court held that this was a competent way of proceeding.[1] (The court also held that he was not personally barred from pursuing the claim.)

His claim succeeded. Perhaps the key passage in the Opinion given by the sheriff is this:[2]

> I would venture to suggest that the position becomes very clear if ... one truncates the time frame. In that event, say the parties had realised within days of purchasing the property that the relationship had failed and that the property had to be sold.[3] They are lucky enough to find that the under-bidder on their purchase is still interested and will match the price of £153,000.00. The defender would then have it that the correct way to distribute the price is to deduct the £118,000.00 mortgage (in this example we will ignore costs) leaving a balance of £35,000.00. She would then expect her share based on the title of 59/153ths that is £13,496.73. This sum would have come entirely from the pursuer's deposit. The pursuer had no intention of donation and such a windfall to the defender is not reasonable or equitable. The parties divided the heritable title in unequal fractions not the heritable security. The parties borrowed the balance of the price from the Halifax PLC equally. The mortgage over time would have reduced to nil.

The pursuer's second head of claim

The pursuer had a second head of claim against Y. After the parties had become estranged, there had been a plan for X to buy out Y and take on sole responsibility for the secured loan. To make it possible for this plan to go ahead, X's father had paid £11,500 to the lender, so as to reduce the total debt to a figure that his son could take on.[4] X argued that in substance he had paid, on his own, a sum (£11,500) which they both (X and Y) should have paid. Hence Y should repay him one half of that figure, ie £5,750. The defender was willing to repay part of the £11,500, but only 59/153, ie £4,434.64. Here too the pursuer was successful.

---

1 The decision is of interest from the standpoint of the law of unjustified enrichment as well as from the standpoint of property law and conveyancing.
2 Paragraph 17. The sheriff was George Way.
3 In fact something very like this happened in *McKenzie v Nutter* 2007 SLT (Sh Ct) 17.
4 The mortgage redemption figure mentioned above, £105,279.82, took account of this. Had it not been for the father's intervention, the redemption figure would have been £11,500 higher (or marginally more than that, because with a higher overall debt more interest might have accrued).

Reflections on the pursuer's first claim

The first point to be made is that the issues arise only where the title shares are unequal. If they are equal then method A and method B will yield the same final result. Traditionally, unequal title shares have been rather unusual, though not unknown. But it may be that they are now becoming commoner, precisely because of the *Esposito* type of case: unmarried couples living together, something that used to be rare but which is now common.[1] Married couples could also split titles unequally, but that seldom happens, presumably because there would normally be no benefit in it. If a married couple break up, there will usually be a divorce, and in a divorce a matrimonial home will normally count as 'matrimonial property' for the purposes of the Family Law (Scotland) Act 1985. As such, what happens to it is subject to the discretion of the court, but the default rule is that matrimonial property is shared equally. The way title is taken does not normally matter. If the matrimonial home is owned solely by one party, it is just as much 'matrimonial property' as if it had been owned in equal shares.

Where the title shares are unequal, is method B right? One element in method B is the allocation of the heritable debt *equally* to X and Y. The sheriff says: 'The parties divided the heritable title in unequal fractions not the heritable security. The parties borrowed the balance of the price from the Halifax PLC equally.'[2] But is that correct? Might it not be argued that X and Y in fact agreed an unequal responsibility for the loan?[3] Since X had a larger share of the title, every £1.53 that either of them paid to the lender would boost his equity by 94p and her equity by only 59p. One could make a case for saying that in the division and sale, the heritable debt should have been deducted from the two pots not 50/50 but in proportion to their respective title shares. Indeed, one could say the same for the expenses of sale, for it is not obvious why there should be an equal division between unequal owners.

On that basis, a modified version of method B – call it method B1 – would look like this:

	X's pot	Y's pot
£173,000 divided by title share	£106,287.57	£66,712.43
Take off expenses and secured loan, rateably (respectively £66,644.32 and £41,829.95)		
Final figure for distribution to owners	£39,643.25	£24,881.47

It will be seen that this works out the same as method A: indeed, mathe-matically, it appears to be the same. We think, however, that it is method B which is right.

---

1 For another example, see *Burnett v Menzies Dougal* 2006 SC 93 (*Conveyancing 2005* Case (40)). Here title was taken 4/5 to the pursuer and 1/5 to her fiancé.
2 Paragraph 17.
3 As between the parties. In relation to the lender, each was liable for the whole, on the footing of joint and several (solidary) liability.

Go back to the way that the parties originally divided the title: 94/153 to X and 59/153 to Y. That apportionment shows that they were thinking that each had contributed one half of the loan. On that basis, method B is correct.

Are *Esposito* and *McKenzie v Nutter*[1] consistent with each other? The issue was not addressed in *Esposito*, for the earlier case was not cited. It is not easy to reconcile the cases. In *Esposito* the proceeds were distributed in accordance with the shares of title; in *McKenzie* they were not. Although in our annual volume for 2006 we described *McKenzie* as 'reasonable'[2] we now incline to doubt its soundness. If two parties agree on a title share, to divide the proceeds of sale according to that title share is not unjustified enrichment: it is simply carrying out the wishes of the parties. If that is right, the only question that remains is how (in cases where the title shares are different) the heritable loan is to be deducted, and on that *Esposito* provides guidance which seems sound.

Reflections on the pursuer's second claim

X's father paid off £11,500 of the heritable debt. If A pays B's debt to C, A can claim back from B what has been paid. So the father was, it seems, entitled to recover this from X and Y. But he did not seek its recovery. Instead, X claimed half of it from Y, on the basis that the sum was owed equally by both of them, so she should contribute half. One of her defences was that there was no title to sue. The money had not been paid by X, but by a third party. This defence was rejected by the sheriff:[3]

> I reject the defender's submission that the pursuer lacked title to sue. The fact that the source of the payment made to reduce the mortgage balance came from his father is irrelevant. The pursuer is the co-obligant and he is entitled to pursue the overpayment against the defender. This is made clear by the case of *Christie's Executrix v Armstrong*[4] where the actual payment to redeem the joint mortgage came from an insurance company but the executor was found entitled to pursue the deceased's co-obligant.

Here we would express some doubt. It was not the son who paid the £11,500. We know that, not only because we know, positively, that the payment was by someone else, but also because we know that the son was not in a position to pay that amount at the time in question. So why should it be the son, rather than the father, who can recover? The learned sheriff cites the *Christie* case, but in that case the payment by the insurance company was a payment of money belonging to one of the parties. That fact is what makes it possible to identify which of the co-debtors could claim the benefit of the payment as against the other. But in *Esposito*, the payment was not made with X's money. It was a pure third-party payment. Arguably Y had just as much right (ie none) to sue X for half of it as X had to sue Y. The only person who could have sued for it was the father. Of course, it would

---

1 2007 SLT (Sh Ct) 17, discussed at p 171 above.
2 *Conveyancing 2006* p 120.
3 Paragraph 23.
4 1996 SC 295.

have been otherwise if the father had assigned his claim to the son, but no such assignation is mentioned in the case.

Varying the figures into negative equity

It may be of interest to see what happens with the two methods – method A and method B – as the sale figure falls so as to produce negative equity for one or possibly both parties. There may be scope for debate about how the two methods work when one moves into negative figures, but the following is how we see it. We give two examples. In the first, the property sells for £140,000. The other facts are the same.

Method A[1]

Gross sale price	£140,000.00
Take off expenses of £3,194.45	£136,805.55
Take off secured loan of £105,279.82	£31,525.73
X's share (94/153 of £31.525.73)	£19,368.75
Y's share (59/153 of £31,525.73)	£12,156.98
Total distributed to X and Y	£31,525.73

Method B

	X's pot	Y's pot
£140,000 divided by title share	£86,013.07	£53,986.93
Take off expenses (£3,194.45), equally	£84,415.85	£52,389.71
Take off secured loan (£105,279.82), equally	£31,775.94	–£250.20
Final figure for distribution to owners	£31,775.94	–£250.20

In method B, Y comes out with a negative figure. But that applies only between X and Y. As far as the bank is concerned, it is entitled to be paid in full. So X would actually receive not £31,775.94, but £31,775.94 minus £250.20 = £31,525.74. X would then have a right against Y (based in the law of unjustified enrichment) to be paid £250.20.

In the example just given, the amount of the secured loan is less than the value of the property, so there is no negative equity in the normal sense. But there is negative equity in respect of Y's share, at least if method B is correct. In the

---

1 The figures brought out by method A are the same as those brought out by method B1. So we do not give the latter.

next example the property sells for £100,000, which is less than the outstanding secured loan, so that the property overall has negative equity. Despite that fact, when applying method B the negative equity applies only to Y's share, and X's share emerges with positive equity.

Method A

Gross sale price	£100,000.00
Take off expenses of £3,194.45	£96,805.55
Take off secured loan of £105,279.82	−£8,474.27
X's share (94/153 of - £8,474.27)	−£5,206.41
Y's share (59/153 of - £8,474.27)	−£3,267.86
Total distributed to X and Y	−£8,474.27

Method B

	X's pot	Y's pot
£100,000 divided by title share	£61,437.91	£38,562.09
Take off expenses (£3,194.45), equally	£59,840.69	£ 36,964.87
Take off secured loan (£105,279.82), equally	£7,200.78	−£15,675.04
Final figure for distribution to owners	£7,200.78	−£15,675.04

The difference between method A and method B is particularly striking. In method A, X and Y come out with a fairly similar position, the difference being only about £2,000, and it is X who suffers more loss than Y. In method B, it is Y who suffers more loss than X, and the difference is large: over £22,000. Is the latter fair? Given that X's 'deposit' has been wiped out, perhaps it is.

But in this example, the fact that the property overall has negative equity may torpedo the sale. For the sale proceeds will not pay off the secured loan (unlike the previous example). So the sale will not go ahead unless the shortfall is found from other resources. If X wishes the sale to go ahead, and if he has the resources, it will be in his interest to pay off the shortfall, and then demand the relevant sum from Y (assuming that Y can be made to pay.)

Presumably parallel issues could arise where a sale happens at the instance of a heritable creditor. In such a case negative equity could not torpedo the sale, for a buyer from a heritable creditor takes an unencumbered title regardless of whether the sale proceeds have paid off all the secured debt.

SERVITUDES

Pedestrian or vehicular access?

Servitudes often comprise a right of 'way' or 'access' without further stipulation. The question is then whether the access can be used by vehicles as well as by pedestrians. The default position, as Cusine and Paisley point out, is for pedestrian use only, because of the presumption for freedom, but this default position can be overcome either by the wording of the deed or by surrounding circumstances such as the width and condition of the road or a history of usage by vehicles.[1] Actual examples, however, are hard to come by in the case law, so that the new case of *Parkin v Kennedy*[2] is particularly welcome.

A terraced house in Port Charlotte, Islay, was feued in 1934 subject to the following servitude:

> But declaring always that a servitude right of way along a passage known as the Back Road running through the subjects hereby disponed and shown on said plan is reserved to the adjoining feuars and tenants, said right of way or passage running along the back of the dwelling house facing Main Street. . . .

That wording, in the context of the deed as a whole, suggested to the Lands Tribunal the existence of a right of access for vehicles:[3]

> [T]he express wording of this right points in our view to vehicular access. It is described as 'along a passage known as the Back Road'. We note the use of capitals in 'Back Road' and we also note the use of the word 'Road'. The western boundary of both the applicants' [servient proprietors'] house and the respondent's is described as being along 'a private road'. The northern boundary of the applicants' house is described as being by a 'road'. Finally in both the applicants' title and the respondent's founding title in 1922 the land in front of the houses is described in both deeds as 'the footpath'. We see nothing in the way the various passage-ways or accesses are described that would indicate any looseness, uncertainty or interchangeability of terms as to what the original disponer intended. In our view, the use of 'footpath' for the area in front of the terrace and the use of the word 'Road' for the area at the rear points clearly to a differentiation between the two areas.

It is true that the road was unsurfaced and was rather narrow for vehicular traffic. 'But that is the character of this locality and these tracks are, in the main, still used for access by cars or small commercial vehicles.'[4] There was evidence of such usage in relation to this particular road – so much so, indeed, that a servitude of vehicular access might have been constituted by positive prescription. All in all, the Tribunal concluded, a servitude of vehicular access was established.

---

1 D J Cusine and R R M Paisley, *Servitudes and Rights of Way* (1998) para 3.03.
2 23 March 2010, Lands Tribunal. The Tribunal comprised K M Barclay FRICS.
3 Paragraph 33.
4 Paragraph 36.

An oddity of this decision is that the Tribunal focused on what seems to be the wrong deed. The servitude was reserved in the split-off writ for the servient tenement in 1934 and this was the deed which the Tribunal considered. But the dominant tenement had apparently been split off earlier, in 1922, and the writ in question contained a declaration that 'my said Disponee and her foresaids have a right to the use of the carriage way at the back of the house'. That grant was sufficient to create the servitude,[1] and, the servitude having already been created in 1922, it could not be created again in 1934.[2] The 1934 deed, therefore, was of little or no relevance. As it happens, however, it is unlikely that a decision based on the 1922 deed would have been any different, for that deed refers expressly to a right over a 'carriage way'.

Extinction by abandonment

It is well understood that servitudes are lost by 20 years' non-use, by virtue of the long negative prescription.[3] But can non-use for a shorter period also result in the extinction of a servitude? Cusine and Paisley draw attention to the doctrine of abandonment.[4] On one view this can come about by non-use alone, but Cusine and Paisley argue that more is needed and in particular that there must be an intention to abandon, whether express or evidenced by acts or omissions. Indeed if this were not so, abandonment would be merely a way of reducing the period of negative prescription.

Pullar v Gauldie[5] is a rare and therefore welcome example of a case in which the issue arose.[6] A servitude was held to have been established by express reservation in a split-off disposition but it was not exercised for the next five years. During this period the owners of the servient tenement did various things to interfere with the route, which ran through sand dunes by way of a rough track. In particular they had extended a bothy in such a way as to block off one variant version of the route, and they had erected a fence across the track with a locked gate.

The sheriff[7] accepted Cusine and Paisley's view that intention was a prerequisite of abandonment. But where was the evidence of intention in the present case?

> [L]ocking a gate does not in my view amount to acceptance by the dominant tenement that the right is no longer available. In my opinion the evidence falls far short of establishing abandonment by the dominant tenement. It is clear from the various

---

1 Under the law then in force a servitude could be created by grant in a split-off conveyance of the dominant tenement, despite the fact that it would not then appear in the title of the servient tenement.
2 Although a *different* servitude could of course have been created. But this was plainly not a different servitude.
3 Prescription and Limitation (Scotland) Act 1973 s 8.
4 Cusine and Paisley, *Servitudes and Rights of Way* para 17.15.
5 25 August 2004, Arbroath Sheriff Court. Although decided in 2004 this unreported case has only recently come to our attention.
6 The doctrine of abandonment was also raised in *Orkney Housing Association Ltd v Atkinson* 15 October 2010, Kirkwall Sheriff Court, a case in which proof before answer was allowed.
7 Ian G Inglis.

cases to which I was referred that abandonment is relatively rarely established. Each case must be looked at in the light of its own facts and in this case I see nothing in the actions of [the dominant proprietor] to show that the right to use the track ... had been abandoned.

As well as confirming the doctrinal basis of abandonment, this decision indicates that the plea will rarely succeed. In most cases a person who has periods of non-use of a road or other facility will have little to fear from this doctrine.

STUDENT TENANTS AND THEIR
HUMAN NEIGHBOURS

Oakfield Avenue, Glasgow, runs north-east from University Avenue to Great Western Road and is thus in the heart of Studentland. No 12 is a tenement, and while some of the flats in it are student flats, others are occupied by humans. Them Properties LLP bought one of the flats and let it out to several students. It did not have an HMO licence,[1] though the previous owner had had such a licence. When it applied for one, two residents in the tenement lodged objections, one of them being in the flat immediately below the flat in question. Eventually the dispute finished up in the Inner House of the Court of Session. We quote from the court's Opinion:[2]

> She[3] raised a number of issues. These included, first, overcrowding; there being between sixteen and twenty students in the tenement during term time. Secondly, there was safety. One student had thrown a wardrobe out of a third floor window into the back court in the early hours of the morning. It had tipped over and broken a bedroom window of the main door flat (number 14). Another incident involved the students being entertained by a fire eater in the back court, again in the early hours of the morning. Thirdly, there was the condition of the flat itself. Fourthly, she complained of noise as follows:
>
> > 'There has been a track record of noisy, inconsiderate tenants in this flat. When it was managed by an agent there was some improvement. But problems persisted and I had to complain on several occasions last year, to the students and eventually to the agent. A persistent problem was loud music and the thump from the bass of a Hi Fi. Worst of all was being kept awake at night by one tenant. He regularly came in during the wee small hours and dropped heavy items on the floor. The sound of heavy items being dragged around the room and doors slamming could be heard. There were loud conversations which lasted until 3.00 or even 5.00 am. This tenant once brought about 20 people back to the flat, after he had been asked about two hours earlier, to quiet down.'

---

1 Civic Government (Scotland) Act 1982 (Licensing of Houses in Multiple Occupation) Order 2000, SSI 2000/177. This will be replaced by part 5 of the Housing (Scotland) Act 2006 when it is brought into force.
2 *Them Properties LLP v Glasgow City Council* [2010] CSIH 51, 2010 SC 690, 2010 Hous LR 69 at para 3. The Opinion of the Court was given by Lord Carloway.
3 One of the human beings in the tenement.

Fifthly, the objector complained of being unable to have common repairs executed because of the number of HMO flats. Sixthly, there was the volume of refuse, often disposed of carelessly. Finally, there was litter in the form of beer cans, bottles etc in the front garden. The second letter dated 7 June 2007, from the occupier of number 14, was much shorter, but it too complained of the wardrobe incident, which had involved the window of her son's bedroom. It referred to the level of noise, which disturbed her children's sleep, and the dumping of items in communal areas. She concluded:

> 'I feel we have our fair share of multiple occupancy in this close and I would like 1 year where I get some uninterrupted sleep and do not have to worry about my children's safety when they are asleep in bed.'

The court's opinion does not disclose whether the residents in question had sufficiently considered, and carried out an ECHR-compliant 'balancing exercise', in relation to the arguments for and against homicide.

Glasgow City Council refused the application for an HMO licence, and the owner appealed to the sheriff court. The sheriff allowed the appeal, holding that the approach taken by the council had been wrong in law, and ordered the council to reconsider the application. The council appealed to the Inner House, which reversed the sheriff's decision, thus restoring the council's decision to refuse to grant an HMO licence. The court added:[1]

> Finally, it is worth commenting that, given the somewhat obvious inherent suitability and convenience of this flat as a HMO for students, should the respondents receive a further application for a licence, in which the appellants are able to demonstrate an ability to control the activities of future student tenants, it may be difficult for the respondents to refuse the application for the reasons previously given. Whether to do so or not, however, remains a matter for them to decide in the first instance.

Thus, the court is saying that it is 'obvious' that the flat is suitable 'as a HMO for students' but is also saying that the owner would have to 'demonstrate an ability to control the activities of future student tenants'. Both statements are interesting. We are not sure of the legal basis for the first. Possibly the view was taken that any flat or house that has the space to take a substantial number of occupants is automatically HMO-suitable. Possibly the reference to students is relevant: perhaps if the flat had not been near a university building the position would have been different. The statutory instrument about HMOs does not state what the criteria are for the grant or refusal of HMO licence applications, with the result that the criteria in schedule 1 to the Civic Government (Scotland) Act 1982 apply.[2] These criteria are rather general, for they govern a variety of activities regulated by the 1982 Act. The present case is only of limited value in determining how the criteria apply to HMO licensing. As for the second statement, it may not be easy for an owner to 'demonstrate' that it has the 'ability' to 'control the activities of future student tenants'.

---

1 Paragraph 15.
2 The legislative provisions about HMOs will be changing as from 31 August 2011. See p 60 above.

Local authorities have extensive powers as against landlords who tolerate antisocial tenants: see part 7 of the Antisocial Behaviour etc (Scotland) Act 2004. Section 81 defines antisocial behaviour thus:

a person engages in antisocial behaviour if the person –

(a) acts in a manner that causes or is likely to cause alarm, distress, nuisance or annoyance; or

(b) pursues a course of conduct that causes or is likely to cause alarm, distress, nuisance or annoyance,

to a person residing in, visiting or otherwise engaging in lawful activity at, or in the locality of, a relevant house.

We have no statistics, but we have doubts as to whether these part 7 powers are much used.

WHAT IS AN 'OBLIGATION RELATING TO LAND'?

Smith v Stuart[1] was another case in which one document binds a party to sign another document. The defender owned land at Denhead in Aberdeenshire. In 1995 he granted this undertaking in favour of the pursuer, his sister:

I, ALEXANDER SHEWAN STUART, hereby confirm that, I will enter into a formal Minute of Agreement with my sister, ELIZABETH ANNE SMITH, Glenloye, Ardo, Whitecairns, Aberdeen to the following effect:

(1) In the event of the sale of the land adjacent to The Stead Inn, Denhead, Potterton for agricultural or development purposes, half of the sale proceeds of the said land will fall to be paid to my sister, the said Elizabeth Anne Smith, and

(2) In the event of the sale of the said land for agricultural purposes, I will effect the sale on the basis that if the purchaser from me were to sell the said land for development purposes, the increase in the value of the said land over agricultural value because of the said sale for development purposes will be paid equally to both myself and my sister, the said Elizabeth Anne Smith.

(3) In the event of the sale of the said land for agricultural purposes and that I do not wish to retain any interest in the future development of the property I will effect the sale on the basis that if the purchaser from me (or any future purchaser thereafter) were to sell the said land for development purposes, one-half of the increase in the value of the said land over agricultural value because of the said sale for development purposes will be paid to my sister, the said Elizabeth Anne Smith.

There was no sale of the land. No minute of agreement was entered into and in 2001 – just over five years later – the sister raised an action to enforce the undertaking. In the sheriff court she was unsuccessful,[2] and she appealed to the

1 [2010] CSIH 29, 2010 SC 490, 2010 SLT 1249.
2 2010 SCLR 131 (digested as *Conveyancing 2009* Case (2)).

Inner House, which has now also held against her. The main issue was whether the obligation had been extinguished by negative prescription, and that in turn depended on whether the five-year or the 20-year period applied. In principle, the five-year prescription applies to unilateral promises, but it is disapplied in respect of 'any obligation relating to land'.[1] The question was whether the obligation in the present case related to land. In the view of the Lord Justice-Clerk (Gill), it did not:[2]

> The expression 'any obligation relating to land' is not defined by the 1973 Act. In *Barratt Scotland Ltd v Keith*[3] the Second Division did not attempt a definition, other than to say that that expression must be given its natural and ordinary meaning. It is clear that the expression is apt to cover a wide range of obligations and that is not limited to those relating to real rights in land. In *Barratt Scotland Ltd v Keith* an obligation in missives to deliver a valid disposition in exchange for the purchase price was held to be an obligation relating to land. But, as the court recognised in that case, there are obligations to which land is only incidental and which cannot properly be said to 'relate' to it.
>   I incline to the view expressed by Johnston (*Prescription and Limitation*, para 6.60) that for para 2(e) of sch 1 to apply, the land must be the main object of the obligation. That, I think, is in line with the approach of the court in *Barratt Scotland Ltd v Keith*.
>   The wording of the undertaking is unambiguous, in my opinion; so extrinsic evidence as to its construction is neither necessary nor admissible. This case can be decided on a straightforward construction of the words themselves.
>   In my opinion, the undertaking does not create an obligation relating to land. The obligation that it creates is an obligation on the part of the respondent to enter into an agreement with the appellant at an unspecified time.

Hence the obligation had prescribed.

The pursuer also sought to argue that 'the undertaking had conferred on the appellant an interest in the land' and that 'the sheriff erred in characterising the undertaking as a promise to share the proceeds of sale. It was a promise to secure payment to the appellant by a third party purchaser'.[4] These submissions are not easy to understand and indeed were not accepted by the court. The pursuer further argued that the undertaking gave a *jus quaesitum tertio* in a future contract that her brother might enter into. This too was rejected.

There seems to have been an acceptance that the prescriptive clock began to tick when the undertaking was signed, and hence that the five-year period had (just) expired. Presumably this was because s 6(3) of the Prescription and Limitation (Scotland) Act 1973 says that the clock begins to tick on 'the date when the obligation becomes enforceable', and the obligation to enter into the minute of agreement became enforceable as soon as the undertaking was signed. Suppose, however, that the undertaking had been drafted differently. Instead of being an undertaking to enter into an undertaking, suppose that it was a direct

---

1 Prescription and Limitation (Scotland) Act 1973 sch 1 paras 1(g), 2(e).
2 Paragraphs 9 to 12.
3 1993 SC 142.
4 Paragraph 8.

undertaking to pay the sister the sums in question in the event of a sale etc. In that case we incline to think that prescription would not begin to run unless and until such a sale did take place.[1] If that is right, the situation is rather unfortunate from the sister's point of view, in that prescription has run against her because of the way the agreement happened to be drafted. There is a parallel here with *Aziz v Whannel* discussed above.[2] If X and Y are formally agreeing today, why have a clause that there *will* be a future agreement between them on defined terms? If the parties have already shaken hands and signed a document, what need is there for another document?

Smith v Stuart turned on the meaning of 'obligation relating to land' for the purposes of the law of negative prescription. This is an issue which crops up in the courts quite often, and 2010 saw another such case, *Warren James (Jewellers) Ltd v Overgate GP Ltd.*[3] Here the action was for damages against a landlord for breach of the terms of the lease. The landlord pled prescription as a defence. Since the breach was more than five years back, the question was whether the five-year or the 20-year period was applicable. It was held that, whilst the obligation in the lease that had been breached was an obligation relating to land, the damages for breach of that obligation could not be classified as an obligation relating to land. Hence the relevant prescriptive period was five years rather than 20. As the Lord Ordinary (Lord Glennie) put it:[4]

> The obligation in clause 4.3 of the lease is clearly an obligation relating to land within the meaning of that expression as used in para 2(e) of Schedule 1 to the Act. However, that is not the end of the matter. The pursuers do not sue to enforce that obligation. They sue for damages for its breach. There is a significant difference between the two. As Lord Coulsfield said in *Lord Advocate v Shipbreaking Industries Ltd (No 1)* 1991 SLT 838 at p 840J–K, an obligation arising out of a breach of an obligation relating to land is not the same thing as an obligation relating to land.

STAMP DUTY LAND TAX AND OTHER TAX ISSUES[5]

The overall tax picture could not be clearer – they want more! The fiscal situation has moved beyond the possibility of relying on concealed, minor taxes and thus there have been significant headline increases. The rise in VAT from 4 January 2011 will do a good deal of the 'heavy lifting' from the tax system, and of course will be a significant property tax increase for those, such as financial and educational institutions, who cannot recover all of their VAT.[6] But it will not affect the vast majority of residential transactions, nor (other than by cashflow) the tax burden

---

1 Because the clock does not begin to tick until 'the date when the obligation becomes enforceable' which would be the date of the sale (if that ever took place).
2 See p 112.
3 [2010] CSOH 57, 2010 GWD 17-348.
4 Paragraph 4.
5 This part is contributed by Alan Barr of the University of Edinburgh and Brodies LLP.
6 Finance (No 2) Act 2010 s 3, amending Value Added Tax Act 1994 s 2(1).

on businesses that can recover all of their VAT. As, however, stamp duty land tax is charged on consideration with the addition of VAT, a VAT increase will also increase the amount of SDLT chargeable on many commercial transactions.

2010 began with a more general increase (or at least restoration) in SDLT, as the nil-rate threshold was restored to £125,000 from its temporarily increased level of £175,000.[1] There had been speculation about the higher threshold being maintained as an economic stimulus, but that came to nothing. The relief for residential property in disadvantaged areas is now relevant again, as the threshold of £150,000 for such property now exceeds the basic threshold.[2]

But tinkering with the nil-rate threshold continued right up to the election. The March 2010 Budget brought an increase to £250,000, but only for first-time buyers of residential property.[3] This applies to transactions on or after 25 March 2010 and is intended to last for two years, but this allows ample time for further alterations. The conditions for this increased threshold may cause some difficulty. *All* of the purchasers (if more than one) must be first-time buyers (which involves never having acquired a major interest in land, whether in the UK or otherwise). They must also intend (presumably at the time of purchase) to occupy the property purchased as their only or main residence.[4] This last condition seems quite loose, and the scheme may be rather difficult to police effectively. Solicitors should take particular care not to be involved in its abuse, as they could have a significant degree of personal responsibility if assisting in completing an incorrect SDLT tax return.[5]

This small silver lining accompanies an impending cloud for transactions at the other end of the scale. With effect from 6 April 2011 the rate of SDLT on residential properties with a consideration over £1 million is to be increased from 4% to 5%.[6] Unlike the increase in the threshold for first-time buyers, there is no sign that this increase is to be time-limited and one cannot help but suspect that a more general increase to a 5% rate for all property may start to look very tempting.

To counter partnership avoidance schemes, the anti-avoidance rules in Finance Act 2003 s 75A are to be applied to SDLT on partnerships.[7]

Looking further ahead, the whole future for SDLT is debatable. It was one of the taxes proposed for further devolution by the Calman Commission. In terms of the Scotland Bill,[8] if it is passed in its current form:

A tax charged on any of the following transactions is a devolved tax –

(a) the acquisition of an estate, interest, right or power in or over land in Scotland;

---

1 Finance Act 2009 s 10(1)(a).
2 See Finance Act 2003 s 57, sch 6.
3 See Finance Act 2010 s 6, inserting ss 57AA and 73CA into the Finance Act 2003 (the latter dealing with alternative property finance – so-called 'Islamic mortgage' – transactions).
4 Finance Act 2003 s 57AA(1)(d).
5 Finance Act 2003 s 96.
6 Finance Act 2010 s 7, amending Finance Act 2003 s 55.
7 Finance Act 2010 s 55.
8 Scotland Bill (No 115 of 2010) cl 28, inserting Chapter 3 into Part 4A of the Scotland Act 1998.

(b) the acquisition of the benefit of an obligation, restriction or condition affecting the value of any such estate, interest, right or power.

While this describes the current form of SDLT, there is no requirement that any Scottish replacement should have the same form. It might be added that the above definition would seem to encompass VAT on land, which it is not intended to devolve.

In relation to other taxes on land, the special rules applicable to furnished holiday lettings have been the subject of proposals for extensive changes, followed by reversals of these proposals and detailed discussion. This process continued throughout 2010. The starting-point was an extension of the special reliefs for furnished holiday lettings, for the year 2009–10, to all property within the European Economic Area. This extension was to meet the UK's obligations under European law, but its announcement was accompanied by an intimation that a simpler consistency would be achieved by complete abolition of the special regime with effect from 2010–11. After consultation, this intention was formally changed from the date of the so-called 'Emergency Budget' after the election – 22 June 2010.[1] The rules continue in their current form for 2010–11, and yet another consultation was launched, with responses due by 22 October 2010. This has now led to draft legislation being published in December 2010. This preserves the basic form of the relief, but loss relief is to be restricted to the same holiday lettings business (from April 2011). From April 2012 the minimum period over which a qualifying property must be available to let to the public during a year would increase from 140 to 210 days, and the minimum period over which a qualifying property must actually be let from 70 days to 105 days. Given the relative short length of the Scottish tourist season, these proposals may cause difficulties – but of course for those who run such accommodation, they represent a substantial improvement on the complete abolition of the special regime.

---

1 A useful 'Questions and Answers' document on Furnished Holiday Lettings was published by HMRC on 22 June 2010.

PART V
TABLES

TABLES

CUMULATIVE TABLE OF DECISIONS ON VARIATION OR DISCHARGE OF TITLE CONDITIONS

This table lists all opposed applications under the Title Conditions (Scotland) Act 2003 for variation or discharge of title conditions. Decisions on expenses are omitted. Note that the full opinions in Lands Tribunal cases are often available at http://www.lands-tribunal-scotland.org.uk/records.html.

Restriction on building

Name of case	Burden	Applicant's project in breach of burden	Application granted or refused
Ord v Mashford 2006 SLT (Lands Tr) 15; *Lawrie v Mashford*, 21 Dec 2007	1938. No building.	Erection of single-storey house and garage.	Granted. Claim for compensation refused.
Daly v Bryce 2006 GWD 25-565	1961 feu charter. No further building.	Replace existing house with two houses.	Granted.
J & L Leisure Ltd v Shaw 2007 GWD 28-489	1958 disposition. No new buildings higher than 15 feet 6 inches.	Replace derelict building with two-storey housing.	Granted subject to compensation of £5,600.
West Coast Property Developments Ltd v Clarke 2007 GWD 29-511	1875 feu contract. Terraced houses. No further building.	Erection of second, two-storey house.	Granted. Claim for compensation refused.
Smith v Prior 2007 GWD 30-523	1934 feu charter. No building.	Erection of modest rear extension.	Granted.
Anderson v McKinnon 2007 GWD 29-513	1993 deed of conditions in modern housing estate.	Erection of rear extension.	Granted.
Smith v Elrick 2007 GWD 29-515	1996 feu disposition. No new house. The feu had been subdivided.	Conversion of barn into a house.	Granted.

Name of case	Burden	Applicant's project in breach of burden	Application granted or refused
Brown v Richardson 2007 GWD 28-490	1888 feu charter. No alterations/new buildings	Erection of rear extension.	Granted. This was an application for renewal, following service of a notice of termination.
Gallacher v Wood 2008 SLT (Lands Tr) 31	1933 feu contract. No alterations/new buildings.	Erection of rear extension, including extension at roof level which went beyond bungalow's footprint.	Granted. Claim for compensation refused.
Blackman v Best 2008 GWD 11-214	1934 disposition. No building other than a greenhouse.	Erection of a double garage.	Granted.
McClumpha v Bradie 2009 GWD 31-519	1984 disposition allowing the erection of only one house.	Erection of four further houses.	Granted but restricted to four houses.
McGregor v Collins-Taylor 14 May 2009	1988 disposition prohibiting the erection of dwellinghouses without consent.	Erection of four further houses.	Granted but restricted to four houses.
Faeley v Clark 2006 GWD 28-626	1967 disposition. No further building.	Erection of second house.	Refused.
Cattanach v Vine-Hall	1996 deed of conditions in favour of neighbouring property. No building within 7 metres of that property.	Erection of substantial house within 2 metres.	Refused, subject to the possibility of the applicants bringing a revised proposal.
Hamilton v Robertson, 10 Jan 2008	1984 deed of conditions affecting five-house development. No further building.	Erection of 2nd house on site, but no firm plans.	Refused, although possibility of later success once plans firmed up was not excluded.
Cocozza v Rutherford 2008 SLT (Lands Tr) 6	1977 deed of conditions. No alterations.	Substantial alterations which would more than double the footprint of the house.	Refused.
Scott v Teasdale 22 Dec 2009	1962 feu disposition. No building.	New house in garden.	Refused.
Hollinshead v Gilchrist 7 Dec 2009	1990 Disposition and 1997 feu disposition. No building or alterations.	Internal alterations.	Granted.

Name of case	Burden	Applicant's project in breach of burden	Application granted or refused
Tower Hotel (Troon) Ltd v McCann 4 March 2010	1965 feu disposition. No building. Existing building to be used as a hotel or dwellinghouse.	No firm plan though one possibility was the building of flats.	Granted.
Corstorphine v Fleming 2 July 2010	1965 feu disposition. No alterations, one house only.	A substantial extension plus a new house.	Granted.
Corry v MacLachlan 9 July 2010	1984 disposition of part of garden. Obligation to build a single-storey house.	Addition of an extra storey.	Refused.

Other restriction on use

Name of case	Burden	Applicant's project in breach of burden	Application granted or refused
Church of Scotland General Trs v McLaren 2006 SLT (Lands Tr) 27	Use as a church.	Possible development for flats.	Granted.
Wilson v McNamee, 16 Sept 2007	Use for religious purposes.	Use for a children's nursery.	Granted
Verrico v Tomlinson 2008 SLT (Lands Tr) 2	1950 disposition. Use as a private residence for the occupation of one family.	Separation of mews cottage from ground floor flat.	Granted.
Matnic Ltd v Armstrong 2010 SLT (Lands Tr) 7	2004 deed of conditions. Use for the sale of alcohol.	Use of units in a largely residential estate for retail purposes.	Granted but restricted to small units and no sale of alcohol after 8 pm.
Clarke v Grantham 2009 GWD 38-645	2004 disposition. No parking on an area of courtyard.	A desire to park (though other areas were available).	Granted.
Hollinshead v Gilchrist 7 Dec 2009	1990 disposition and 1997 feu disposition. No caravans, commercial or other vehicles to be parked in front of the building line.	Parking of cars.	Granted and claim for compensation refused.
Perth & Kinross Council v Chapman 13 Aug 2009	1945 disposition. Plot to be used only for outdoor recreational purposes.	Sale for redevelopment.	Granted.

Flatted property

Name of case	Burden	Applicant's project in breach of burden	Application granted or refused
Regan v Mullen 2006 GWD 25-564	1989. No subdivision of flat.	Subdivision of flat.	Granted.
Kennedy v Abbey Lane Properties 29 March 2010	2004. Main-door flat liable for a share of maintenance of common passages and stairs.	None.	Refused.
Melville v Crabbe 19 Jan 2009	1880 feu disposition. No additional flat.	Creation of a flat in the basement.	Refused.

Sheltered and retirement housing

Name of case	Burden	Applicant's project in breach of burden	Application granted or refused
At.Home Nationwide Ltd v Morris 2007 GWD 31-535	1993 deed of conditions. On sale, must satisfy superior that flat will continue to be used for the elderly.	No project: just removal of an inconvenient restriction.	Burden held to be void. Otherwise application would have been refused.

Miscellaneous

Name of case	Burden	Applicant's project in breach of burden	Application granted or refused
McPherson v Mackie 2006 GWD 27-606 rev [2007] CSIH 7, 2007 SCLR 351	1990. Housing estate: maintenance of house.	Demolition of house to allow the building of a road for access to proposed new development.	Discharged by agreement on 25 April 2007.

Applications for renewal of real burdens following service of a notice of termination

Name of case	Burden	Respondent's project in breach of burden	Application granted or refused
Brown v Richardson 2007 GWD 28-490	1888 feu charter. No buildings.	Substantial rear extension.	Refused.

Name of case	Burden	Applicant's project in breach of burden	Application granted or refused
Council for Music in Hospitals v Trustees for Richard Gerald Associates 2008 SLT (Lands Tr) 17	1838 instrument of sasine. No building in garden.	None.	Refused.

Applications for preservation of community burdens following deeds of variation or discharge under s 33 or s 35

Name of case	Burden	Respondent's project in breach of burden	Application granted or refused
Fleeman v Lyon 2009 GWD 32-539	1982 deed of conditions. No building, trade, livestock etc.	Erection of a second house.	Granted.

Applications for variation of community burdens (s 91)

Name of case	Burden	Applicant's project in breach of burden	Application granted or refused
Fenwick v National Trust for Scotland 2009 GWD 32-538	1989 deed of conditions.	None. The application was for the complete discharge of the deed with the idea that a new deed would eventually be drawn up.	Refused.

Servitudes

Name of case	Servitude	Applicant's project in breach of burden	Application granted or refused
George Wimpey East Scotland Ltd v Fleming 2006 SLT (Lands Tr) 27 and 59	1988 disposition. Right of way.	Diversion of right of way to allow major development for residential houses.	Granted (opposed). Claim for compensation for temporary disturbance refused.
Ventureline Ltd, 2 Aug 2006	1972 disposition. 'Right to use' certain ground.	Possible redevelopment.	Granted (unopposed).

Name of case	Servitudes	Applicant's project in breach of burden	Application granted or refused
Graham v Parker 2007 GWD 30-524	1990 feu disposition. Right of way from mid-terraced house over garden of end-terraced house to the street.	Small re-routing of right of way, away from the burdened owner's rear wall, so as to allow an extension to be built.	Granted (opposed).
MacNab v McDowall, 24 Oct 2007	1994 feu disposition reserved a servitude of way from the back garden to the front street in favour of two neighbouring house.	Small re-rerouting, on to the land of one of the neighbours, to allow a rear extension to be built.	Granted (opposed).
Jensen v Tyler 2008 SLT (Lands Tr) 39	1985 feu disposition granted a servitude of way.	Re-routing of part of the road in order to allow (unspecified) development of steading.	Granted (opposed).
Gibb v Kerr 2009 GWD 38-646	1981 feu disposition granted a servitude of way.	Re-routing to homologate what had already taken place as a result of the building of a conservatory.	Granted (opposed).
Parkin v Kennedy 23 March 2010	1934 feu charter. Right of way from mid-terraced house over garden of end-terraced house.	Re-routing to allow extension to be built, which would require a restriction to pedestrian access.	Refused (opposed).
ATD Developments Ltd v Weir 14 September 2010	2002 disposition granted a servitude right of way.	Narrowing the servitude so as to allow gardens for proposed new houses.	Granted (unopposed).
Colecliffe v Thompson 2010 SLT (Lands Tr) 15	1997 disposition granted a servitude of way.	None. But the owners of the benefited property had since acquired a more convenient access, secured by a new servitude.	Granted (opposed).
G v A 26 Nov 2009	1974 disposition granted a servitude of way.	None. But the owners of the benefited property had since acquired a more convenient access (although not to his garage).	Granted (opposed) but on the basis that the respondent should apply for compensation.

Name of case	Servitudes	Applicant's project in breach of burden	Application granted or refused
Graham v Lee 18 June 2009	2001 disposition granted (a) a servitude of way and (b) of drainage.	None.	(a) was granted provided the applicants discharged a reciprocal servitude of their own, and compensation was considered. (b) was refused.
McKenzie v Scott 19 May 2009	Dispositions from 1944 and 1957 granted a servitude of bleaching and drying clothes.	None. But the servitude had not in practice been exercised for many years.	Granted (opposed).
Chisholm v Crawford 17 June 2010	A driveway divided two properties. A 1996 feu disposition of one of the properties granted a servitude of access over the driveway.	None. But the applicant was aggrieved that no matching servitude appeared in the neighbour's title.	Refused.

CUMULATIVE TABLE OF APPEALS

A table at the end of *Conveyancing 2008* listed all cases digested in *Conveyancing 1999* and subsequent annual volumes in respect of which an appeal was subsequently heard, and gave the result of the appeal. This table is a continuation of the earlier table, beginning with appeals heard during 2009.

Aberdeen City Council v Stewart Milne Group Ltd
[2009] CSOH 80, 2009 GWD 26-417, 2009 Case (6) *affd* [2010] CSIH 81, 2010 GWD 37-755, 2010 Case (9)

Euring David Ayre of Kilmarnock, Baron of Kilmarnock Ptr
[2008] CSOH 35, 2008 Case (82) *rev* [2009] CSIH 61, 2009 SLT 759, 2009 Case (93)

Christie Owen & Davies plc v Campbell
2007 GWD 24-397, Sh Ct, 2007 Case (53) *affd* 18 Dec 2007, Glasgow Sheriff Court, 2007 Case (53) *rev* [2009] CSIH 26, 2009 SLT 518, 2009 Case (82)

Martin Stephen James Goldstraw of Whitecairns Ptr
[2008] CSOH 34, 2008 Case (81) *rev* [2009] CSIH 61, 2009 SLT 759, 2009 Case (93)

Hamilton v Dumfries and Galloway Council
[2008] CSOH 65, 2008 SLT 531, 2008 Case (37) *rev* [2009] CSIH 13, 2009 SC 277, 2009 SLT 337, 2009 SCLR 392, 2009 Case (50)

Hamilton v Nairn
[2009] CSOH 163, 2010 SLT 399, 2009 Case (51) *affd* [2010] CSIH 77, 2010 SLT 1155, 2010 Case (44)

Holms v Ashford Estates Ltd
2006 SLT (Sh Ct) 70, 2006 Case (40) *affd* 2006 SLT (Sh Ct) 161, 2006 Case (40) *rev* [2009] CSIH 28, 2009 SLT 389, 2009 SCLR 428, 2009 Cases (19) and (52)

Kerr of Ardgowan, Ptr
[2008] CSOH 36, 2008 SLT 251, 2008 Case (80) *rev* [2009] CSIH 61, 2009 SLT 759, 2009 Case (93)

Luminar Lava Ignite Ltd v Mama Group plc
[2009] CSOH 68, 2009 GWD 19-305, 2009 Case (91) *rev* [2010] CSIH 1, 2010 SC 310, 2010 SLT 147, 2010 Case (77)

Mehrabadi v Haugh
June 2009, Aberdeen Sheriff Court, 2009 Case (17) *affd* 11 January 2010 Aberdeen Sheriff Court, 2010 Case (15)

Multi-link Leisure Developments Ltd v North Lanarkshire Council
[2009] CSOH 114, 2009 SLT 1170, 2009 Case (70) *rev* [2009] CSIH 96, 2010 SC 302, 2010 SLT 57, 2010 SCLR 306, 2009 Case (70) *affd* [2010] UKSC 47, 2011 SLT 184, 2010 Case (52)

R & D Construction Group Ltd v Hallam Land Management Ltd
[2009] CSOH 128, 2009 Case (8) *affd* [2010] CSIH 96, 2011 GWD 2-85, 2010 Case (4)

Royal Bank of Scotland plc v Wilson
2008 GWD 2-35, Sh Ct, 2008 Case (61) *rev* 2009 CSIH 36, 2009 SLT 729, 2009 Case (75) *rev* [2010] UKSC 50, 2010 SLT 1227, 2010 Hous LR 88, 2010 Case (66)

Scottish Coal Company Ltd v Danish Forestry Co Ltd
[2009] CSOH 171, 2009 GWD 5-79, 2009 Case (9) *affd* [2010] CSIH 56, 2010 SC 729, 2010 Case (3)

Sheltered Housing Management Ltd v Bon Accord Bonding Co Ltd
2007 GWD 32-533, 2006 Cases (24) and (35), 11 October 2007, Lands Tribunal, 2007 Case (21) *rev* [2010] CSIH 42, 2010 SC 516, 2010 SLT 662, 2010 Case (25)

Smith v Stuart
2009 GWD 8-140, Sh Ct, 2009 Case (2) *affd* [2010] CSIH 29, 2010 SC 490, 2010 SLT 1249, 2010 Case (10)

Tuley v Highland Council
2007 SLT (Sh Ct) 97, 2007 Case (24) *rev* [2009] CSIH 31A, 2009 SC 456, 2009 SLT 616, 2009 Case (48)

Wright v Shoreline Management Ltd
Oct 2008, Arbroath Sheriff Court, 2008 Case (60) *rev* 2009 SLT (Sh Ct) 83, 2009 Case (74)

TABLE OF CASES DIGESTED IN EARLIER VOLUMES BUT REPORTED IN 2010

A number of cases which were digested in *Conveyancing 2009* or earlier volumes but were at that time unreported have been reported in 2010. A number of other cases have been reported in an additional series of reports. For the convenience of those using earlier volumes all the cases in question are listed below, together with a complete list of citations.

A W D Chase de Vere Wealth Management Ltd v Melville Street Properties Ltd
[2009] CSOH 150, 2010 SCLR 521

Braes v Keeper of the Registers of Scotland
[2009] CSOH 176, 2010 SLT 689, 2010 SCLR 202

Colecliffe v Thompson
2010 SLT (Lands Tr) 15

Ferro Finance UL plc v Akintola
2010 Hous LR 28

Fotheringham v Hillcrest Housing Association Ltd
2010 SLT (Lands Tr) 13, 2009 Hous LR 99

Frank Houlgate Investment Co Ltd v Biggart Baillie LLP
[2009] CSOH 165, 2010 SLT 527, 2010 SCLR 527

Garson v McLeish
2010 SLT (Sh Ct) 131

Hamilton v Nairn
[2009] CSOH 163, 2010 SLT 399

Matnic Ltd v Armstrong
2010 SLT (Lands Tr) 7

McCoach v Keeper of the Registers of Scotland
2010 GWD 7-123

Multi-link Leisure Developments Ltd v North Lanarkshire Council
[2009] CSIH 96, 2010 SC 302, 2010 SLT 57, 2010 SCLR 306

Patersons of Greenoakhill Ltd v SP Transmission Ltd
[2009] CSOH 155, 2010 SLT 115

Smith v Stuart
2010 SCLR 131

Taylor v Renfrewshire Council
2010 SLT (Lands Tr) 2